William Graham Sumner
[*1895*]

WAR AND OTHER ESSAYS

WAR AND OTHER ESSAYS

BY

WILLIAM GRAHAM SUMNER

EDITED WITH INTRODUCTION

BY

ALBERT GALLOWAY KELLER

AMS PRESS
NEW YORK

Reprinted from the edition of 1911, New Haven
First AMS EDITION published 1970
Manufactured in the United States of America

Library of Congress Catalog Card Number: 78-108124
SBN: 404-06304-7

AMS PRESS, INC.
New York, N.Y. 10003

CONTENTS

INTRODUCTION

In 1872, when the author of the essays here assembled was elected professor of political and social science in Yale College, he was, to use his own words, "a young and untried man." He was selected for his position, not as a specialist, but because he was what he was. Someone in those days must have been an excellent judge of men. "I have tried," Sumner wrote, in 1881, "to justify their [the Corporation's] confidence. I threw myself into the work of my department and of the college with all my might. I had no other interest or ambition." He could have repeated these words, with equal truth, at the end of his incumbency; for the prime interest in Sumner's professional career from his election to the day of his retirement, in June, 1909, was the scrupulously faithful discharge of his academic duties; and to this end he spent freely the powers of a sturdy frame and an eager mind. His teaching and the many administrative tasks that fell to him always occupied his attention to the subordination of what he might have preferred to do, or of what might have been to his personal interest to do. Of a consequence his writings and public utterances represented extra labor, out of hours. The only one of his books not written at the behest of a publisher, he once told me, was the *Folkways*. In addition to the engrossing activities which I have mentioned, there was yet another factor which held back systematic enterprises on the large scale; left to himself, Sumner's tendency was to wait on further acquisition and on organization of his knowledge rather than to hasten his output. This was particularly evident in respect to his purely sociological work. A dozen years ago a breezy young reporter is said to have asked him why he did not publish on sociology, and to have received the gruff rejoinder: "Because

I would rather correct my own mistakes than have other people do it for me."

In view of these circumstances it is natural that the shorter writings and lectures of Professor Sumner should have been more characteristic of him than are most of his books — however weighty the latter in their scholarship and however highly esteemed by his colleagues in the social sciences. The most characteristic of all his activities was his teaching, for this was his absorbing interest; but next to that, I think, come his occasional essays — with which I should class the two little volumes on *Protectionism* and *What Social Classes Owe to Each Other*. Sumner had time for essays where he was sure to be hurried on his books; his consecutive leisure came in small fragments. And he could improve such shorter periods with great success, for he was remarkably rapid in his composition; his ideas were in order from his much teaching, and he could go ahead, he once told me, as fast as he could drive the pen.

These are the main reasons why Sumner's essays form a more spontaneous, characteristic, and finished product than his longer writings; and so he has been known, if not to scholars, at any rate to the general public, better through them than through his books.

No one who has the interests of American education at heart can regret that Sumner's fidelity to duty prevented him from writing more — or even from completing what he had begun. His enduring output is the human document, the awakened minds of many young men, which is a product that can only roll up in significance as time passes, and is incapable of being antedated or superseded. It was the influence of a mind and character that could not harbor the small and mean which made Sumner such a power in his world. This was true throughout his career, and neither the force of his intellect nor that of his character ever deserted him, even in the shadow of the end. It is the Sumner of the later years whom the present writer knew; and I have been asked, as a close associate and co-worker, to afford his friends and admirers some idea of his activities, and of the man himself, particularly in this his latter phase.[1] I am aware that, in these days, so soon after his death, anything that I may write of him is sure to betray a personal feeling for the man, one which grew ever stronger as I knew him better.

Of Sumner's labors one might say in general that they were as unremitting as strength would allow, whereas before his illness of the early nineties they had been virtually incessant. There seems to have been in this man such intellectual eagerness, such a very mania for discovering the truth, coupled with so strong a power of will, that he wore out a robust physique untimely — for with his vigorous frame and sound constitution he might well have lived out the life of a Humboldt. As it was, Professor Sumner retained his large elective courses and ruled them with iron discipline, up to a few years before his retirement; and to the very end of his active service he remained an incomparable leader in the college faculty. We younger men are told that at a crisis the leadership has been wont to creep into his hand as by some inherent urge; he hit about him rather regardlessly in the preliminary skirmishes, but as others grew hot he grew cool and took command of the situation. One who seeks to account for what Yale College has become, and who realizes that such an institution is not built of bricks and stones, but of men, cannot leave out of reckoning the often determinative influence wielded for nearly forty years by Professor Sumner. He did not fumble about in the mazes of compromise, and he was unafraid. Even during the last years of his life he never lost his characteristic power of cutting straight to the core of an issue; nor, indeed, was he deprived, until the latest days, of his joy in battle. He remained, as he had been in his prime, the redoubtable debater, confronting opposition with a combination of manner, matter, and method with which few ever successfully coped. But the fight, though Homeric in its tactics, was always fair; Sumner took his wounds in front, and as one observer remarked, always shouted, "Look out! I'm com-

[1] A considerable portion of what immediately follows is quoted or adapted from a letter of mine in the New York Nation for April 21, 1910.

ing for you!" before he charged. The greatest immediate loss involved in Professor Sumner's retirement and death, excluding the bereavement of those who loved him, is that sustained by the faculty of Yale College. It is no derogation to anybody to say that he was *sui generis* and can have no successor. What the larger Yale College thought of him was finely expressed in the demonstration of June, 1909, when Yale accorded him the doctorate of laws — when fathers and sons united in applauding the great teacher of two generations. This affected him, as he admitted, to tears; and during the succeeding summer he received many letters expressive of gratitude and affection, which made him feel, as he told me, that the world was using him well.

But whatever may be said of his intellectual qualities, yet the most attractive and the grandest aspect of Sumner's latter years was that, not of his mind, but of his character. He was a Roman soul among us; he lived before his students and colleagues as the embodiment of honesty and fearlessness. Duty always preceded all else with him; the memory of his performance of what some would call hackwork, even when he was ill, would have been pathetic if it had not been done with such unconsciousness and simple dignity. Until the aid he would not ask for was almost forced upon him, he used to grade between three hundred and five hundred test papers every week. He was to the end the uncompromising foe of hypocrisy, sham, ostentation, and weak sentiment — which last he curtly denominated "gush." Further, he was in character a humble man. He seemed at all times positive and even intellectually arrogant, but his personal opinion of his own services and work was entirely self-depreciatory. In personal relations he was unassuming, helpful, excessively grateful for small services rendered, but beset by the fear that he would cause anybody else some trouble. In many respects his character was strangely like that of Charles Darwin. He was ready at all times with kindly counsel and sympathy — and the counsel was that of deep wisdom and the sympathy that of a warm heart. I have somewhat enlarged upon this side of his nature, because in appearance and to slight acquaintance he was stern, often gruff, seemingly without human feelings. But this was all a matter of externals. He was a strong hater and a strong lover, as must happen where the essence of a man's character is strength.

It was in characteristic response to the call of duty that Professor Sumner's last efforts and energy were expended. He was scheduled for the presidential address [1] of the American Sociological Society; and he dragged himself off to New York, ill and weak, but as determined as ever, in the snowstorm of Monday, December 27, 1909, with his manuscript carefully prepared, typewritten and corrected, in his valise. No remonstrances could have stopped him. He struggled up nearly to the battle-line, prepared to discharge his duty, as of old, but there was no strength remaining. "How characteristic of Sumner!" was the common remark at the tidings of his fall. One could scarcely wish for a more graphic summing-up of his character and career.

The essays which now lie before the reader suggest many a comment for which the necessary brevity of this introduction may not provide space. Within the last months I have heard and read a number of expressions whose general tenor was: If Sumner had only lived a little longer to receive something of the belated honor of the prophet amongst his own people! It would be interesting to select from the following essays and from Sumner's books passages of an almost prophetic nature; but the fact that they are such — and many are too profound in their insight to have yet attained recognition — is not at all a marvel of second-sight; it is only the inevitable emergence of the truth that makes them seem so. Wisdom has often ere this been sought out with intense labor and ardent mind, first to be dubbed "academic" by the ignorant, preoccupied, or prejudiced, and then to be wondered at and referred to as a sort of supernatural product. The historic ascription wrung from ignorance by knowledge has been that of wizardry.

[1] "Religion and the Mores," pp. 129-146 of this volume.

But no one need commiserate Sumner because he did not receive full meed of deserved recognition while he lived. It is not that he was unappreciative of praise; he was deeply sensitive to it, contrary to the impression which not a few have derived. No man is all iron. But if one reads the *Folkways* with understanding he will see that its author was in possession of a point of view and of a philosophy of life which rendered him, though humanly appreciative of kindly expression, essentially independent of the commendation or blame accorded to him by his time. He used sometimes to refer in his quizzical way to some historical character (I think it was not Saint Paul) whose aim was to be "all things to all men," in the sense of pleasing everybody; and he used to conclude, dryly, "It is not reported that he succeeded."

No one could say that Sumner himself strove to be all things to all men. He never hesitated to strike out against the tide, and he did not fear to be alone in so doing; nor, indeed, did it affect his composure and resolution if he made no headway, but was overborne by the current. This attracted to him, among the strong men of his time, many admirers, of whose sentiments he was probably uninformed; for instance, the late Mr. Hammond Lamont once wrote of him: "Professor Sumner's valiant fight for free trade — almost single-handed it seemed at one time — has won him my especial respect." He thought protectionism, currency-inflation, and imperialism wrong and hateful, and assailed them at sight, in all times and places, irrespective of the sentiment of the age. No man ever had a profounder faith in the possibility of attaining to truth by study and thought, and few have had such power — which goes with strength of conviction and unassuming courage — literally to infect others with the same belief. These were the chief of the factors that made him so compelling a teacher; one of the grandest traits of young men is their generous enthusiasm for intellectual honesty and ardor, and for uncalculating fearlessness in following conviction, once attained, wherever it leads; and Sumner fairly radiated these qualities. One may wish for him that he could have had the personal gratification of seeing his ideas, for which he had suffered unpopularity and abuse, recognized; but he had the greater satisfaction of looking back upon a life of spotless honor, undeviating in its sincerity and intrepidly true to truth where truth seemed to be. That a wave of popular sentiment might roll up to exalt part of what he stood for, he well knew; but he was fortified to expect that, in the complex play of human interests, the "mores" would presently swing off toward some new form of the irrational, or even back to the old follies again.

It is plain, from the evidence of these essays, that Sumner was always a sociologist, that is, he always reached out spontaneously to an interpretation of societal phenomena broader than the purely economic or political one. The issues attacked in these essays are approached with a breadth of vision which goes with a general science of society and not with any single one of its subdivisions. Nobody who has studied the science of society with Sumner ever has any doubts about there being such a science; what persuaded us that there was one, was the actual demonstration set before us in the classroom. There was something that appealed to us as superlatively vital and enthralling, but of which no antecedent discipline had given us more than an oblique glimpse. Until the memory of his breadth and inclusiveness of vision as to human reaction and motive has faded quite away, it will be an arduous task to prove to one of Sumner's students that there is no general science of society. No amount of mere formal analysis and intellectual fence-building can stand against demonstration.

Sumner was a path-breaker by nature and circumstance; but he had his impulsion, as is the way of men, from the hand of another.[1] To judge by his own comments, he derived from Herbert Spencer some such intellectual awakening as he later gave to many. But it is wrong and shallow to class Sumner

---

[1] There is, in the Popular Science Monthly for June, 1889 (pp. 261-268), a *Sketch of William Graham Sumner*, which is largely autobiographical and which deserves re-publication. It touches upon several of the points noticed in this Introduction.

as a thick-and-thin adherent of the Spencerian system; he was not adapted to discipleship. He accepted a number of Spencer's ideas — some of which were sure to appeal to him temperamentally — notably those leading to the *laissez-faire* attitude and to distrust of socialistic tendencies; but he parted company with Spencer in the latter author's most characteristic and fundamental point of view. Spencer was essentially a philosopher and not a scientist, seeking in his evolutionary studies, carried through the bulky volumes of the *Synthetic Philosophy*, for an inclusive formula. But this is not what science is looking for, and Sumner's sympathies and respect were all for science — in particular for natural science. He abhorred and eschewed the metaphysical and intuitional; he studied philosophy much as a young man, but as he once expressed it, he "had been engaged in heaving that whole cargo overboard ever since." I have never heard in his conversation or seen in his writings anything to indicate that he accepted the essence of the Spencerian system; on the contrary, he never advised us to read the *First Principles* or other parts of the *Synthetic Philosophy*, except, perhaps, the *Principles of Biology*, and used often to say that the *Principles of Sociology* represented the only large part of Spencer's work destined to live, because here Spencer was forced to collect his data and so "get down to facts." Among scientists Darwin was Sumner's hero, as he generally is to the real scientist; his honor of Darwin is indicated, for instance, by his often expressed perplexity as to how Darwin, otherwise well-nigh impeccable, could have made a bad slip in his description of Tierra del Fuego and its inhabitants.

I feel impelled to refer in this place to the belief of some of Sumner's admirers that he made a mistake when he retired from political economy and took up the more general science of society. As well say that there is an error in the development from the blade to the ear and the full corn in the ear. The obituary notices of a year ago recalled the Sumner of the seventies and eighties rather than the tranquil student of more recent years — Sumner the political economist rather than

Sumner in his latest and ripest period. The popular tendency in thinking of him is to hark back to his vigor as the embattled champion of free trade and sound money, and if something is said of the latter part of his career, it is likely to have to do with his opposition to the imperialistic movement. Popular mention of the book destined to be his last, the *Folkways*, is generally perfunctory and vague. Such an attitude is natural enough, for Sumner's activities of thirty years ago were such as to leave a lasting impression upon his friends, and an even more persistent recollection, if that were possible, in the minds of those whom he assailed.[1] Upon this period of tremendous vigor, in the classroom, in the faculty councils, in publication, and on the platform, there ensued, in the early nineties, a breakdown in health which coincided with Professor Sumner's withdrawal from the field of political economy, and which, in the eyes of the public, seemed to mark the end of his effective career. Many of us would be happy enough to conclude a career with the renown which Sumner enjoyed as a political economist, especially if we include several substantial volumes on economic subjects, published in the later nineties and taken by some to be signs of the closing up of a lifework. But to him the end of labors in this field merely marked the termination of one more phase of a full life. And the later and final mode was there already and had been from the beginning. I have said that Sumner was always a sociologist; this is reported to have been evident even in his clerical period, but more definitely it dates, as has been remarked, from his acquaintance with Spencer. For he had read *The Study of Sociology* at the time of its publication in the early seventies, and used frequently to mention the sense of intellectual assent and emancipation which broke over him upon making acquaintance with this and the larger sociological works of Spencer.

---

[1] Says "the distinguished American economist," quoted in the *Sketch* previously referred to: ". . . the results of his experience in the discussion of the relative merits and advantages of the systems of free trade and protection have been such that probably no defender of the latter would now be willing to meet him in a public discussion of these topics."

It was characteristic of Sumner that he must not only know the truth, but pass it on; and, after some conflict with the entrenched conservatism of the day, he finally set before Yale College men the first course in sociology ever presented in an American college curriculum.[1] He was moving, as was his wont, steadily and safely from the special to the general. His interest in the general science steadily increased, his second inspiration dating from the reading, in the late eighties, of Julius Lippert's *Kulturgeschichte*. His breakdown in health precipitated the change which had been preparing; and, upon his partial recovery, he ceased to teach political economy to undergraduates and developed his classic course in what the students came to call "Sumnerology." In those days a Yale man was hardly supposed to have won a genuine B.A. if he had not had "Billy Sumner." Within a few years the graduate courses also in political economy had been superseded by others in the science of society, and Professor Sumner had ceased altogether to teach the specialty of his young manhood. Many, I say, have regretted this change, but it was inevitable; the only legitimate regret is that he did not live to reap in full from the sowing of a lifetime — he himself wished that he had been able to surrender political economy sooner. For his interests had outgrown the sub-science and reached out toward the more comprehensive study of the life of society in all its phases. The idea that Sumner's career was over, when, in the early nineties, he retired from political economy, has always been a source of irritation to the men who worked with him in his latter years. As a matter of fact, some of us had been taken to his study and had viewed with amazement the serried rows of classified notes on anthropology and the science of society, and we knew what not many outsiders did, that the old-time

---

[1] "I formed a class," he says, "to read Spencer's book in the parts as they came out, and believe that I began to interest men in this important department of study, and to prepare them to follow its development, years before any such attempt was made at any other university in the world." *Sketch*, p. 266.

industry and vigor had not lessened; we used to believe that if Spencer had had such a collection of materials, the *Principles of Sociology* would have been far more strongly buttressed, and would more nearly have resembled the irresistible *Origin of Species*. Equipped linguistically, as I shall later describe, for the collection of materials, he had plunged into the field marked off by Tylor, Lubbock, Spencer, and others, and had read an incredible number of books, journals, and other sources. The first public indication of this research, and of his long reflection upon its results, was the appearance, in 1907, of *Folkways, a Study of the Sociological Importance of Usages, Manners, Customs, Mores, and Morals*. I cannot go into this publication except to say (as bearing upon what immediately precedes) that it has astonished scholars by the range of its survey over a field to which the author had been able to give exclusive attention for so comparatively short a time. The bibliography of this book covers fifteen closely printed pages, and yet includes scarcely any titles of systematic works, and practically no references to the author's extensive economic reading. To his fellow-scientists *Folkways* revealed the fact that Sumner's scholarly labors, under conditions of ill-health and of declining strength, had in later years even surpassed those of his prime. Further, and more important, it is thought by many that *Folkways* represents a fundamental step in the development of any sound science of society. Sumner used to say that he had found, in the conception of the mores, "either a gold-mine or a big hole in the ground," and that it must be left to the future to determine which.

To understand the bearing of this book on the treatise covering the science of society (of which, in the preface to the *Folkways*, Professor Sumner speaks as his next task), one must realize that the idea of the "folkways" or "mores" was one which he came to regard as entirely fundamental to any scientific system of sociology. He had written for five years, more or less, on his projected general treatise on the *Science of Society* before he came to what he called the "section on the mores"; and this section it was which developed, under the title *Folk-*

ways, into a separate volume to precede the major treatise. It is entirely regrettable that the latter could not have been completed, but if a choice could have been made, it would have been better that *Folkways* should receive the preference. Since its publication the scientific recognition accorded to it has been steadily increasing. What place it will finally make for itself cannot yet be said; but no other of Professor Sumner's books has approached it in profundity and in lasting importance.

Like Darwin, Sumner was an indefatigable collector of facts. His industry was truly discouraging to those about him. Steadily, relentlessly, day by day, year in and year out, he explored his literature until the sum of his readings was almost incredible; a friend, he told me, asked him how he had ever found time to read the multitude of books and articles referred to in *Folkways*, and he had answered that he did not himself know. And his bibliographies were never padded by the inclusion of matter which he had only scanned; nor were the references to publications in the more remote foreign languages second-hand or gotten by way of a translator and then listed as from personal reading. As bearing on the industry and the insatiable scientific curiosity of the man, his attainment of control over languages is extraordinary evidence. The late Prof. Edward Bourne used to tell how, in the middle eighties, Sumner was apparently unfamiliar with other modern foreign languages than French and German; for upon a certain occasion he had said doubtfully of the word "naranja" that he supposed that it was Spanish for "orange." But shortly thereafter he apparently felt that he must extend his range, for certain of his dictionaries, Dutch, Danish, Portuguese, and others, bear acquisition dates of the late eighties. Within a few years he had acquired the two Scandinavian tongues, Dutch, Spanish, Portuguese, Italian, Russian, and Polish. None of these, apparently, was begun before the age of forty-five; and it was perfectly characteristic of Sumner that he "ground the paradigms," as he said, in all cases, and even went to the extent of translating all the exercises in his grammars; not only, for example, the Swedish-into-English exercises, but those from English into Swedish. The excellent Balbus may have begun Greek at seventy, but among moderns such a display of energy and industry at middle age is sufficiently remarkable. It should not be forgotten that Sumner, as his maiden publication witnesses, was a good Hebrew scholar, and that he knew Greek and Latin well. So that his control of languages, though he used to say that he was not quick at learning them, extended to some thirteen or fourteen; and of these he had an exact and precise grammatical control. It may be added that at about the same time he was acquiring a knowledge of calculus in order to see for himself what there was in mathematical economics. And all this while writing, lecturing, teaching a heavy schedule, and taking a leading part in faculty labors.

One of the characteristics of Sumner's mode comes out quite unmistakably in his essays; and that is his simplicity and clearness. He struck straight at the heart of a matter. He used to say that there were three questions to be asked about any production: What is it? How do you know it? *What of it?* Upon the last inquiry he laid particular emphasis; but, granted that there was any use in doing a piece of work, he was keen about his other two criteria: that it should be set forth so it could be understood, — that one should tell, with brevity and clearness, what it was that he had found, — and that he should give good and sufficient reason for his opinions. He used to prune the theses written under him of verbiage and slash out inexact expressions, usually making careful emendations, until the pages were scarcely recognizable. For himself, he abjured latinity and chose the tersest and most rugged of Anglo-Saxon terms, using, for an extreme example, a word like leech-craft in place of a more indirect and ponderous term. He hated long and involved sentences, and urged us all to be sure to translate German passages that looked as if they were significant, to see if they really were; for, as he said, "the German language and style lend themselves easily to bathos." He believed that if the thought were clear the expression would be, and where the latter was rambling and disordered he looked for turgidity of thought. His own clarity and epigrammatic expression were probably a reflection of his own nature, for he spoke simply and vigorously, using homely phrases that stuck in the mind — he certainly got so that he thought in a way corresponding to this graphical, forceful phraseology. But as qualities of style he also recognized and cultivated brevity and curt precision; in his collections are several envelopes filled with slips of paper, such as he used to carry about in his pocket for jotting, covered with tersely expressed thought on a variety of topics. His original sketch of an essay or part of a book, at least in his latter years, was likely to contain strings of short sentences, which he then pieced together to some extent in his many re-writings. The volleys of short sentences in some of his writings — especially those originally in lecture-form — are unquestionably a literary defect, however much the avoidance of involution may conduce to clearness. He grew ever more impatient of verbosity in writing and of vagueness in thought.

Some have said that Sumner's clarity was due to the fact that he never saw but one side to a question, and therefore was not bothered by the need of hedging and shading. It certainly conduces to clarity to see an issue in that way; but it would not be fair to one who has stood to so many as a champion and exponent of fairness to let this offhand version go unchallenged. The Commencement orator of 1909, when Sumner received the Yale doctorate of laws, said: "Like all great teachers and real leaders of men, he is intensely dogmatic; but his dogmas are not the result of narrowness or prejudice; they come from prolonged study and profound thought." This sentence contains, implicitly at least, the *rationale* of Sumner's dogmatism. He was always teaching the elements of social science to beginners, whether they sat in his classes or not; and in the teaching of the elements dogmatism is necessary. Any teacher who knows his business is aware that some well-defined standpoint must be gained before the balancing of theories can be profitably begun.

Hence Sumner was, in his teaching and essays, very positive; and the worth of this pedagogical device is vouched for by many — even by those who now dispute the positions upheld by Sumner. I do not mean to say that Sumner did not thoroughly believe in what he said; he was intellectually honest to the extent of refusing to support in debate the easier, more plausible, but to him wrong side of a question. His flatly stated opinions were the result of long study; what he presented was, as it were, the building without the scaffolding. This could readily be seen by his more advanced students, for in his graduate classes he opened up to us his doubts and perplexities in the frankest manner; and no one could talk with him as man to man without becoming aware that he held all his scientific opinions open to revision. His mind was essentially hospitable to new truth; but pending its emergence he clung with great loyalty to what he regarded as already demonstrated. Above all, he clave to "common sense," and used often to urge us to hold in abeyance any theory which seemed to conflict with it; for correspondence with common sense was, to him, an ultimate test.

Sumner's attitude toward his profession was marked by a certain austerity. He would sometimes regret that he had not gone into law, but was never apologetic as respects his profession, though he used in private to joke about it in a grim sort of way. This quality of austerity was especially happy in a man who stood for sociology; for if any modern science needs the austere exponent, it is precisely that one. "The field of sociology," Sumner once said to me, "is so raw that any crank can fasten on it from any angle." Here was an apt arena for a man whose grand message to his students was, as one of them crystallized it: Don't be a damn fool! He had no use for the sensationalist or the man with the programme, and it was partly for this reason that he paid so little attention to "practical sociology" and reiterated in his lectures and in the announcements of his courses that the science of society as he taught it was based upon the facts of ethnography and history. He had comparatively little faith in systematic works on sociology and paid but slight attention to them; if I take his attitude rightly, it was not that of "intellectual arrogance," as some have asserted, but resulted from the belief that extended theorizing and ambitious attempts at systematization are not suited to the early phases of a new science. There is too much else to do.

This whole attitude of austerity bespoke the high·esteem in which he held the subject of the science of society; he regarded it as of an importance so great as not to admit of any treatment save the most careful and conscientious. The result was that his utterances in the classroom were marked by a seriousness, almost a severity, which was relieved only by the recurrent play of a grim humor and a picturesque and stinging satire. He brought to these lectures, as I have said above, a manner, matter, and method to which we had never been introduced. The manner was authoritative and compelling, and was never tainted by the slightest sensationalism, whatever distortions of his sayings may have reached the press; and it was marked by a most delicate propriety of expression, for this powerful man had, as respects sensitiveness and purity, the mind of a woman. The matter was rich and thought-enkindling. The method was direct and unadorned, the embodiment of the conviction that truth plainly set forth would come to its own. There was no placation of the hearer, no device to hold attention, no oratory — nothing but the man and the word. And these seemed to be one; before those who knew Sumner and who later read his writing there arises the reminiscence of a broad-shouldered, powerful frame, leaning forward a little from the lecture chair; a head whose baldness and close-clipped fringe of hair seemed, in what they revealed, appropriate; a stern, lined face; a level eye, deep-pouched and redoubtable to meet; a long, bony, upraised forefinger; a "voice of iron," an enunciation deep, almost harsh in its ruggedness, and with impressive pauses. To this figure of the man the words he spoke seemed entirely congruous; and as one who sat under Sumner reads the essays which follow he cannot dispel, if he would, the memory of a commanding personality.

Many of us have enjoyed in times past the occasional essay of Professor Sumner, and have wished that we could have it conveniently at hand, either for our own re-reading or that we might the more readily introduce a friend to a sturdy and dauntless personality in the world of thought. It is in response mainly to desires of this order that the present collection has been assembled. I am aware that an occasional favorite will not be found here; some will seek in vain for the haunting phrase or pungent, half-remembered epigram that he would gladly con again. A great deal of Sumner's writing was in the form of short articles, hot from the forge, in newspapers and magazines; but all of these could not be collected and included in the present volume. His famous retort to the youthful socialist — to which no reply was forthcoming — was hard to leave out; so was the laconic Foreword to Professor Cutler's *Lynch Law*, where Sumner says of lynching, in his characteristic way: "It would be a disgrace to us if amongst us men should burn a rattlesnake or a mad dog. The badness of the victim is not an element in the case at all. Torture and burning are forbidden, not because the victim is not bad enough, but because we are too good." But these shorter treasures could not well go in, and the selection was finally limited to the longer essays. One is the more reconciled to the omissions in the hope that a *Life and Letters* may at some time see the light, where the many isolated "Sumnerisms" may find appropriate place.

As arranged, the following seventeen essays fall under three main heads, both topicwise and, to a large degree, chronologically as well. Of the first seven all but one are products of the last years of Professor Sumner's life, and all but two were published in 1909 and 1910; the next group (five) run between 1887 and 1894 and have to do chiefly with the practical applications of sociological principles to problems of the time; the following four come between 1896 and 1900, all bearing upon the "predominant issue" of that period, imperialism. To these groups is added a single essay on American colleges, dating from 1884 and constituting in the main an attack on the then preferred position of the classical studies, but including much that is of a more than local or temporary value. The better to preserve their character, certain of these essays have been left in their original lecture-form. The date given at the head of each essay will indicate its setting and thus clear up local references that occur.

All of Sumner's sociological writings exhibit the strong, sane mind which many have followed admiringly in the economic and political field, traversing the broadest and most comprehensive phases of social life. But the dominating idea in the thought of his latter years was that of the "folkways" or "mores," and the rest of his later writings should all be read in the light of his last book. The *Status of Women* and *Witchcraft* are really abbreviated chapters, originally intended for *Folkways*, as the preface to that volume indicates. The whole of the unfinished *magnum opus*, on the *Science of Society*, was to be re-written upon the basic idea of the mores; for Sumner regarded these as the germ and matrix of all societal institutions. Anyone who knew Sumner personally, or through his writings, will realize that his fundamentals of societal life would be simple and profound, non-metaphysical, and based upon the quintessence of common sense. The *Folkways* is a repository of shrewd observation and epigrammatic statement, based upon broad scholarship, clear vision, and ripe wisdom. It can be read by the scholar with the scholar's profit; by the layman with the result of enrichment of thought and life; and by any former student of Sumner, whoever he may be, with all that others may get, and, in addition, with the impressions which attend the raising of a host of memories — such memories as throng to the mind when it recalls the quickening influence of the loved and honored.

ALBERT GALLOWAY KELLER.

NEW HAVEN, June 27, 1911.

WAR

ESSAYS OF WILLIAM GRAHAM SUMNER

I

WAR

[1903]

WE have heard our political leaders say from time to time that "War is necessary," "War is a good thing." They were trying to establish a major premise which would suggest the conclusion, "Therefore let us have a little war now," or "It is wise, on general principles, to have a war once in a while." That argument may be taken as the text of the present essay. It has seemed to me worth while to show from the history of civilization just what war has done and has not done for the welfare of mankind.

In the eighteenth century it was assumed that the primitive state of mankind was one of Arcadian peace, joy, and contentment. In the nineteenth century the assumption went over to the other extreme — that the primitive state was one of universal warfare. This, like the former notion, is a great exaggeration. Man in the most primitive and uncivilized state known to us does not practice war all the time; he dreads it; he might rather be described as a peaceful animal. Real warfare comes with the collisions of more developed societies.

If we turn to facts about the least civilized men we find proofs that they are not warlike and do not practice war if they can help it. The Australians have no idea

NOTE. — It has seemed best to the editor to retain the original lecture form in which it was written.

[3]

of conquest or battle. Their fights do not lead to slaughter or spoils or other consequences of victory.[1] Sometimes a fight takes the form of a friendly trial of skill with weapons between two parties who, one by one, cast their weapons at each other. Quarrels between tribes are sometimes settled by a single combat between chiefs. "Real fighting rarely takes place unless the women arouse the men," and even then it is only carried on by taunts and wrestling. "The first wound ends the combat." It is often followed by a war of words, hair-pulling, and blows with yam-sticks between the women.[2] The Australians have no war because they have no property that is worth pillaging; no tribe has anything to tempt the cupidity of another. They have no political organization, so there can be no war for power.[3] Each group appropriates hunting grounds, and over these war arises only with the increase of population. An Englishman who knew them well said that he knew of serious wounds, but he had known of but one death from their affrays.[4]

Neither are the Papuans of New Guinea warlike in all parts of the island. Like other men on the same grade of civilization, they may be assassins, but they are not warriors, and if two bodies of them meet in hostility, we are told that "there is a remarkably small death-roll at the end of the battle."[5] Of another group of them we are told that they have no offensive weapons at all, but live without disturbance from neighbors and without care for the future.[6] Their children rarely quarrel at play, and if they do, it ends in words. We are told

[1] Curr, E. M.: The Australian Race, I, 86.
[2] Dawson, J.: Australian Aborigines, 77.
[3] Semon, R.: In the Australian Bush, etc., 225.
[4] Smyth, R. B.: Aborigines of Victoria, I, 156, 160.
[5] Abel, C. W.: Savage Life in New Guinea, etc., 130.
[6] Krieger, M.: Neu-Guinea, 205.

that they lack the courage, temper, and concentration
of will which would be necessary for a good schoolboy
fight. Perhaps the converse would be true: they have
no schoolboy fights and therefore have no courage, temper, and concentration of will. We are not astonished
to hear that they develop excessive tyranny and cruelty
to those who are weaker than themselves, especially to
women, and even to their mothers.[1] These people are
excessively distrustful of each other and villages but a
little distance apart have very little intercourse. This is
attributed in great part to head-hunting and cannibalism.
In general they know the limits of their own territory
and observe them, but they quarrel about women.[2] The
people in German Melanesia are of the same kind; they
are cowardly and mean, make raids on each other's land
to destroy and plunder, when they think they can do it
safely, but they will not join battle.[3] On some of the
small islands war is entirely unknown.[4]

The Chatham Islanders sometimes quarreled over
booty won in pursuing seals or whales, but they had a law
that the first drop of blood ended the fight.[5] The Khonds
in Madras became insubordinate a few years ago and a
police force was sent against them; they prepared stones
to roll down the hill in front of their village, but left the
rear unguarded, and when the police entered by the rear
the Khonds protested against the unfairness of this movement after they had taken such precautions in front.

[1] Pfeil, J.: Studien und Beobachtungen aus der Südsee, 23.
[2] Hagen, B.: Unter den Papua's, etc., 250.
[3] Pfeil, J.: l. c., 125.
[4] Kubary, J.: Beitrag zur Kenntnis der Núkuóro- oder Monteverde-Inseln, 20; Ibid.: Ethnographischer Beitrag zur Kenntnis des Karolinen Archipels, 94; Bastian, A.: Die mikronesischen Kolonien, etc., 4.
[5] Weiss, B.: Mehr als fünfzig Jahre auf Chatham Island, 18.
[6] Journal of the Asiatic Society of Bombay ("J.A.S.B."), I, 240.

The Rengmahs on the Assam hills attach to the body a
tail of wood eighteen inches long, curved upwards, which
they use to wag defiance at an enemy.[1] Such people
evidently could never have had much experience of war.
The Mrú on the Chittagong hills are peaceable, timid,
and simple; in a quarrel they do not fight, but call in an
exorcist to take the sense of the spirits on the matter.[2]

Livingstone says that the tribes in the interior of South
Africa, where no slave trade existed, seldom had any war
except about cattle, and some tribes refused to keep
cattle in order not to offer temptation. In one case
only had he heard of war for any other reason; three
brothers, Barolongs, fought over one woman, and their
tribe had remained divided, up to the time of writing, into
three parties. During his residence in the Bechuana
country he never saw unarmed men strike each other.
They quarrel with words, but generally both parties
burst into a laugh and that ends it.[3] By an exception
among the Canary islanders, the people of Hierro knew
no war and had no weapons, although their long leaping-
poles could be used as such when occasion demanded.

A Spanish priest, writing an account, in 1739, of the
Aurohuacos of Colombia,[5] says that they have no weapons of offense or defense. If two quarrel they go out to
a big rock or tree and each with his staff beats the rock
or tree with vituperations. The one whose staff breaks
first is the victor; then they embrace and return home
as friends. Even our American Indians, who appear in

[1] Journal of the Anthropological Institute of Great Britain and Ireland
("J.A.I."), XI, 197.

[2] Lewin, T. H.: Wild Races of South-Eastern India, 232.

[3] Livingstone, D.: Missionary Travels and Researches in South Africa, I,
232; II, 503.

[4] American Anthropologist, N. S., II, 475.

[5] Ibid., N. S., III, 612.

our legends to be so bloodthirsty and warlike, always appreciated the blessings of peace. Wampum strings and belts were associated with peace-pacts and with prayers for peace.

In contrast with these cases we find others of extreme warlikeness which account for the current idea that primitive men love war and practice it all the time. But if we examine the cases of peacefulness or unwarlikeness which have been cited, we see that only two or three seem to present evidence of Arcadian peace and simplicity, such as, in the imagination of the eighteenth century philosophers, characterized men in a state of nature. Probably if we had fuller knowledge these few instances would be much modified. What we see is that men have always quarreled. The cases which have been selected are some of them also those of people who have been defeated, broken, and cowed down. Another set of examples consists of those in which abstinence from war is due to cowardice, and with it go the vices of cowardice — tyranny and cruelty to the weak. These cases are calculated to delight the hearts of the advocates of strenuosity. What our testimonies have in common is this: they show that we cannot postulate a warlike character or a habit of fighting as a universal or even characteristic trait of primitive man.

When we undertake to talk about primitive society we should conceive of it as consisting of petty groups scattered separately over a great territory. I speak of groups because I want a term of the widest significance. The group may consist, as it does amongst Australians and Bushmen, of a man with one or possibly two wives and their children, or it may have a few more members, or it may be a village group as in New Guinea, or a tribe or part of a tribe as amongst our own Indians. It is to be observed that this ultimate unit is a group and not an individual. Every individual excludes every other in the competition of life unless they can by combining together win more out of nature by joint effort than the sum of what they could win separately. This combination is what makes groups and brings about industrial organization. When a man and woman unite in the most elementary group known, they do it for economic reasons, because they can carry on the struggle for existence better together than apart. In time this turns into a kin-group, united "by blood." This remains undivided as long as its organization gives advantages, but breaks up when it grows too big for the existing economic system. As soon as it breaks, the fractions begin to compete with each other. If by greater culture a higher organization becomes possible, two groups coalesce by intermarriage or conquest, competition gives way to combination again, and the bigger unit enters into competition with other composite units. Thus at all stages throughout the history of civilization competition and combination forever alternate with each other.

These groups are independent of each other, their size being determined by their mode of life, because the number who can live together economically is limited by the possibilities of the food-quest. When a group outgrows this limit, it breaks up and scatters. The fact of former association is long remembered and there is a bond of kinship and alliance which may at times draw former associates together again for festivals and religious observances, but after they separate the tendency is to become entirely independent and to fall under the type just described; *viz.*, scattered groups each with its individuality, yet in a certain neighborhood to each other. Their remoter relationship does not keep them from quarreling and fighting. In the book of Judges [1] we see cases of war between tribes of Israel in spite of the higher bond which united them with each other and separated them from the Gentiles.

All the members of one group are comrades to each other, and have a common interest against every other group. If we assume a standpoint in one group we may call that one the "we-group" or the "in-group"; then every other group is to us an "others-group" or an "out-group." The sentiment which prevails inside the "we-group," between its members, is that of peace and cooperation; the sentiment which prevails inside of a group towards all outsiders is that of hostility and war. These two sentiments are perfectly consistent with each other; in fact, they necessarily complement each other. Let us see why that is so.

War arises from the competition of life, not from the struggle for existence. In the struggle for existence a man is wrestling with nature to extort from her the means of subsistence. It is when two men are striving side by side in the struggle for existence, to extort from nature the supplies they need, that they come into rivalry and a collision of interest with each other takes place. This collision may be light and unimportant, if the supplies are large and the number of men small, or it may be harsh and violent, if there are many men striving for a small supply. This collision we call the competition of life. Of course men are in the competition of life with beasts, reptiles, insects, and plants — in short, with all organic forms; we will, however, confine our attention to men. The greater or less intensity of the competition of life is a fundamental condition of human existence, and the competition arises between those ultimate unit

[1] Chapters 12, 20.

groups which I have described. The members of the unit group work together. The Australian or Bushman hunter goes abroad to seek meat food, while the woman stays by the fire at a trysting place, with the children, and collects plant food. They cooperate in the struggle for existence, and the size of the group is fixed by the number who can work together to the greatest advantage under their mode of life. Such a group, therefore, has a common interest. It must have control of a certain area of land; hence it comes into collision of interest with every other group. The competition of life, therefore, arises between groups, not between individuals, and we see that the members of the in-group are allies and joint-partners in one interest while they are brought into antagonism of interest with all outsiders. It is the competition of life, therefore, which makes war, and that is why war always has existed and always will. It is in the conditions of human existence. In the cases which have been cited of nature peoples who have no war, we have heard mention already of division of hunting grounds and of quarrels which arise about them. Wherever there is no war, there we find that there is no crowding, as among the scattered Eskimo, or that, after long fighting, treaties and agreements have been made to cover all relations of interest between the groups. These we call peace-pacts, and it is evident that they consist in conventional agreements creating some combination between the groups which are parties to the agreement.

Each group must regard every other as a possible enemy on account of the antagonism of interests, and so it views every other group with suspicion and distrust, although actual hostilities occur only on specific occasion. Every member of another group is a stranger; he may be admitted as a guest, in which case rights and security are granted him, but if not so admitted he is an enemy. We can now see why the sentiments of peace and cooperation inside are complementary to sentiments of hostility outside. It is because any group, in order to be strong against an outside enemy, must be well disciplined, harmonious, and peaceful inside; in other words, because discord inside would cause defeat in battle with another group. Therefore the same conditions which made men warlike against outsiders made them yield to the control of chiefs, submit to discipline, obey law, cultivate peace, and create institutions inside. The notion of rights grows up in the in-group from the usages established there securing peace. There was a double education, at the same time, out of the same facts and relations. It is no paradox at all to say that peace makes war and that war makes peace. There are two codes of morals and two sets of mores, one for comrades inside and the other for strangers outside, and they arise from the same interests. Against outsiders it was meritorious to kill, plunder, practice blood revenge, and to steal women and slaves; but inside none of these things could be allowed because they would produce discord and weakness. Hence, in the in-group, law (under the forms of custom and taboo) and institutions had to take the place of force. Every group was a peace-group inside and the peace was sanctioned by the ghosts of the ancestors who had handed down the customs and taboos. Against outsiders religion sanctioned and encouraged war; for the ghosts of the ancestors, or the gods, would rejoice to see their posterity and worshipers once more defeat, slay, plunder, and enslave the ancient enemy.

The Eskimos of Bering Strait think it wrong to steal from people in the same village or tribe; a thief is publicly reproached and forced to return the thing stolen. But to

steal from an outsider is not wrong unless it brings harm
on one's own tribe.[1]   Strabo[2] says of the Scythians that
they were just and kind to each other, but very savage towards all outsiders.   The sentiment of cohesion,
internal comradeship, and devotion to the in-group, which
carries with it a sense of superiority to any out-group and
readiness to defend the interests of the in-group against
the out-group, is technically known as ethnocentrism.   It
is really the sentiment of patriotism in all its philosophic
fullness; that is, both in its rationality and in its extravagant exaggeration.   The Mohaves and the Seri of southern California will have no relations of marriage or trade
with any other people; they think themselves superior.
The Mohaves are wild and barbarous and the Seri are
on a lower grade of civilization than any other tribe in
America.   Therefore, we see that ethnocentrism has
nothing to do with the relative grade of civilization of any
people.   The Seri think that "the brightest virtue is the
shedding of alien blood, while the blackest crime in their
calendar is alien conjugal union."[3]   Perhaps nine-tenths
of all the names given by savage tribes to themselves
mean "Men," "The Only Men," or "Men of Men";
that is, We are men, the rest are something else.   A
recent etymology of the word Iroquois makes it mean
"I am the real man."[4]   In general Indians held that
they were a favored race, due to a special creation.[5]
Nansen[6] gives a letter written by an Eskimo in 1756
when he heard of the war between England and France.
He burst into a rhapsody about Greenland.   "Your
unfruitfulness makes us happy and saves us from moles-

[1] Bureau of American Ethnology, 18, I, 293.   [2] 300, 302.
[3] Bur. Eth., 17, I, 11; Am. Anth., N. S., IV, 279.
[4] Am. Anth., N. S., IV, 558.
[5] Bur. Eth., VIII, 36.   [6] Eskimo Life, 180.

tation." The writer was surprised that the Christians
had not learned better manners amongst the Eskimo,
and he proposed to send missionaries to them. A trav-
eler in Formosa says that the Formosans thought foreigners barbarians, "civilization being solely within the
dominion of the Celestial Emperor. All the rest of the
world — if there was any poor remainder — was be-
nighted, and but the home of 'barbarians,' not 'men.'" [1]
This is the language of ethnocentrism; it may be read
in the newspapers of any civilized country to-day.

We find then that there are two sentiments in the minds
of the same men at the same time. These have been
called militancy and industrialism. The latter term does
not seem to be a good one and it is not apt until we
reach high civilization; what we want is a term to express
the peace sentiment in antithesis to militancy, but industrialism has obtained currency and it has this much justification, even for savage life, that, inside the group, the
needs of life must be provided for by productive labor.
Generally that is left to the women and the men practice
militarism.

It would not be possible for neighboring groups to
remain really isolated from each other. One has in its
territory stone or salt, water or fuel, limited fruits, melons,
nuts, fish, or perhaps other natural materials which the
others need. They also take wives from each other, generally, but not always. Hence arise treaties of *commercium*
and *connubium*, which bring about a middle state of things
between war and peace. These treaties are the origin of
international law. A comparison of modern municipal
and international law will show that the difference between the relations of members of the in-group with each
other, and of the groups with each other, still exists.

[1] Pickering, W. A.: Pioneering in Formosa, 136.

If now we turn back to the question with which I started, whether men began in a state of peace or a state of war, we see the answer. They began with both together. Which preponderated is a question of the intensity of the competition of life at the time. When that competition was intense, war was frequent and fierce, the weaker were exterminated or absorbed by the stronger, the internal discipline of the conquerors became stronger, chiefs got more absolute power, laws became more stringent, religious observances won greater authority, and so the whole societal system was more firmly integrated. On the other hand, when there were no close or powerful neighbors, there was little or no war, the internal organization remained lax and feeble, chiefs had little power, and a societal system scarcely existed.

The four great motives which move men to social activity are hunger, love, vanity, and fear of superior powers. If we search out the causes which have moved men to war we find them under each of these motives or interests. Men have fought for hunting grounds, for supplies which are locally limited and may be monopolized, for commerce, for slaves, and probably also for human flesh. These motives come under hunger, or the food-quest, or more widely under the economic effort to win subsistence. They have fought for and on account of women, which we must put partly under love, although the women were wanted chiefly as laborers and so, along with the slaves, would come under the former head. They have fought to win heads, or scalps, or other trophies, and for honor or dignity, or purely for glory; this comes under the operation of vanity. They have fought for blood revenge, to prevent or punish sorcery, and to please their gods; these motives belong under the fear of superior powers. It was reserved for modern

civilized men to fight on account of differences of religion,
and from this motive the fiercest and most persistent
wars have been waged.

Is there anything grand or noble in any of these motives
of war? Not a bit. But we must remember that the
motives from which men act have nothing at all to do
with the consequences of their action. Where will you
find in history a case of a great purpose rationally adopted
by a great society and carried through to the intended
result and then followed by the expected consequences in
the way of social advantage? You can find no such thing.
Men act from immediate and interested motives like these
for which they have waged war, and the consequences
come out of the forces which are set loose. The consequences may be advantageous or disadvantageous to men.
The story of these acts and consequences makes up
human history. So it has been with war. While men
were fighting for glory and greed, for revenge and superstition, they were building human society. They were
acquiring discipline and cohesion; they were learning cooperation, perseverance, fortitude, and patience. Those are
not savage virtues; they are products of education. War
forms larger social units and produces states; of the North
American Indians, those had the intensest feeling of
unity who were the most warlike.[1] The Netherlands form
a striking example in modern history of the weakness of
a state which is internally divided; the best historian
of Dutch civilization tells us that the internal disintegration was always greatest in times of truce or of peace.[2]
There can be no doubt that the Germans of to-day owe
their preeminence in industry and science to the fact

[1] Am. Anth., N. S., IV, 279.
[2] Van Duyl, C. F.: Overzicht der Beschavingsgeschiedenis van het Neder-
landsche Volk, 190.

that they are a highly disciplined nation. A Portuguese sociologist says that "War is the living fountain from which flows the entire society." [1] If we fix our minds on the organic growth and organization of society, this assertion is not exaggerated. An American sociologist[2] says that "in spite of the countless miseries which follow in its train, war has probably been the highest stimulus to racial progress. It is the most potent excitant known to all the faculties." The great conquests have destroyed what was effete and opened the way for what was viable. What appalls us, however, is the frightful waste of this process of evolution by war — waste of life and waste of capital. It is this waste which has made the evolution of civilization so slow.

Here, then, let us turn back and see how the peace-element develops alongside the war-element. We shall find that peace-rules and peace-institutions have been established, from the earliest civilization, even for the relations of groups with each other. House-peace is perhaps the simplest form. The nature-people very often bury a man under his own fireplace, and from this usage radiate various customs, all of which go to associate the ghosts of the dead with the hearthstone of the living. It follows that quarreling, brawling, or violence near the hearth is an insult to the ghosts. Hence arises a notion of religious sacredness about the hearth an atmosphere of peace is created, and the women who live in the house and work at the hearth profit by it. The householder has a dignity and prerogative in his house, however humble his social position may be; hence the maxim that a man's house is his castle goes back to the beginning of civilization. It may be only a wind-shelter, but

[1] Martins, J. P. Oliveira: As Raças Humanas, etc., II, 55.
[2] Brinton, D. G.: Races and Peoples, 76.

the ghosts protect it; and any stranger, fugitive, sup-
pliant, even an enemy, if admitted, comes under the house
protection and hospitality while there. As the house
becomes larger and better the peace-taboo extends from
the fireplace to the whole house and then to the yard or
enclosure. This is the house-peace.

If any group which possesses deposits of salt, flint-
stone fit for implements, pipe-stone, water supply, or
special foods should try to prevent others from having
access to the same, all others would join in war against
that one until an agreement was made and established
by usage. This agreement is either one of peaceful
access to natural supplies or one of trade. Tribes also
agree to take wives from each other. We often have
reason to be astonished at the institution-making power
of nature-men when disagreeable experience has forced
them to find relief. The Tubu of the Sahara are warlike
and distrustful even of each other to such an extent that
they scarcely form a society; even in their villages they
quarrel and fight. It is a very noteworthy feature that
these people have no notion of rights. It is the in-
group as a peace-group which is the school of rights;
as we have seen, there can be peace and order inside only
by law (using this term in its broadest sense); but a law
creates and enforces rights. Now these Tubu have been
forced to make a law that inside the village no weapons
may be worn,[1] so that here already we find an institutional arrangement to limit warlikeness. When Nachtigal, visiting the Tubu, complained of their ill usage of
himself and threatened to go away, they pointed out to
him that as soon as he had left their territory he would
be at their mercy.[2] This shows that even they had an
idea of some rights of a guest inside their group as com-

[1] Nachtigal, G.: Sahara und Sudan, I, 439.   [2] *Ibid.*, I, 276.

pared with his status outside, when he would be protected by nothing. The Beduin have the same notion. They are ruthless robbers and murderers, but a guest in the tent is perfectly safe and entitled to their best hospitality. When he leaves it he is fair game, whether enemy, friend, or neighbor.[1]

The West-Australians have a usage that any man who has committed a wrong according to their code must submit to a flight of spears from all who think themselves aggrieved, or he must allow a spear to be thrust through his leg or arm. There is a tariff of wounds as penalties for all common crimes.[2] We understand that this is an in-group usage. It is a common custom in Australia that a man who has stolen a wife from an out-group must submit to a flight of spears from her group-comrades; this is now only a ceremony, but it is a peace-institution which has set aside old warfare on account of stolen women. As we have seen, the Australians live in very small groups, but they assemble from time to time in large kin-groups for purposes of festivals of a religious character. The kin-groups are not peace-groups,[3] because they are loose and have no common life. At the assemblies all the sacred objects are brought into the ceremonial ground, but on account of the danger of quarrels, no display of arms is allowed anywhere near the sacred objects.[4] Bearers of messages from one tribe to another are regarded as under a peace-taboo in eastern Australia; women are under a peace-taboo and hence are employed as ambassadors to arrange disputes between tribes. After a quarrel there is a corroboree, to make and

[1] Burchardt, J. L.: Notes on the Bedouins, etc., 90.

[2] Grey, G.: Journals of Two Expeditions of Discovery in North-West and Western Australia, II, 243.

[3] Curr: Australian Race, I, 69.

[4] Spencer, B., and Gillen, F. J.: Native Tribes of Central Australia, 135.

confirm peace.[1] These usages are institutional. They
are positive rules of an arbitrary character, depending
upon agreement and usage, but are devised to satisfy
expediency. In Queensland no fighting at all is allowed
at night in camp; those who want to fight must go
outside, and after a fight the victor must show to his comrades that he had a real grievance. If he does not con-
vince them of this they force him to submit to the same
mutilation from his victim that he has inflicted. The
women fight with their yam-sticks, which are about four
feet long. One woman allows the other to strike her
on the head; the second must then submit to a blow;
thus they go on until one does not want any more.[2]
What we have to notice here is that the fight, inside the
group, is under regulations, which fact makes it institutional. The duel is a similar case of a conventionalized
fight in the midst of a peaceful civil order. In all these
cases we see that war is admitted inside of a peace-group
when individuals are wronged or offended by comrades,
but only in conventionalized and regulated form, so that
it is a kind of lawful war.

We also find war between groups under some regulation and conventionalization when there is a bond of
kinship or religion uniting the two groups. It appears
that this is the origin of the rules of war by which its
horrors are reduced. On the island of Tanna in the New
Hebrides the eight thousand inhabitants are divided into
two groups, one at each end of the island, and each group
is subdivided into villages. If two villages in the same
division fight, as they often do, the fighting is not intense

[1] Mathews, R. H.: Message-sticks used by the Aborigines of Australia, in
Am. Anth., X, 290; Smyth, R. B.: Aborigines of Victoria, I, 165, 181; Curr,
Australian Race, I, 92.

[2] Roth, W. E.: Ethnological Studies among the North-West-Central Queensland Aborigines, 141.

and there is no cannibalism; but between the two big
divisions there is blood revenge, and if they fight there is
no limit to the ferocity, cannibalism being then practiced.[1]
On the Mortlock Islands when two tribes go to war each
warrior must select as his antagonist on the other side
one who is not in the same kin-group with himself.[2]
Amongst certain Sumatrans if a man of one village has
a grievance against a man of another, the men of the
former go into the fields of the other, where they are
met by the local chief, who asks their errand.   They
answer that they have come to destroy the plantation
of the man in the village who has injured a man of
theirs.   The chief admits that this is just, but proposes
to avoid violence; so he brings to them fruit from the
plantation of the offender and, if the offense was great,
he allows them to destroy a certain number of trees on it.
They also burn down the offender's house "ceremonially"
— a little hut is built of light material on his field and
with triumphant cries is set on fire by the offended party.
Generally an agreement is reached, but if not, long hostilities endure between two neighboring villages.[3]

The Christian states have always professed to moderate
somewhat the horrors of war when they went to fighting
with each other, and so we have laws of war which are
good between the states agreeing to them, but not with
outsiders.   This makes a limited peace-group of all the
states which unite now to make international law.   Let us
follow these peace-institutions up into higher civilization.

The Scandinavian people spread in small bodies over
their territory, and these bodies often engaged in war with
each other.   They had a common sanctuary at Upsala at

[1] Australian Association for the Advancement of Science, 1892, 648.
[2] Finsch, O.: Ethnologische Erfahrungen und Belegstücke aus der Südsee,
III, 311.
[3] Snouck-Hurgronje, C. S.: De Atjèhers, I, 81–83.

which there were annual festivals. This religious bond
kept up a certain sense of national unity, which, however,
has never produced national sympathy. At the festivals at
Upsala peace was enforced for the time and place[1]; disputes were settled and fairs held, and there were also feasts
and conferences. The Swedes in the thirteenth century
formed kin-groups which adopted rules of mutual succor
and defense.[2] The dwellings of kings also came to have
in so far the character of sanctuaries that peace was
maintained around them.[3] The ancient Germans maintained by law and severe penalties peace for women as to
person and property; the penalties for wrong to a woman
varied in the laws of the different German nations, but
were two or three times as great as for wrongs to men.[4]
The house-peace was also very fully developed in German
law.[5] The Peace of God was perhaps the most remarkable case in history of a law to establish a time-taboo
against war and violence. In the tenth century the
church tried to curb the robber barons and to protect
merchants; the attempts were often repeated with little
result, but the "Truce of God" was at last established
in 1041 by the Bishop of Arles and the Abbot of Cluny,
and it won some acceptance throughout France. There
was to be no fighting between Wednesday evening and
Monday morning; later these limits were changed.[6]
No such law was ever obeyed with any precision and it
never became a custom, much less an institution, but it
had some influence. As the kings gained real power and
prestige in the feudal states they made the king's peace

[1] Geijer, E. G.: Svenska Folkets Historia, I, 12, 112.
[2] Montelius, O.: Sveriges Historia, I, 461.
[3] Folklore, 1900, 285.
[4] Stammler, C.: Ueber die Stellung der Frauen im alten deutschen Recht, 9.
[5] Osenbrüggen, E.: Der Hausfrieden.
[6] Van Duyl, C. F.: Beschavingsgeschiedenis, etc., 110.

a great reality; it went with the development of the modern state. The king's peace was a name for a central civil authority which could put down all private war and violations of public order and establish a peace-group over a great extent of territory, within which rights, law, and civil authority should be secured by competent tribunals. In the Holy Roman Empire of the German nation the public general peace of the empire was introduced in 1495, but the emperors never had the means to enforce it, and it did not exist until 1873. We can see how the king's peace grew by the following case: Canute the Dane made a law in England that, if any unknown man was found dead, he should be assumed to be a Dane and a special tax, called *murdrum*, should be paid for him to the king. William the Conqueror followed this example, only the unknown man was assumed to be a Norman; if it could be proved that he was an Englishman ("proving his Englishry") then the murderer or the hundred had nothing to pay to the king but only the legal compensation to the family of the deceased, if he had one.[1] This means that the king first extended his peace over his own countrymen by a special penalty on the murder of one of them, while Englishmen were left only under the old law of compensation for blood revenge; but in time equal protection was extended to all his subjects. Again, at the time of the Conquest all crimes committed on the roads which ran through a city (Canterbury, for instance) were crimes against the king's peace — which also extended one league, three perches, and three feet beyond the city gate. This means that the high roads which ran through a town were first brought under the king's peace, and this peace also extended beyond the royal burgh for an extent which

[1] Inderwick, F. A.: The King's Peace, 27.

was measured with droll accuracy. What was a crime
elsewhere was a greater crime there, and what was not
a crime elsewhere might be a crime there. King Edmund
forbade blood revenge in his burgh[1]; that is, he delimited
an in-group in which there must be law and an administration of justice by his tribunal; Jews and merchants
bought the protection of the king's peace throughout
his realm. From this germ grew up the state as a peace-
group and the king's peace as the law of the land; we
Americans call it the peace of the people.

One of the most remarkable examples of a peace-
group which could be mentioned is the League of the
Iroquois which was formed in the sixteenth century;
it deserves to be classed here with the peace-institutions
of civilized states. This league was a confederation of
five, afterwards six tribes of Indians, to maintain peace.
By Indian usage blood revenge was a duty; but the
Iroquois confederation put a stop to this, as between its
members, by substituting laws and civil authority. It
was, for its stage, fully as marvelous a production of
statesmanship as are these United States — themselves
a great peace-confederation. Compared with Algonkins
and Sioux the Iroquois were an industrial society. They
tried to force others to join the confederacy — that is,
to come into the peace-pact or to make an alliance with
it; if they would do neither, war arose and the outside
people was either exterminated or absorbed.[2] Hiawatha
was the culture-hero to whom the formation of the league
was attributed The constitution was held in memory
by strings of wampum, and at annual festivals there were
confessions and exhortations. The duties inculcated were

[1] Maitland, F. W.: Domesday Book and Beyond, 184.

[2] Hale, H.: The Iroquois Book of Rites (in Brinton, D. G.: Library of Abo-
riginal American Literature, No. II), 68, 70, 92; Morgan, L. H.: League of the
Iroquois, 91.

those of a warrior towards outsiders and of tribal brother-
hood towards insiders. "The duty of living in harmony
and peace, of avoiding evil-speaking, of kindness to the
orphan, of charity to the needy and of hospitality to all,
would be among the prominent topics brought under
consideration" at the annual assemblies.[1]

We have now found a peace of the house, of the sanctuary, of religion, of the market, of women, of the popular
assembly, and of the king, all of which were legal and
institutional checks upon war and an introduction of
rational and moral methods in the place of force. Let
us see next what has been the relation between religion
on the one side and peace or war on the other.

Those who perform the rites of worship towards the
same ancestors or the same gods come into the same cult-
group, but no religion has ever succeeded in making its
cult-group into a peace-group, although they all try to
do it. The salutation of members of a cult-group to
each other is very generally "Peace," or something
equivalent. Quakers call themselves "Friends" and
always have a closer bond to each other than to the
outside world. Such a peace-group is only an ideal for
all who profess the same religion; in most of the great
religions down to the seventeenth century, dissenters or
heretics were always treated with great severity, because
it was thought that they would bring down the wrath
of the ghost or the god not only on themselves but also
on the whole community. The New England Puritans
had this notion that the sins of some would bring down
the wrath of God on the whole. Religion has always
intensified ethnocentrism; the adherents of a religion
always think themselves the chosen people or else they

[1] Morgan, L. H.: League of the Iroquois, 190; Hale, H.: Iroquois Book of
Rites, 32.

think that their god is superior to all others, which
amounts to the same thing. The Jews looked down upon
all non-Jews as Gentiles; the Mohammedans despise all
infidels — their attitude towards non-Mussulmans is one
leading to aggression, plunder, and annihilation. The
Greeks looked down on all non-Greeks as barbarians,
but in their case the sentiment was only partly religious;
they themselves were never united by their own religion.
In the thirteenth and fourteenth centuries, when Mohammedanism threatened to overwhelm Christendom, Latin
Christians were inflamed with greater rage against Greek
Christians than against Mohammedans. Nicholas V in
1452 gave to Alfonso V of Portugal authority to subjugate
any non-Christians, having in view especially people of
the west coast of Africa, and to reduce them to servitude
(*illorum personas in servitutem*), which probably did not
mean slavery, but subjection.[1] The Spaniards and Portuguese of the sixteenth century treated all aborigines with
ruthlessness because the aborigines were outside of
Christianity and entitled to no rights or consideration.
When the American colonies revolted, the English were
amazed that the colonists could ally themselves with
Frenchmen against the mother-country, although the
French were Roman Catholics in religion, absolutists
in the state, and of an alien nationality. Buddhism is
characterized by a pervading peacefulness, but no religion has ever kept its adherents from fighting each
other. The instances which have been cited suffice to
show that religion has been quite as much a stimulus to
war as to peace; and religious wars are proverbial for
ruthlessness and ferocity.

Christianity has always contained an ideal of itself
as a peace-group. The mediæval church tried to unite

[1] Raynaldus, O.: Annales Ecclesiasticae, etc., 18, 423.

all Christendom into a cult- and peace-group which should reach over all the disintegration and war of the feudal period. This was the sense of mediæval Catholicity. Churches, convents, and ecclesiastical persons were put under a peace-taboo. The church, however, at the same time, entered into an alliance with the feudal nobles and adopted militant methods; heretics were dealt with as outside the fold. The modern state, as it began to take definite form, entered into a contest with the church for the control of society and for the guardianship of peace, because the church had failed to secure peace.

The United States presents us a case quite by itself. We have here a confederated state which is a grand peace-group. It occupies the heart of a continent; therefore there can be no question of balance of power here and no need of war preparations such as now impoverish Europe. The United States is a new country with a sparse population and no strong neighbors. Such a state will be a democracy and a republic, and it will be "free" in almost any sense that its people choose. If this state becomes militant, it will be because its people choose to become such; it will be because they think that war and warlikeness are desirable in themselves and are worth going after. On their own continent they need never encounter war on their path of industrial and political development up to any standard which they choose to adopt. It is a very remarkable fact, and one which has had immense influence on the history of civilization, that the land of the globe is divided into two great sections, the mass of Europe, Asia, and Africa on the one side and these two Americas on the other, and that one of these worlds remained unknown to the other until only four hundred years ago. We talk a great deal about progress and modern enlightenment and democracy and

the happiness of the masses, but very few people seem
to know to what a great extent all those things are consequences of the discovery of the new world. As to this
matter of war which we are now considering, the fact
that the new world is removed to such a distance from
the old world made it possible for men to make a new
start here. It was possible to break old traditions, to
revise institutions, and to think out a new philosophy to
fit an infant society, at the same time that whatever
there was in the inheritance from the old world which
seemed good and available might be kept. It was a
marvelous opportunity; to the student of history and
human institutions it seems incredible that it ever could
have been offered. The men who founded this republic recognized that opportunity and tried to use it. It
is we who are now here who have thrown it away; we
have decided that instead of working out the advantages of it by peace, simplicity, domestic happiness,
industry and thrift, we would rather do it in the old way
by war and glory, alternate victory and calamity, adventurous enterprises, grand finance, powerful government,
and great social contrasts of splendor and misery. Future
ages will look back to us with amazement and reproach
that we should have made such a choice in the face of
such an opportunity and should have entailed on them
the consequences — for the opportunity will never come
again.

Some illustration of our subject has, however, been
furnished by the internal history of our peace-group.
The aborigines of this continent have never been taken
into our peace-bond, and our law about them is, consequently, full of inconsistencies. Sometimes they have
been treated as comrades in the in-group; sometimes as
an out-group with which our group was on a footing of

hostility. Another question seems to be arising with respect to the negroes; we have been trying, since the Civil War, to absorb them into our peace-bond, but we have not succeeded. They are in it and not of it now, as much as, or more than, in the days of slavery, for the two races live more independently of each other now than they did in those former days. The Southern States do not constitute true societies because they lack unity of interest and sentiment, on account of the race difference which divides them. This discord may prove worse and more fatal to the internal integrity of the peace-group than such old antagonisms of interest as disturb Ireland, the national antagonisms which agitate Austria-Hungary, or the religious antagonisms which distract Belgium. In short, a state needs to be a true peace-group in which there is sufficient concord and sympathy to overcome the antagonisms of nationality, race, class, etc., and in which are maintained institutions adequate to adjust interests and control passions. Before even the great civilized states have reached this model, there is yet much to be done.

If we look at these facts about peace-laws and institutions and the formation of peace-groups in connection with the facts previously presented about the causes of war and the taste for war, we see that militancy and peacefulness have existed side by side in human society from the beginning just as they exist now. A peaceful society must be industrial because it must produce instead of plundering; it is for this reason that the industrial type of society is the opposite of the militant type. In any state on the continent of Europe to-day these two types of societal organization may be seen interwoven with each other and fighting each other. Industrialism builds up; militancy wastes. If a railroad is built, trade and intercourse indicate a line on which it ought to run; military

strategy, however, overrules this and requires that it
run otherwise. Then all the interests of trade and intercourse must be subjected to constant delay and expense
because the line does not conform to them. Not a discovery or invention is made but the war and navy bureaus
of all the great nations seize it to see what use can be
made of it in war. It is evident that men love war;
when two hundred thousand men in the United States
volunteer in a month for a war with Spain which appeals
to no sense of wrong against their country, and to no
other strong sentiment of human nature, when their
lives are by no means monotonous or destitute of interest,
and where life offers chances of wealth and prosperity,
the pure love of adventure and war must be strong in our
population. Europeans who have to do military service
have no such enthusiasm for war as war. The presence
of such a sentiment in the midst of the most purely industrial state in the world is a wonderful phenomenon. At
the same time the social philosophy of the modern civilized world is saturated with humanitarianism and flabby
sentimentalism. The humanitarianism is in the literature; by it the reading public is led to suppose that
the world is advancing along some line which they call
"progress" towards peace and brotherly love. Nothing
could be more mistaken. We read of fist-law and constant war in the Middle Ages and think that life must
have been full of conflicts and bloodshed then; but
modern warfare bears down on the whole population with
a frightful weight through all the years of peace. Never,
from the day of barbarism down to our own time, has
every man in a society been a soldier until now; and the
armaments of to-day are immensely more costly than ever
before. There is only one limit possible to the war
preparations of a modern European state; that is, the

last man and the last dollar it can control. What will come of the mixture of sentimental social philosophy and warlike policy? There is only one thing rationally to be expected, and that is a frightful effusion of blood in revolution and war during the century now opening.

It is said that there are important offsets to all the burden and harm of this exaggerated militancy. That is true. Institutions and customs in human society are never either all good or all bad. We cannot adopt either peacefulness or warlikeness as a sole true philosophy. Military discipline educates; military interest awakens all the powers of men, so that they are eager to win and their ingenuity is quickened to invent new and better weapons. In history the military inventions have led the way and have been afterwards applied to industry. Chemical inventions were made in the attempt to produce combinations which would be destructive in war; we owe some of our most useful substances to discoveries which were made in this effort. The skill of artisans has been developed in making weapons, and then that skill has been available for industry. The only big machines which the ancients ever made were battering-rams, catapults, and other engines of war. The construction of these things familiarized men with mechanical devices which were capable of universal application. Gunpowder was discovered in the attempt to rediscover Greek fire; it was a grand invention in military art but we should never have had our canals, railroads, and other great works without such explosives. Again, we are indebted to the chemical experiments in search of military agents for our friction matches.

War also develops societal organization; it produces political institutions and classes. In the past these institutions and classes have been attended by oppression and by the exploitation of man by man; nevertheless, the more highly organized society has produced gains for all its members, including the oppressed or their posterity. The social exploitation is not essential to the organization, and it may be prevented by better provisions. In long periods of peace the whole societal structure becomes fixed in its adjustments and the functions all run into routine. Vested interests get an established control; some classes secure privileges and establish precedents, while other classes form habits of acquiescence. Traditions acquire a sacred character and philosophical doctrines are taught in churches and schools which make existing customs seem to be the "eternal order of nature." It becomes impossible to find a standing-ground from which to attack abuses and organize reform. Such was the case in France in the eighteenth century. By war new social powers break their way and create a new order. The student is tempted to think that even a great social convulsion is worth all it costs. What other force could break the bonds and open the way? But that is not the correct inference, because war and revolution never produce what is wanted, but only some mixture of the old evils with new ones; what is wanted is a peaceful and rational solution of problems and situations—but that requires great statesmanship and great popular sense and virtue. In the past the work has been done by war and revolution, with haphazard results and great attendant evils. To take an example from our own history: the banking and currency system of the United States, in 1860, was at a deadlock; we owe the national bank system, which was a grand reform of currency and banking, to the Civil War. It is impossible to see how else we could have overcome the vested interests and could have extricated ourselves from our position. It was no purpose of the war to reform the currency, but it gave an incidental opportunity and we had to win from it what we could.

There is another effect of war which is less obvious but more important. During a period of peace, rest, and routine, powers are developed which are in reality societal variations, among which a certain societal selection should take place. Here comes in the immense benefit of real liberty, because, if there is real liberty, a natural selection results; but if there is social prejudice, monopoly, privilege, orthodoxy, tradition, popular delusion, or any other restraint on liberty, selection does not occur. War operates a rude and imperfect selection. Our Civil War may serve as an example; think of the public men who were set aside by it and of the others who were brought forward by it, and compare them in character and ideas. Think of the doctrines which were set aside as false, and of the others which were established as true; also of the constitutional principles which were permanently stamped as heretical or orthodox. As a simple example, compare the position and authority of the president of the United States as it was before and as it has been since the Civil War. The Germans tell of the ruthless and cruel acts of Napoleon in Germany, and all that they say is true; but he did greater services to Germany than any other man who can be mentioned. He tore down the relics of mediævalism and set the powers of the nation to some extent free from the fetters of tradition; we do not see what else could have done it. It took another war in 1870 to root out the traditional institutions and make way for the new ones. Of course the whole national life responded to this selection. The Roman state was a selfish and pitiless subjugation of all the rest of mankind. It was built on slavery, it cost inconceivable blood and tears, and it was a grand system of extortion and plunder, but it gave security and peace under which the productive powers of the provinces expanded and grew. The Roman state gave discipline and organization and it devised institutions; the modern world has inherited societal elements from it which are invaluable. One of the silliest enthusiasms which ever got control of the minds of a great body of men was the Crusades, but the Crusades initiated a breaking up of the stagnation of the Dark Ages and an emancipation of the social forces of Europe. They exerted a selective effect to destroy what was barbaric and deadening and to foster what had new hope in it by furnishing a stimulus to thought and knowledge.

A society needs to have a ferment in it; sometimes an enthusiastic delusion or an adventurous folly answers the purpose. In the modern world the ferment is furnished by economic opportunity and hope of luxury. In other ages it has often been furnished by war. Therefore some social philosophers have maintained that the best course of human affairs is an alternation of peace and war.[1] Some of them also argue that the only unity of the human race which can ever come about must be realized from the survival of the fittest in a war of weapons, in a conflict of usages, and in a rivalry issuing in adaptability to the industrial organization. It is not probable that aborigines will ever in the future be massacred in masses, as they have been in the past, but the case is even worse when, like our Indians for instance, they are set before a fatal dilemma. They cannot any longer live in their old way; they must learn to live by unskilled labor or by the mechanic arts. This, then, is the dilemma: to enter into the civilized industrial organization or to die

[1] Gumplowicz, L.: Grundriss der Sociologie, 125.

out. If it had been possible for men to sit still in peace without civilization, they never would have achieved civilization; it is the iron spur of the nature-process which has forced them on, and one form of the nature-process has been the attack of some men upon others who were weaker than they.

We find, then, that in the past as a matter of fact war has played a great part in the irrational nature-process by which things have come to pass. But the nature-processes are frightful; they contain no allowance for the feelings and interests of individuals — for it is only individuals who have feelings and interests. The nature-elements never suffer and they never pity. If we are terrified at the nature-processes there is only one way to escape them; it is the way by which men have always evaded them to some extent; it is by knowledge, by rational methods, and by the arts. The facts which have been presented about the functions of war in the past are not flattering to the human reason or conscience. They seem to show that we are as much indebted for our welfare to base passion as to noble and intelligent endeavor. At the present moment things do not look much better. We talk of civilizing lower races, but we never have done it yet; we have exterminated them. Our devices for civilizing them have been as disastrous to them as our firearms. At the beginning of the twentieth century the great civilized nations are making haste, in the utmost jealousy of each other, to seize upon all the outlying parts of the globe; they are vying with each other in the construction of navies by which each may defend its share against the others. What will happen? As they are preparing for war they certainly will have war, and their methods of colonization and exploitation will destroy the aborigines. In this way the human race

WAR   35

will be civilized — but by the extermination of the
uncivilized — unless the men of the twentieth century
can devise plans for dealing with aborigines which are
better than any which have yet been devised. No one
has yet found any way in which two races, far apart in
blood and culture, can be amalgamated into one society
with satisfaction to both. Plainly, in this matter which
lies in the immediate future, the only alternatives to
force and bloodshed are more knowledge and more reason.

Shall any statesman, therefore, ever dare to say that
it would be well, at a given moment, to have a war, lest
the nation fall into the vices of industrialism and the
evils of peace? The answer is plainly: No! War is never
a handy remedy, which can be taken up and applied by
routine rule. No war which can be avoided is just to the
people who have to carry it on, to say nothing of the
enemy. War is like other evils; it must be met when it is
unavoidable, and such gain as can be got from it must
be won. In the forum of reason and deliberation war
never can be anything but a makeshift, to be regretted;
it is the task of the statesman to find rational means to
the same end. A statesman who proposes war as an
instrumentality admits his incompetency; a politician
who makes use of war as a counter in the game of parties
is a criminal.

Can peace be universal? There is no reason to believe
it. It is a fallacy to suppose that by widening the peace-
group more and more it can at last embrace all mankind.
What happens is that, as it grows bigger, differences, discords, antagonisms, and war begin inside of it on account
of the divergence of interests. Since evil passions are a
part of human nature and are in all societies all the time,
a part of the energy of the society is constantly spent in
repressing them. If all nations should resolve to have

no armed ships any more, pirates would reappear upon
the ocean; the police of the seas must be maintained.
We could not dispense with our militia; we have too frequent need of it now. But police defense is not war
in the sense in which I have been discussing it. War, in
the future will be the clash of policies of national vanity
and selfishness when they cross each other's path.

If you want war, nourish a doctrine. Doctrines are
the most frightful tyrants to which men ever are subject,
because doctrines get inside of a man's own reason and
betray him against himself. Civilized men have done
their fiercest fighting for doctrines. The reconquest of
the Holy Sepulcher, "the balance of power," "no universal dominion," "trade follows the flag," "he who holds
the land will hold the sea," "the throne and the altar,"
the revolution, the faith — these are the things for which
men have given their lives. What are they all? Nothing but rhetoric and phantasms. Doctrines are always
vague; it would ruin a doctrine to define it, because then
it could be analyzed, tested, criticised, and verified; but
nothing ought to be tolerated which cannot be so tested.
Somebody asks you with astonishment and horror whether
you do not believe in the Monroe Doctrine. You do not
know whether you do or not, because you do not know
what it is; but you do not dare to say that you do not,
because you understand that it is one of the things which
every good American is bound to believe in. Now when
any doctrine arrives at that degree of authority, the name
of it is a club which any demagogue may swing over
you at any time and apropos of anything. In order to
describe a doctrine we must have recourse to theological
language. A doctrine is an article of faith. It is something which you are bound to believe, not because you
have some rational grounds for believing it true, but

because you belong to such and such a church or denomination. The nearest parallel to it in politics is the "reason of state." The most frightful injustice and cruelty which has ever been perpetrated on earth has been due to the reason of state. Jesus Christ was put to death for the reason of state; Pilate said that he found no fault in the accused, but he wanted to keep the Jews quiet and one man crucified more or less was of no consequence. None of these metaphysics ought to be tolerated in a free state. A policy in a state we can understand; for instance it was the policy of the United States at the end of the eighteenth century to get the free navigation of the Mississippi to its mouth, even at the expense of war with Spain. That policy had reason and justice in it; it was founded in our interests; it had positive form and definite scope. A doctrine is an abstract principle; it is necessarily absolute in its scope and abstruse in its terms; it is a metaphysical assertion. It is never true, because it is absolute, and the affairs of men are all conditioned and relative. The physicists tell us now that there are phenomena which appear to present exceptions to gravitation which can be explained only by conceiving that gravitation requires time to get to work. We are convinced that perpetual motion is absolutely impossible within the world of our experiences, but it now appears that our universe taken as a whole is a case of perpetual motion.

Now, to turn back to politics, just think what an abomination in statecraft an abstract doctrine must be. Any politician or editor can, at any moment, put a new extension on it. The people acquiesce in the doctrine and applaud it because they hear the politicians and editors repeat it, and the politicians and editors repeat it because they think it is popular. So it grows. During the recent difficulty between England and Germany on one side and Venezuela on the other, some newspapers here began to promulgate a new doctrine that no country ought to be allowed to use its naval force to collect private debts. This doctrine would have given us standing-ground for interference in that quarrel. That is what it was invented for. Of course it was absurd and ridiculous, and it fell dead unnoticed, but it well showed the danger of having a doctrine lying loose about the house, and one which carries with it big consequences It may mean anything or nothing, at any moment, and no one knows how it will be. You accede to it now, within the vague limits of what you suppose it to be; therefore you will have to accede to it to-morrow when the same name is made to cover something which you never have heard or thought of. If you allow a political catchword to go on and grow, you will awaken some day to find it standing over you, the arbiter of your destiny, against which you are powerless, as men are powerless against delusions.

The process by which such catchwords grow is the old popular mythologizing. Your Monroe Doctrine becomes an entity, a being, a lesser kind of divinity, entitled to reverence and possessed of prestige, so that it allows of no discussion or deliberation. The President of the United States talks about the Monroe Doctrine and he tells us solemnly that it is true and sacred, whatever it is. He even undertakes to give some definition of what he means by it; but the definition which he gives binds nobody, either now or in the future, any more than what Monroe and Adams meant by it binds anybody now not to mean anything else. He says that, on account of the doctrine, whatever it may be, we must have a big navy. In this, at least, he is plainly in the right; if we have the doctrine, we shall need a big navy. The Monroe Doctrine is an exercise of authority by the United States over a controversy between two foreign states, if one of them is in America, combined with a refusal of the United States to accept any respon-sibility in connection with the controversy. That is a position which is sure to bring us into collision with other States, especially because it will touch their vanity, or what they call their honor — or it will touch our vanity, or what we call our honor, if we should ever find ourselves called upon to "back down" from it. Therefore it is very true that we must expect to need a big navy if we adhere to the doctrine. What can be more contrary to sound statesmanship and common sense than to put forth an abstract assertion which has no definite relation to any interest of ours now at stake, but which has in it any number of possibilities of producing complications which we cannot foresee, but which are sure to be em-barrassing when they arise!

What has just been said suggests a consideration of the popular saying, "In time of peace prepare for war." If you prepare a big army and navy and are all ready for war, it will be easy to go to war; the military and naval men will have a lot of new machines and they will be eager to see what they can do with them. There is no such thing nowadays as a state of readiness for war. It is a chimera, and the nations which pursue it are falling into an abyss of wasted energy and wealth. When the army is supplied with the latest and best rifles, someone invents a new field gun; then the artillery must be pro-vided with that before we are ready. By the time we get the new gun, somebody has invented a new rifle and our rival nation is getting that; therefore we must have it, or one a little better. It takes two or three years and several millions to do that. In the meantime somebody proposes a more effective organization which must be introduced; signals, balloons, dogs, bicycles, and every other device and invention must be added, and men must be trained to use them all. There is no state of readiness for war; the notion calls for never-ending sacrifices. It is a fallacy. It is evident that to pursue such a notion with any idea of realizing it would absorb all the resources and activity of the state; this the great European states are now proving by experiment. A wiser rule would be to make up your mind soberly what you want, peace or war, and then to get ready for what you want; for what we prepare for is what we shall get.

THE FAMILY AND SOCIAL CHANGE

II

THE FAMILY AND SOCIAL CHANGE

[1909]

WE currently speak of the "institution" of marriage. We also use marriage instead of wedding, nuptials, or matrimony. The result is confusion. A wedding or even nuptials occur as a ceremony or festival, on a day, and as the commencement of wedlock or matrimony. Wedlock may be an institution, but a wedding is not, for a wedding lacks the duration or recurrence which belongs to an institution. It does not provide for an enduring necessity and has no apparatus for the repeated use of the same couple. Wedlock is a permanent relation between a man and a woman which is regulated and defined by the mores. It brings the pair into cooperation for the struggle for existence and the procreation and nurture of children. Wedlock therefore forms a family, and a family seems to satisfy our idea of an institution far better than marriage or matrimony. The family institution existed probably before marriage; a woman with an infant in her arms is what we see as far back as our investigations lead us. She was limited and burdened in the struggle for existence by her infant. The task of finding subsistence was as hard for her as for a man, and, in addition to this the infant was a claimant to her time and labor. Her chance of survival lay in union and cooperation with a man. Undoubtedly this gives us the real explanation of the primitive inferiority of women; they needed the help of men more than men needed theirs, and if a union was made it was made on terms under which the woman got the disadvantage.

It certainly is a great mistake to believe that the women were put down because the men were always physically stronger. In the first place the men are not always stronger; perhaps it is, as a rule, the other way. Mr. H. H. Johnston says of the Andombies on the Congo that the women, though working very hard as laborers in general, lead a happy existence; they are often stronger than the men and more finely developed, some of them having splendid figures. Parke, speaking of the Manyuema of the Arruwimi in the same region, says that they are fine animals, and the women very handsome. They are as strong as the men. In North America an Indian chief once said to Hearne, "Women were made for labor; one of them can carry, or haul, as much as two men can do." Schellong says of the Papuans in the German protectorate of New Guinea that the women are more strongly built than the men.[1] According to Kubary,[2] a man has the right to beat his wife, but the women are so robust that a man who tries to do it may well find that he will get the worse of it. Fights between men and women are not rare in savage life, and the women prevail in a fair share of them; Holm mentions a case where a Greenland Eskimo tried to flog his wife, but she flogged him.[3] We hear of a custom in south-eastern Australia that fights between the sexes were provoked when "there were young women who were marriageable but were not mated, and when the eligible bachelors were backward. The men would kill a totem animal of the

---

[1] Ellis, H.: Man and Woman, 4.
[2] Beitrag zur Kenntnis der Núkuóro- oder Monteverde-Inseln, 35.
[3] Ethnologisk Skizze af Angmagsalikerne, 55.

women or the women would kill a totem animal of the men. This led to a fight of the young men and young women; then, after the wounds healed they would pair off and the social deadlock would pass away." [1] Another case, from higher civilization, shows how the woman was weakened by considerations of another kind. Sieroshevski, a Pole, who lived for twelve years among the Yakuts, says that he knew a Yakut woman who was constantly abused by her husband, although she was industrious and good-natured. At last the European asked her why she did not fight. He assured her that she would succeed and he argued with her that if she would once give her husband a good beating he would not misuse her any more. She, however, answered that that would never do, that her husband's companions would deride him as the man whose wife beat him, and their children would be derided by the other children for the same reason. She would not do anything which would produce that consequence and would make her worse off. This case has many parallels. A characteristic incident occurred at the Black Mountain station on the Snowy River about the years 1855–56. "A number of Theddora (Ya-itma-thang) blacks had come across from Omeo and there met a woman, known to me as Old Jenny, of their tribe, who had broken their law by becoming the wife of a man to whom she stood in the tribal relationship of *Najan* (mother). She had been away for some years, and this was the first time that her kindred had encountered her. The wife of one of them attacked her first with a digging-stick, but she defended herself so well with the same weapon that the woman had to desist, and her husband continued the attack on Old Jenny, who had divested herself of all but one small

[1] Howitt, A. W.: South Eastern Australia, 149.

garment. He commenced with a club, but finding he could not hit her, changed it for a curved club with which he tried to 'peck' her on the head over guard. After a time he also had to give it up, and they had to make friends with the invincible woman. This is an instance of the manner in which the women are able to defend themselves with their weapon, the yam-stick, being no mean opponents of a man armed only with a club." [1]

The status of woman was generally sad and pathetic in savage life, but we may accept it as an established fact that this was not because she was physically inferior to man, but was due rather to inferiority in the struggle for existence on account of maternity. In the family the man often tyrannized over the woman, and the woman came into the family unwillingly, driven by a greater necessity, but the family was not a product of force. It was a product of contract. It was controlled by the mores which soon established notions of the right way to behave and of rights and duties which would be conducive to prosperity and happiness.

In this primitive society the family became the arena in which folkways were formed and taught, traditions were handed down, myths were invented, and sympathies were cultivated. The mother and the children were in the closest association and intimacy. The instruction of example without spoken command or explanation was the chief instruction. It makes little difference whether we think of a family in a horde or of monandrous family of Australians or Bushmen. The children learned from their mothers the usages which were domestic and familiar, which underlie society and are moral in their character. At puberty the boys went with their fathers into the political body and became

[1] Howitt, A. W.: *l.c.*, 197.

warriors and hunters. Then they were disciplined into the life of men and left the family. They got wives and founded families, but the father, in his own family, was an outsider and a stranger with few functions and little authority.

Mohammed gave approval to the father-family, which seems to have been winning acceptance in his time. Islam is founded on the father-family. In the Koran women are divided into three classes in respect to marriage: first, wives, that is, status-wives with all the rank, honor, and rights which the name implies; second, concubines, that is, wives of an inferior class, in a permanent and recognized relation, but without the rank and honor of wives; third, slaves, whose greatest chance of happiness was to "find favor" in the eyes of their master or owner. This classification of the wives was also a classification of the mothers, and it produced jealousy and strife of the children. Only men of rank and wealth could have households of this complex character. Those of limited means had to choose which form of wife they would take. The full status-wife could make such demands that she became a great burden to her husband, and it appears that the Moslems now prefer concubines or slaves. In Mohammedan royal families the jealousies and strifes of children, where the son of a slave might be preferred and made heir by the father, have reduced kingdoms and families to bloodshed and anarchy.

In general, in the mother-family, the domestic system must have lacked integration and discipline. The Six Nations or Iroquois had the mother-family in well-developed form. Each woman with her husband and children had a room about seven feet square in the "long house." This room was separated from others inhabited by similar families, not by a partition, but only by a pole three or four feet

from the floor, over which skins were hung. Each family
shared fire with another family opposite, and evidently
privacy was only imperfectly secured. Any man who
did not bring in what was considered his fair share of
food-supply could be expelled at any time. A husband
had to satisfy not only his wife, but all her female relatives if he was to be in peace and comfort. He could
withdraw when he chose, but he must leave his children,
for they belonged to his wife. He must also keep the
peace with all the other husbands in the house, although
it is easy to see that frequent occasions of quarrel would
occur. In short, the man had constant and important
reasons to be dissatisfied with the mother-family. He
always had one alternative: he could capture a woman
outside the group. If he did this he distinguished himself by military prowess and the woman was a trophy.
He was not limited in his control of her or of their children
by any customs or traditions, and he could arrange his
life as he pleased. We should expect that great numbers
of men would try this alternative, but it does not appear
that many did so. If they had done so they would have
speedily introduced man-descent and the father-family.
As we well know, uncivilized men do not freely reflect
on their experience or discuss reforms or speculate on
progress; they accept custom and tradition and make the
best of it as they find it. The change to the man-family
was brought about by some great alteration in the conditions of the struggle for existence or by the invention of
a new tool or weapon used by the men or by war with
powerful neighbors. This much, however, can be said
with confidence about the family under woman-descent:
it was the conservative institution of that form of society
and in it traditions were cherished and education was
accomplished. It did not encourage change or cherish

reforms, but preserved what had been inherited and protected what existed.

Probably the change from mother-family to father-family was by far the greatest and most important revolution in the history of civilization. This was so because the family, especially in primitive society, is such a fundamental institution that it forces all other societal details into conformity with itself. Miss Kingsley, speaking of the negroes of West Africa, describes societal details as follows: "The really responsible male relative is the mother's older brother. From him must leave to marry be obtained for either girl or boy; to him and the mother must the present be taken which is exacted on the marriage of a girl; and should the mother die, on him and not on the father lies the responsibility of rearing the children. They go to his house and he treats and regards them as nearer and dearer to himself than his own children, and at his death, after his own brothers by the same mother, they become his heirs."[1] These details are all consistent with the mother-family and are perfectly logical deductions from its principles. There never was any such thing as woman-rule, if by that it should be understood that women administered and conducted in detail the affairs of house or society, directing the men what they should do or not do; but the women of the Iroquois regulated the house life; they owned the land, in the only sense in which Indians could conceive of land-owning, because they tilled it; they established the reputation of warriors, and so determined who should be elected war chief in any new war, and they decided the treatment of captives. Women, however, never made a state, and war, so long as the woman-family existed, was always limited and imperfect. It was never

[1] Travels in West Africa, etc., 224.

decided whether a man must fight with his wife's people
or go back to the clan in which he was born and fight
with that. War was oftenest about women or about
blood revenge. It was, as among our Indians, a raid
and not a persistent campaign; it was mean, cowardly,
savage, and marked by base bloodshed.

Much of this seems strange and inverted to us, because
our society has long been characterized by the father-
family. The state has long been the institution, or set
of institutions, on which we rely for our most important
interests and our notions of kinship, of rights, of moral
right or wrong; and our ways of property, inheritance,
trade, and intercourse have all been created by or adjusted to the system of man-descent. We can see what
a great revolution had to be accomplished to go over
from woman-descent to man-descent. Christian missionaries often find themselves entangled in this transition. In West Africa the native tie between mother
and children is far closer than that between father and
children, and the negro women do not like the change
which white culture would bring about. In native law
husband and wife have separate property, so that if white
man's law was introduced, the woman would lose her
property and would not get her husband's. The man also
objects to giving his wife any claim on his property, while
at the same time he does not want the children saddled
on him. It seems to him utter absurdity that it should
be his duty to care more for his wife than for his mother
and sister.[1] At every point, in going over to the father-
family, there is a transfer of rights and power and a
readjustment of social theory.

In the long history of the man-family men have not
been able to decide what they ought to think about

[1] Kingsley, M. H.: West African Studies, 377.

women. It has been maintained that woman is man's
greatest blessing and again that she is a curse. Also
the two judgments have been united by saying that she
is a cheat and a delusion, that is, she looks like a blessing
while she is a curse. Each of those exaggerated views
supports the other. Every blessing may appear doubtful,
under circumstances; every curse will sometimes appear
to be a blessing. What was most important about both
these views was that man was regarded as independent
and complete in the first place and the woman was brought
to him as a helpmeet or assistant; at least as an inferior
whose status and destiny came from her position as an
adjunct. That was the position of woman in the man-
family. We have abandoned part of the harshness of
this construction of the status of woman and all the
unkind deductions from it; the moral inferences, however, remain, and we regard them as self-evident and
eternal. Loyalty to her husband is the highest virtue
of a woman, and devotion to her family and sacrifice for
it are the field of heroism for her. We speak of the
Christian family as the highest form of the family, and
in our literature and our current code the Christian
family is considered as furnishing women with their
grand arena for self-culture and social work. I cannot
find that Christianity has done anything to shape the
father-family; of the Jewish form the Old Testament
tells us hardly anything. In Proverbs we find some
weighty statements of general truths, universally accepted, and some ideal descriptions of a good wife.
The words of Lemuel in chapter 31 are the only didactic
treatment of the good wife in the Old Testament; she
is described as a good housekeeper, a good cook, and a
diligent needlewoman. Such was the ideal Jewish
woman. In the New Testament there is no doctrine

of marriage, no description of the proper family, and no exposition of domestic virtues. Down to the time of Christ it appears that each man was free to arrange his family as he saw fit. The rich and great had more than one wife or they had concubines. The Talmud allowed each man four wives, but not more. In fact, at the birth of Christ, among Jews, Greeks, and Romans, all except the rich and great had no more than one wife each, on account of the trouble and expense of having more. Yet if circumstances, such as childlessness, seemed to make it expedient, anyone might take a second wife. Therefore it became a fact of the mores, of all but the rich and great, that all practiced pair-marriage and were educated in it.

Christianity took root in the lowest free classes. It got the mores from them and in later centuries gave those mores authority and extension, and this is the origin and historical source of the Christian family. The Pharisees are credited with introducing common sense into domestic relations. They made the Sabbath an occasion of "domestic joy," bringing into increasing recognition the importance and dignity of woman as the builder and guardian of the home. They also set aside the seclusion of women at childbirth, in spite of the law.[1] A leader of the Pharisees introduced the *Ketubah*, or marriage document, "to protect the wife against the caprice of the husband." The Shammaites would not permit a wife to be divorced except on suspicion of adultery, but the Hillelites allowed more easy divorce, for the "welfare and peace of the home."[2] The ancient Romans practiced pure monogamy, but after they developed a rich leisure class, in the second century B.C., they developed a luxurious polygamy. The

[1] Lev. 12 : 4–7; 15 : 19–24.   [2] Jewish Encyclopedia, IX, 663 f.

traditions which came down into the Christian church were confused and inconsistent and various elements have from time to time got the upper hand in the history of the last nineteen hundred years. Gide says: "In a word, the law of the gospel accomplished a radical revolution in the constitution of the family. It broke domestic tyranny and recomposed the unity of the family by uniting all its members under mutual duties. It elevated and ennobled marriage by giving it a heavenly origin, and it made of marriage a union so intimate and so holy that God alone can break it."[1]

This is a good literary statement of what is generally taught and popularly believed, but it is impossible to verify it. We cannot tell what was the origin of our modern pair-marriage, but it grew up in the mores of the humble classes in which Christianity found root. In the first centuries of the Christian era the leading classes at Rome went through rapid corruption and decay, but the laboring classes had little share in this life. Christian converts could easily hold aloof from it. During the first four centuries Christians believed that the world was about to perish, and evidently this belief affected the whole philosophy of life, for marriage lost sense and the procreation of children lost interest.[2] It also helps to explain the outburst of asceticism and extravagant behavior, such as the renunciation of conjugal intimacy by married people. Paul also, as is well known, discusses the renunciation of marriage, but he speaks with remarkable restraint, and urges objections. John of Asia Minor appears in tradition as the apostle of virginity, and the glorification of virgins[3] confirms this view of his; but

---

[1] Étude sur la condition privée de la Femme dans le droit ancien et moderne, 195.

[2] This may be seen in I Cor., chap. 7.   [3] Apoc. 14: 4.

54   ESSAYS OF WILLIAM GRAHAM SUMNER

it is something quite different from this when false
teachers are said in the Pastoral Epistles to hinder marriage.[1] Procreation as such was considered sin, and the
cause of death's domination. Christ came to break away
from it.[2] On the other hand, we have the idealizing
of Christian motherhood[3]; woman may fall into sin, but
shall be saved through child-bearing. Sexual impulse is
a foul frenzy, something devilish[4]; stories of the lust of
the devil and his companions after beautiful women make
up the gnostic romances. The horribleness and insatiable-
ness of the sensual passions are illustrated by all sorts of
terrible tales.[5] It may indeed have happened, as the
Acts of Thomas report, that bride and bridegroom from
the very marriage-day renounced wedlock, and man and
wife separated from one another; in particular, the
continually recurring narratives of a converted wife
avoiding common life with her unbelieving husband seem
to be taken from life. We have the express witness,
not only of Christian apologists, but also of the heathen
physician Galen, that among the Christians many women
and men abstained all their life from the intercourse of
sex. It is not possible for us to estimate the actual
spread of this kind of absolute renunciation.[6]

On the one hand the women are little thought of. In
the Clementine homilies (3 : 22) it is expressly declared
that the nature of woman is much inferior to that of
man. Women, except the mother of Clement, play
almost no rôle in this romance.[7] Professor Donaldson[8]
shows the error of supposing that Christianity raised the

[1] I. Tim. 4 : 3.
[2] Satornil *apud* Iren., i, 34. 3; Tatian, *ibid.*, 38. 1; Gospel of the Egyptians.
[3] I Tim. 2 : 15.   [4] Act Joh., 113, 213.
[5] Dobschütz, E. von: Christian Life in the Primitive Church, 261, 262.
[6] *Ibid.*   [7] *Ibid.*, 263.
[8] Contemporary Review, September, 1889.

status of women. "It is rather a formulation due to dogmatic than historical interests to assert that the worth of women came to recognition first in Christianity and in Christianity from the very beginning." [1]

Renan says that Christianity, in the second century of the Christian era, "gave complete satisfaction to just those needs of imagination and heart which then tormented the populations" around the Mediterranean. It offered a person and an ideal, and made no such demand on credulity as the old mythologies which had now lost their sense. It joined stoicism in hostility to idols and bloody sacrifices, and the faith in Jesus superseded ritual. Renan thinks it a wonder that Christianity did not sooner win control, but at Rome all the civil maxims were against it. [2] The latest scholars also recognize the strong rivalry between Christianity and Mithraism.

Tertullian (born 160 A.D.) was an extremist among Christian ascetics, but he was one of the ablest and most influential men of his time. Addressing women he says [3]: "Woman, thou shouldst always be dressed in mourning and in rags, and shouldst not offer to the eyes anything but a penitent drowned in tears and thus shouldst thou pay ransom for thy fault in bringing the human race to ruin! Woman, thou art the gate by which the demon enters! It was thou who corruptedst him whom Satan did not dare to attack in face [man]. It is on thy account that Jesus Christ died." It was the doctrine of the church fathers who lived about 400 A.D. that marriage is a consequence of original sin, and that, but for the first sin, God would have provided otherwise for the maintenance of the human species. [4] "Let us cut up by

[1] Zscharnack, L.: Der Dienst der Frau in den ersten Jahrhunderten der christlichen Kirche, 5.   [2] Renan, E.: Marc-Aurèle, 582–85.
[3] De Cultu Feminarum, I, 1.   [4] See Chrysostom: De Virginitate, I, 282.

the roots," said Jerome, "the sterile tree of marriage. God did indeed allow marriage at the beginning of the world, but Jesus Christ and Mary have now consecrated virginity." Virginity thus furnished the ideal in the church, and not honest wedlock.

Juvenal and Tacitus give us pictures of Roman (heathen) society in the first centuries of the Christian era which would make us doubt if there was any family at all, but some of our later historians have well pointed out that we ought not to take the statements in Juvenal and Tacitus as characteristic of all Roman society. Let me quote two or three passages from Dill about Roman women of the empire: "Tacitus, here and there, gives glimpses of self-sacrifice, courageous loyalty, and humanity, which save his picture of society from utter gloom. The love and devotion of women shine out more brightly than ever against the background of baseness. Tender women follow their husbands or brothers into exile, or are found ready to share their death. Even the slave girls of Octavia brave torture and death in their hardy defence of her fair fame. There is no more pathetic story of female heroism than that of Politta, the daughter of L. Vetus. . . . Vetus himself was of the nobler sort of Roman men, who even then were not extinct. When he was advised, in order to save the remnant of his property for his grandchildren, to make the emperor chief heir, he spurned the servile proposal, divided his ready money among his slaves, and prepared for the end. When all hope was abandoned, father, grandmother, and daughter opened their veins and died together in the bath. . . .

"The bohemian man of letters [Juvenal] had heard many a scandal about great ladies, some of them true, others distorted and exaggerated by prurient gossip, after passing through a hundred tainted imaginations. In his own modest class, female morality, as we may infer from the *Inscriptions* and other sources, was probably as high as it ever was, as high as the average morality of any age. There were aristocratic families, too, where the women were as pure as Lucretia or Cornelia, or any matron of the olden days. The ideal of purity, both in men and women, in some circles was actually rising. In the families of Seneca, of Tacitus, of Pliny, and of Plutarch, there were not only the most spotless and high-minded women, there were also men with a rare conception of temperance and mutual love, of reverence for a pure wedlock, to which S. Jerome and S. Augustine would have given their benediction. Even Ovid, that 'debauchee of the imagination,' writes to his wife, from his exile in the Scythian wilds, in the accents of the purest affection. . . .

"Dion Chrysostom was probably the first of the ancients to raise a clear voice against the traffic in frail beauty which has gone on pitilessly from age to age. Nothing could exceed the vehemence with which he assails an evil which he regards as not only dishonoring to human nature, but charged with the poison of far-spreading corruption. Juvenal's ideal of purity, therefore, is not peculiar to himself. The great world was bad enough; but there was another world beside that whose infamy Juvenal has immortalized. . . .

"From the days of Cornelia, the mother of the Gracchi, to the days of Placidia, the mother of Honorius, Roman women exercised, from time to time, a powerful, and not always wholesome, influence on public affairs. The politic Augustus discussed high matters of state with Livia. The reign of Claudius was a reign of women and freedmen. Tacitus records, with a certain distaste for the innovation, that Agrippina sat enthroned beside Claudius on a lofty tribunal, to receive the homage of the captive Caractacus.   Nero emancipated himself from the grasping ambition of his mother only by a ghastly crime. The influence of Cænis on Vespasian in his later days tarnished his fame. The influence of women in provincial administration was also becoming a serious force. . . . Thus Juvenal was fighting a lost battle, lost long before he wrote. For good or evil, women in the first and second centuries were making themselves a power."[1]

The Christian emperors made the dower of the wife not simply the property of the two spouses. It was the endowment of the new household, a sort of reserve fund which the law assures to the children which they would find intact in spite of the ruin of their family, if it should occur. The dower was offset also by the gift *propter nuptias* which the man must give. The law also provided that the dower and the gift *propter nuptias* should be equal and that the spouses should have the same rights of survivorship.[2] These seem to be distinct improvements on the dotal system, but that system has dropped out of popular use in modern times and the advantage of this legislation has been lost with it.

The family was more affected by the imperial constitutions of the fourth century, which enacted the views and teachings of the clergy of that time. Constantine endeavored to put an end to concubinage, and the power of mothers over their children as to property and marriage was made equal to that of fathers.[3] It appears that the collapse of the ancient society and the decay of the old religion with the rise of Christianity and Mithraism with new codes of conduct and duty produced

---

[1] Dill, S.: Roman Society from Nero to Marcus Aurelius, 48, 49, 76, 77, 81.   [2] Gide: *l.c.*, 215.   [3] Cod. Theod., IV, 9.

anarchy in the mores, which are the everyday guides of
men as to what they ought to do. On the one side we
find asceticism and extreme rigor and then by the side
of it, in the Christian church, extravagant license and
grotesque doctrine. What element conquered, and why,
it seems impossible to say. The society of western
Europe emerged from the period of decay and rejuvena-
tion in the twelfth century with some wild passions and
dogmas of commanding force. Overpopulation produced
social pressure and distress with the inevitable tragedy
in human affairs. The other world was figured by un-
restrained imagination and religion went back to primitive daimonism.

Out of this period came the canon law. "Of all civil
institutions, marriage is the one which the canon law
most carefully regulated, and this is the idea from which
all its prescriptions were derived; *viz.*, marriage is a
necessary evil which must be tolerated, but the practice
of which must be restrained."[1] The doctrine of this
law is that "woman was not made in the image of God.
Hence it appears that women are subordinated to men,
and that the law meant them to be almost servants in
the household."[2] From this starting-point the law went
on rationally, although it contained two inconsistent
ideas, the merit of wedlock and the merit of celibacy.
The product of such inconsistency was necessarily base.
Some parts of the literary record which remain to us
would lead us to believe that the whole society was brutal
and vicious, but when we think of the thousands of
families who died without ever making a mark on the
record we must believe that domestic virtue and happiness were usual and characteristic of the society. The
best proof of this is presented by the efforts at reform

---

[1] Gide, *l.c.*, 202.   [2] Can. 13–19, caus. xxxiii, qu. 5.

throughout the fifteenth century and the vigor of the
reformation of the sixteenth century. The hot disputes
between Protestants and Catholics turned chiefly on the
doctrine of the mass and on sacerdotal claims, but they
contained also an element of dissatisfaction with inherited
mores about marriage and the family. The Protestants
denounced the abuses which had grown up around the
monasteries and the gratuitous misery of celibacy. They,
however, lost the old ideas about marriage and divorce
and the Catholics denounced them for laxity and vice.
At the Council of Trent, in 1563, the Catholics made a
new law of marriage, in which they redefined and strengthened the ritual element.

Out of all that strife and turmoil our modern family
has come down to us. The churches and denominations
are now trying to win something in their rivalry with
each other by the position they adopt in regard to marriage and divorce and the family. The family in its
best estate, now among us, is a thing which we may
contemplate with the greatest satisfaction. When the
parents are united by mutual respect and sincere affection and by joint zeal for the welfare of their children,
the family is a field of peace and affection in which the
most valuable virtues take root and grow and character
is built on the firmest foundation of habit. The family
exists by tradition and old custom faithfully handed on.
Our society, however, has never yet settled down to
established order and firm tradition since the great convulsion of the sixteenth century. Perhaps the family
still shows more fluctuation and uncertainty than any
other of our great institutions. Different households
now differ greatly in the firmness of parental authority
and the inflexibility of filial obedience. Many nowadays
have abandoned the old standards of proper authority

and due obedience. The family has to a great extent lost its position as a conservative institution and has become a field for social change. This, however, is only a part of the decay of doctrines once thought most sound and the abandonment of standards once thought the definition of good order and stability. The changes in social and political philosophy have lowered the family. The family has not successfully resisted them. Part of the old function of the family seems to have passed to the primary school, but the school has not fully and intelligently taken up the functions thrown upon it. It appears that the family now depends chiefly on the virtue, good sense, conception of duty, and spirit of sacrifice of the parents. They have constantly new problems to meet. They want to do what is right and best. They do not fear change and do not shrink from it. So long as their own character is not corrupted it does not appear that there is any cause for alarm.

THE STATUS OF WOMEN IN CHALDEA, EGYPT, INDIA, JUDEA, AND GREECE TO THE TIME OF CHRIST

III

THE STATUS OF WOMEN IN CHALDEA, EGYPT, INDIA, JUDEA, AND GREECE TO THE TIME OF CHRIST

[1909]

IN general, the status of women has been controlled, in all civilization up to the highest, by their power to help in the work of life. Where women have had important functions they have been valued; where they have needed protection and support, and have not been able to contribute much, they have been treated with contempt. If the economic situation is strong, so that each man can pay a good price for a wife, girls are valuable; in the contrary case female infanticide arises. If the women's contribution to the food supply is essential, women are well treated; while if the men are warlike meat-eaters, they treat women as drudges, tempering the treatment with respect for them as necessary mothers of warriors. Among nomads the status of women is low, and women, children, and the aged are regarded as burdens. The two former are necessary, but all are treated capriciously. Under agriculture women win a position of independent cooperation. When towns are built women incur dangers on the streets and complications arise; their position in rural life is then far more free than in towns. Public security in the latter once more changes the case. When women are valued for grace and beauty and are objects of affection, not means of gain, they win, as compared with earlier stages. An Arabic Jew of the

tenth century, Ibrahim Ibn Jakub, says of Poland at
that time that grain was cheap and the bride-price for
wives high. Therefore, if a man had many daughters,
he was rich; if he had many sons he was poor.[1] The
interplay of interests under the forms of material gain,
sex-passion, and vanity is here most complicated and
fierce; but the interference of philosophy and religion is
noticeably slight. The phases are many, and there is
not a feeling of the human heart which does not bear
upon the sex-relation in one way or another. Masculine
love of rule and domination, and masculine generosity
to an object of affection, have modified every status.
Fuegians prefer boys, who when they grow up will be a
means of strength and protection to their parents.[2] The
Amarr-Bambala celebrate the birth of a boy with a ban-
quet; boys will become the strength of the country as
hunters and warriors.[3] The Ossetes celebrate the birth
of boys only.[4] Such is the usual sentiment, but in frequent cases girls are preferred. The Basutos find it a
financial calamity if a woman bears all boys, for girls are
salable and constitute a capital.[5] In Kamerun a girl is
preferred because she will soon bring a bride-price.[6]
Amongst Hindus, "when a son is born there is great
rejoicing in the family and friends come with their con-
gratulations, but on the birth of a daughter there are
no sounds indicative of gladness in the house."[7] When
a boy is born the conch shell is blown to call all the
neighbors to rejoice; when a girl is born the conch shell is

[1] Geschichtschreiber der deutschen Vorzeit, XXXIII, 141.
[2] A Voice from South America, XIII, 201.
[3] Vannutelli, L., e Citerni, C.: L'Omo, 195. This tribe is located about
38° E., $5\frac{1}{2}$° N.
[4] Haxthausen, A. F. von: Transkaukasia, II, 54.
[5] Archivio per la Antrop., XXXI, 459.   [6] Globus, LXXXVI, 393.
[7] Wilkins, W. J.: Modern Hinduism, 339.

silent and neighbors offer condolences.[1] "It is believed by an average Hindu that a male child is the fruit of the propitiation of ancestors." [2] The Aryans thought daughters a sorrow, sons the father's pride and glory.[3]

The status of women is therefore a symptom of the mores because all the interests and feelings of man converge in it. It furnishes one of the most prominent illustrations of the traditional persistence of the mores through ages, even in spite of changes in interests, and of the ultimate triumph of interests in the mores. The phenomena are intricate and perplexing, but it is certain that we can never understand them unless we follow those indications in them which show us the mores as their ultimate explanation.

The remotest stage of civilized society which is known to us is that represented in the laws of Hammurabi as existing in the Euphrates valley 2500 years before Christ. In those laws men and women appear to be on an equality of personal rights. Three classes, wives, concubines, and slaves, are recognized.[4] The laws of Hammurabi and the laws of Moses point back to a common law of the Semitic peoples of Western Asia (Müller traces this out), and the society is evidently an old one, with well-established folkways, which are codified in these laws. Winckler [5] is able to show, from the position of the vernal equinox in the signs of the zodiac, that Chaldean culture must date back to the fifth millennium B.C., and Barton fixes dates as far back as 6000 B.C. The code of Hammurabi is elaborate and systematic,

[1] Wilkins, W. J.: Modern Hinduism, 10.

[2] Journal of the Asiatic Society of Bombay, V, 72.

[3] Zimmer, H.: Altindisches Leben, 318.

[4] The story of Abraham, Sarah, and Hagar conforms exactly to the law of Hammurabi (Müller, D. H.: Die Gesetze des Hammurabis, 140).

[5] Die Babylonische Kultur, etc., 30.

and so it can hardly have been the first one. Back of
it there must have been a long period of usage and custom. It is assumed in the laws of Hammurabi that a
man will have but one wife, but as to concubines and
slaves he arranges his affairs as he judges expedient for
his own welfare. The laws define the rights of the parties in certain contingencies, and thus make wedlock a
legal status, not a contract. The status, however, is
plainly the product of mores which have been matured
through a long period. The marriage gifts also show
that long usage had produced elaborate customs. The
bridegroom pays a bride-price (a survival of primitive
purchase), but he also gets a dowry with his wife; furthermore the bride's father gives her a gift which is a
peculium of hers — pin money — and the groom also
gives her a present. Men can repudiate their wives at
will, but they must provide for the wives if the latter
are not guilty. If the woman is childless, the relation
has failed of its primary purpose and is dissolved as a
matter of course. A woman who has borne a child to
a man, even if she is only a slave, has a claim on him
and security by his side. Women can also leave their
husbands, if the latter fail of the duties of a husband.
There were consecrated women under religious vows, but
not vowed to virginity, and public women. Müller[1]
thinks that perhaps these two classes are priests who
dress in woman's dress and women who dress in man's
dress — two classes of hierodules. The former were provided for under a system which was equivalent to life-
annuity.[2] Among the Tel-el-Amarna tablets[3] (1500 B.C.)
there is a story of a god and his wife. He abuses her,

---

[1] Gesetze des Hammurabis, 144.

[2] Winckler, H.: Die Gesetze Hammurabis, Königs von Babylon um 2250
v. Chr., 22.   [3] No. LXXXVI.

but when she remonstrates they make up the quarrel and "whatsoever she wished to have done was done from that time forth forever more."

The laws of Hammurabi show that the problems of matrimony were the same 2500 years before Christ that they are now, and have been ever since. It is asserted that the excavations of Telloh show that the mother-family existed in Chaldea in the third millennium B.C.; that the wife was "goddess of the home," and that she could expel her husband from it.[1] Later, perhaps through Semitic influence, the man got control and the institutions of the father-family were fully developed; *e.g.*, *patria potestas*, sacrifices by the father to ancestors. A son could take only a concubine, not a wife, without the father's consent. A slave woman would resent it if her master took no notice of her; the popular poetry represented her case, and there was reason to fear her arts and magic.[2]

In the old Babylonian kingdom the husband could dismiss his wife at will by giving her a bill of divorcement, and frequent injunctions not to do it show that it often occurred; consequently the woman was powerless and rightless against her husband, although her dignity and authority in the house and over her children were great. If repudiated she could marry again.[3] Repudiated wives, however, were the "strange women" of antiquity; wandering adventuresses, without husbands or status where they were met with, and living by vice.[4] As wealth and social activity increased in the Euphrates valley, polygamy became commoner, women were se-

---

[1] Harper's Magazine, No. 524, 201.
[2] Maspero, G.: Histoire Ancienne des Peuples de l'Orient, I, 735.
[3] Meissner, B.: Beiträge zum Altbabylonischen Privatrecht, 14.
[4] Erman, A.: Ægypten und Ægyptisches Leben im Alterthum, I, 223.

cluded more and more, and they lost their primitive
independence of status. In Chaldea all women of the
higher classes were cloistered in the harem and never
appeared by the side of husbands and brothers as they
did in Egypt.[1] The harem system, at least for Western
Asia and Europe, originated here. The contracts of the
period of Babylonian and Assyrian glory show that
wives were then rarely bought; one such contract only
from that period is known, but the terms in it are more
crassly commercial than in the contracts of the old Babylonian period.[2] A wife brought a dowry to her husband,
or there were no gifts, or each father stated in the contract
what he would give to the young people; if there was
a dowry the ownership remained in the wife, but the
husband had the use; if a man refused his approval to
the marriage of his son, the woman whom the son took
became a slave. Married women could do business and
make contracts without the intervention of their husbands in any way.[3] A very important device, which
helped to produce monogamy, was the stipulation in the
contract that, if the man took a second wife, he should
pay a specified amercement. Many contracts have been
found in which slave concubinage and prostitution are
provided for in the most matter-of-fact, commercial
terms.[4] The Assyrians were fierce and cruel; the Babylonians were more poetical, industrial, and artistic.[5] The
former represent on their monuments very rarely any
domestic scenes; a queen is once shown feasting with the
king,[6] but the only other women on the monuments are

[1] Maspero: *l.c.*, I, 707.   [2] Marx, V.: Die Stellung der Frauen in
Babylonien gemäss den Kontrakten aus der Zeit von Nebukadnezar bis
Darius, in Beiträge zur Assyriologie, IV, 6.   [3] *Ibid.*, 11, 30, 49.

[4] Kohler, J., und Peiser, F. E., Aus dem babylonischen Rechtsleben, I, 7, 8;
IV, 28 ff.

[5] Rogers, R. W.: A History of Babylonia and Assyria, II, 316.

[6] Rawlinson, G.: Five Great Monarchies, I, 492.

captives. Female charms are rarely noticed. We must, however, note that the monuments are all from public buildings.[1] In Babylonia every woman must, once in her life, submit to a stranger, in the temple of Melitta (Venus), for money, which was put in the temple treasury.[2]

Wherever women are treated with tyranny and cruelty, and are denied rights, that is, redress, they kill their husbands. In the laws of Hammurabi a woman who killed her husband was to be either hanged or impaled, the meaning of the word being uncertain.[3] With increasing wealth and the distinction of classes, the mores for rich and poor diverged, for women who had property could defend their interests. They held and administered property, made contracts, etc. In the poem of Gilgamesh, the hero, addressing the ghost of his friend and enumerating the miseries of the dead, says: "Thou canst no longer embrace the wife whom thou lovest, nor beat the wife whom thou hatest." [4] We must take this to represent the mores of the highest classes. Women of the lower classes in Chaldea, whether legitimate wives or not, went about the streets freely unveiled, while those of the upper classes lived in seclusion, or, if they went out, were surrounded by attendants.[5] In all societies women of the poorer classes have to encounter annoyances and have to protect themselves, while seclusion becomes, for the richer, a badge of superiority and a gratification of vanity. Usages which were devised to cherish and pet women become restraints on their liberty and independence, for when they are treated as unequal to the risks and tasks of life by men who take care of them, the next stage is that the men treat them as in-

---

[1] Tiele, C. P.: Babylonische-Assyrische Geschichte, 596.
[2] Herodotus, I, 199.   [3] Müller: Gesetze des Hammurabis, 128.
[4] Maspero: l.c., I, 588.   [5] Ibid., 739.

ferior and contemptible, and will not grant them dignity and respect. When they escape responsibility they lose liberty. Nevertheless, the customs, if introduced by the higher classes, spread downward by imitation; so it must have been with clositering and veiling. Men got security without care, women got the sense of refinement and elegance and of aristocratic usage; the interest of men and the vanity of women thus cooperated to establish the folkways which lowered the status of the latter.

In the early Aryan society the status of a wife depended on whether she was childless, bore daughters, or bore sons. In the first case she was blamed, being considered guilty, and was treated accordingly; in the last case she enjoyed honor.[1]

In that form of the religion of India which appears in the laws of Manu, and in the Mahabharata (about the beginning of the Christian era), fathers chose husbands for their daughters and proposed the marriage, but women also proposed to men who pleased them. Manu allows them to choose, but disapproves of it because the motive would be sexual desire, and for the same reason he classes love marriages as a bad form of marriage.[2]

"Husband-selections" were public ceremonies at which the suitors of princesses entered into competition for them, although the woman could, to some extent at least, set aside the result.[3] Devayani was given as a wife by her father to Yayati; he also gave her maid with her, telling Yayati to honor her, but not to make her his wife. Yayati begot two sons by his wife and three by the maid, and therefore Devayani went home to her father, saying: "Yayati has learned what duty is [from the Veda] and yet he has committed sin."[4] In the Nal episode the

[1] Ihering, R.: The Evolution of the Aryan, 343.   [2] III, 39.
[3] Holtzmann, A.: Indische Sagen, I, 254.   [4] Ibid., II, 108.

hero, charmed by the consent of the heroine, promises her life-long fidelity.[1] "The best medicine of the physicians is not so good for a man, in any ill, as a faithful and beloved wife." [2] There are, in the poem, very striking love stories, especially about the fidelity and sacrifice of lovers, but one woman says that a wife turns away from a husband who has cherished her as soon as he gets into trouble. A little trouble, it is said, outweighs in the minds of women long happiness; they have fickle hearts, and no great virtues can win them to fidelity.[3] The law of India is full of hostile expressions against the female sex; it not only puts them in a position of inferiority to men, but even refuses them the position of persons˜ endowed with independent rights. Manu[4] says: "It is the nature of woman to seduce man in this world"; "women are able to lead astray in this world, not only a fool, but even a learned man, and to make him a slave of desire and anger." A woman is to be always under tutelage; she can have no property, give no testimony, maintain no suit, make no contracts, and conduct no affairs. The books, however, contain also expressions of praise of women, and these fundamental principles are traversed to some extent by more humane ideas. "Where women are honored there the gods are pleased, but where they are not honored no sacred rite yields reward"; "in that family where the husband is pleased with his wife and the wife with her husband, happiness will assuredly be lasting." [5] In the early philosophical period women were freely admitted to hear and share in the discussion of theological and philosophical questions.[6]

The law-givers conceive of woman as a necessary evil.

---

[1] Holtzmann, A.: Indische Sagen, II, 18.
[2] Ibid., II, 27.   [3] Ibid., II, 266.
[6] Hopkins, E. W.: The Religions of India, 382-384.
[4] Manu, II, 213.
[5] Ibid., III, 56, 60.

She is the soil which man requires to produce the desired offspring of marriage. This is one of the many cases in which the status of woman has been influenced by the accepted notions about the respective shares of the sexes in procreation. Marriage is the only sacrament in India in which woman has a share. The essentials of the wedding are the ceremonial of joining hands and taking seven steps together around the sacred fire with recital of formulas of blessing. The ceremony was entirely domestic and the parties married themselves. Marriage by purchase is one of the honorable forms, but Manu says[1]: "No man who knows the law must take even the smallest gratuity for his daughter; for a man who, through avarice, takes a gratuity is a seller of his offspring." The bride-price is to be construed otherwise. Other texts recognize this form of marriage with less reserve. Jolly says that the apparent revulsion against purchase was not in the mores, but was a symptom of a more friendly tone of mind of the lawgiver toward women. In southern India purchase is at the present time almost the only form of marriage. In the Vedic hymns the relation of husband and wife is represented as one of intimate affection, confidence, and cooperation. The place of the wife was especially marked by the fact that she participated with her husband in the household sacrifices, and in the house she was in authority over all the inmates. Only one could occupy this position. Manu's[2] precepts for a wife are that, although the husband is destitute of virtue, or seeks pleasure elsewhere, she is to regard him as a god, and is to make no vow or sacrifices apart from him. Manu also expresses the "one flesh" idea: "Learned Brahmins propound this maxim likewise: 'The husband is declared to be one with the wife.'"[3]

[1] III, 51.   [2] Ibid., V, 154.   [3] Ibid., IX, 45.

The jurists expressed this mystical unity in the provisions that man and wife could not go surety for each other, bear witness, contract debts, maintain suits, or divide property with each other. These are necessary corollaries of the "one flesh" doctrine. In respect to joint property there has been an important development toward the independence of women.[1] In the wedding ceremony the groom led the bride around the domestic fire-altar three times, saying: "I am male; thou art female. Come, let us marry. Let us possess offspring. United in affection, illustrious, well-disposed toward each other, let us live for a hundred years."[2] Although this formula was here directed only to procreation, it is an interesting historical parallel to the Roman formula and to a German formula, which latter ones had relation to rights.

"We shall not err if we understand that women in Iranian antiquity had substantially the same status as in Vedic India, or amongst the ancient Germans, or in the Homeric age of Greece. In all these cases we meet with the same conditions"[3]; that is to say, that in the ultimate forms of civilized society the status of women which we find is the same.

In the Zendavesta the sexes appear equal in rights and honor, but they never were so in fact in historical times. Zoroaster, according to the tradition, had three wives.[4] Each man had concubines and slaves according to his means and his own judgment of his personal welfare, as was the case throughout the whole ancient world. The most remarkable feature of the Iranian social system

[1] Jolly, J.: Ueber die rechtliche Stellung der Frauen bei den alten Indern, etc., 421–439; Zimmer, H.: Altindisches Leben, 315–318.

[2] Monier-Williams, M.: Brahmanism and Hinduism, 363.

[3] Geiger, W.: Ostiranische Kultur, etc., 243.

[4] Jackson, A. V. W.: Zoroaster, 20.

was the injunction to practice the closest incestuous marriages as the most meritorious.[1] This is a very interesting case of the survival of primitive mores into a later religion, and the reason for it was intense desire to maintain the blood-purity of a caste, a desire which had become a predominant motive.[2] For this reason, although courtesans existed, intercourse with them was strongly disapproved, and the mores imposed strict rules on women of the nation.[3] A man was praised for giving his daughter in marriage and ordered to do so as penance for his own sins; thus the interests of the daughter might be subordinated to those of the father. The wedding ceremony was a union of hands with prayers and formulas of words, in which, and in the ceremonies of transfer to her husband's house, the bride is spoken of as the comrade and equal of her husband and as his companion in the household.[4] On the one hand, these rules imposed on a man a status-wife, and on the other hand, as in all such cases, they caused love unions with foreigners and defeated their own purpose. Marriage was encouraged and premiums were given for large families, which seems to show that the premiums were necessary.[5] There are historical cases in which Persians showed very great attachment to their wives.[6]

The status of women in the Old Testament is that which has been described as prevailing in Western Asia in the earlier form. Very little is said about women; they play no rôle, and have no function in religion. Ruth is a heroine because when she, as a widow, had a right

[1] Darmestetter, J.: The Zendavesta, 126.

[2] Tiele-Gerich: Geschichte der Religion im Altertum, etc., II, 1, 165.

[3] Geiger, W.: Ostiranische Kultur, 337.   [4] *Ibid.*, 241.

[5] Spiegel, F.: Eranische Alterthumskunde, III, 679; Darmestetter, J.: Zendavesta, I, 46.

[6] Herodotus, 9, 111; Plutarch: Artaxerxes.

to return to her home and people, she chose to remain with her husband's family and nation and to adhere to his religion. Esther is a political heroine, while Athaliah and Jezebel seize power, as women did upon occasion in other states. In the Proverbs we hear what a good thing a good woman is; what a bad thing a bad woman or wife is. This might all be equally well said of husbands, but it is not said, because it was not in the mores to think of men in the same light. The model woman[1] is an industrious housewife. Woman is a coadjutor to man, though, according to the story in Genesis, she brought woe upon him. "The status of woman is characterized by the fact that she was always the property of some man"; she was the property of her father, who sold her to her husband. Her duty was to bear children and do household work. The man was not bound to exclusive fidelity; the woman was, under penalty of death. A priest might not mourn for his wife,[2] for she was not as near to him as his family kin, including his unmarried sister. This excluded his married sister, as if she went into the kin of her husband, which is inconsistent. A widow did not inherit from her husband, but the heir must care for her. A woman's vow required the confirmation of her father or husband.[3]

A man could have concubines and slaves; it was, however, a very important effect of the later strict endogamy of the Jews that these could be only Jews, and were, therefore, in a protected status, and were nationally equal to the wife; but the case of a war-captive, necessarily a foreigner, at the mercy of the captor, is allowed for.[4] Polygamy was the current usage[5]; divorce was easy at

[1] Prov. 31. [2] Lev. 21 : 1; Ezek. 44 : 25.
[3] Num. 30 : 4; cf. Buhl, D. F.: Die socialen Verhältnisse der Israeliten, 30.
[4] Deut. 21 : 10. [5] Deut. 21 : 15.

the will of the man; motherhood was the chief function
of women. Throughout the canon of the Old Testament
violation of the sex-taboo is earnestly condemned and
made a subject of warning and of prohibition in the name
of Yahveh. Sex-vice, including abortion, exposure of
infants, and child sacrifice, are set forth as the distin-
guishing traits of the heathen, and an abomination to
Yahveh. The prophets were constantly fighting the
mores of the Jews, which coincided with those of the
other people of Western Asia.[1] The Jews who returned
to Judea were a selection of those who had the strongest
national feeling and who thought that the captivity
had been a chastisement of Yahveh. In the rabbinical
period, with intenser national feeling, the antagonism to
heathenism and sex-vice was even more strongly emphasized, and they often hold the first place in ethical
exhortation and discussion. The importance attached,
in the New Testament, to eating things offered to idols
might not seem comprehensible, but it is conjoined with
denunciation of sex-vice, and sex-vice and heathenism
went together, and were the antipodes of Christianity.
These sentiments entered deeply into the Jewish mores
of the rabbinical period, while the standard of marital
life, the conception of matrimony, and the status of
women remained about on the level of the surrounding
nations. Women were held to be inferior, as agents of
seduction and evil; a father or husband had a hard task
to keep daughter or wife from evil.

In Esdras [2] is an interesting argument to prove that
woman is the most powerful thing amongst men; she is
alluring and may be wicked, and is classed with wine as
a cause of ruin to men.[3] All the wisdom of all the ages

[1] Ezek. 8 : 6–11; 22 : 9–11.
[2] I, 3 : 13.   [3] Eccles., chaps. 9, 19, 25, and 26.

and nations reiterates the same few propositions. The woman was held to strict fidelity in marriage, but not the man. The rule of divorce in Deut. 24: 1 was greatly enlarged, although sects differed about it. Hardly anywhere in the rabbinical writings do we find any high conception of wedlock [1]; in the rabbinical period there was a tendency to depreciate all sex-relations, as a consequence of the strong antagonism to heathenism; there is even some glorification of virginity and of long widowhood,[2] and a legend that Rachel withdrew from conjugal life and chose continency.[3] The Essenes, beginning in the second century B.C., rejected marriage and depended on new adherents to continue their sect. The Therapeuts did not reject marriage, but they honored celibacy.[4] The Talmudists said that a man might marry as many wives as he could support, but he was exhorted to take not more than four; it appears doubtful if many men in that period (early centuries of the Christian era) took more than one.[5] Polygamy was put under definite taboo in 1020 A.D.; women were also given more and more definite right of divorce, and divorce by the man from caprice or malice was restrained. Still dicta are quoted which allow wide freedom of divorce to both.[6]

The biblical scholars [7] now tell us that the story of the creation of woman in the second chapter of Genesis dates from about 775 B.C. It is very primitive myth-making. The processes and machinery are all described. So the woman is made out of a rib of man, and the man

[1] Cf. I Cor. 11 : 9–15.   [2] Luke 2 : 36.

[3] Bousset, D. W.: Die Religion des Judenthums im neutestamentlichen Zeitalter, 401–404.

[4] Ibid., 443, 445.

[5] Bergel, J.: Die Eheverhältnisse der alten Juden, etc., 10.

[6] Klügmann, N.: Die Frau im Talmud, 37–46.

[7] Smith, H. P.: Old Testament History.

perceives that he and she were "one flesh." Then follows the enigmatical utterance that the man shall leave father and mother and go to his wife. In what social horizon could that rule arise? Nobody in the father-family ever did it, except heiress-husbands.[1] However, but for this rule there would be no establishment of pair-marriage in this text. If the husband goes to the wife he will have but one, unless it be exceptionally or by some confusion of usages. The first chapter of Genesis is held to have been written not before 500 B.C. It is very simple and direct, and is written as history, not myth; the human race is created in two sexes, and nothing states or implies pair-marriage. It cannot be supposed that the man was said to go to the woman, in opposition to almost universal usage, in order to suggest pair-marriage. Then modern men have read their own mores into these texts, and established such a tradition that we do not perceive that the text does not contain the institution. How could the Jews practice polygamy through their whole history if on the first page of the law stood an injunction of pair-marriage? They did not see it there because it is not there.

The position of women amongst the Jews at the time of Christ was what it was generally in the Greco-Roman world; their place was domestic and their chief function was to bear children. The New Testament Gospels contain very little about women, but later Christian hagiology created myths about the two Marys and Martha to satisfy the demand. The Epistles contain doctrines of marriage which are not fully consistent. One view is that marriage is a *pis aller* for sin.[2] The most important question is that of the effect on a pre-

---

[1] As in Num. 36.

[2] I Cor. 7; the same doctrine appears in Rev. 14 : 4.

existing marriage of conversion of husband or wife to Christianity. The rabbis held the current contemptuous opinion of women; Hillel is quoted as saying, "More women, more witchcrafts." [1] Woman, according to the current belief, was not saved through the Law, but through child-bearing.[2] Philo gives as the reason why the Essenes did not marry that "a wife is a selfish creature, immoderately smitten with jealousy, terrible at shaking to their foundations the natural habits of a man, and bringing him under power by continual beguilements. For as she practices fair false speeches and other kinds of hypocrisy, as it were upon the stage, when she has succeeded in alluring eyes and ears, like cheated servants, she brings cajolery to bear upon the sovereign mind. Moreover, if there are children she begins to be puffed up with pride and license of tongue, and all the things which before she speciously offered in a disguised manner in irony, she now summons forth with a more daring confidence, and shamelessly forces her way into actions, every one of which is hostile to communion. For the man who is bound under spells of wife or children, being made anxious by the bond of nature, is no longer the same person toward others, but is entirely changed, having become, without being aware of it, a slave instead of a free man." [3]

The status of women in Egypt was so free that the Greeks ridiculed the Egyptians as woman-ridden; Herodotus [4] says that the women went to market and the men wove at home. Descent was through women and was marked by the mother's name, which the child bore, while the tie of father and child was slight.[5] In the tombs of the old kingdom (before 2000 B.C.) the wife and

---

[1] Cook, K.: The Fathers of Jesus, II, 127.   [2] I Tim. 2 : 15.
[3] Philo: Apology of the Jews, frag. *apud* Eusebius; Cook: *l.c.*, II, 7.
[4] II, 35.   [5] Maspero: *l.c.*, I, 51.

mother of the deceased are represented; hardly ever the
father. A very peculiar arrangement was that a man's
next heir was his grandson by his eldest daughter, and
that a boy's next friend and protector was his maternal
grandfather. This arrangement was very ancient and
was deeply rooted in the mores.[1] The women of the
harem of Thothmes III got up a conspiracy against him
(about 1600 B.C.) and were able to organize a large force
of men and officers in it.[2] From about 740 B.C. a college
of priestesses at Thebes became the political authority
in that city, the chief priestess concentrating the political
power in herself.[3] Some of these features of society seem
to be survivals of the mother-family, but Herodotus saw
341 statues of successive priests in descent from father
to son, which covered, as the Egyptians said, 11,340
years,[4] and would indicate father descent for that period.
Herodotus [5] reports that each man had but one wife,
"like the Greeks," but Diodorus [6] says that only priests
were restricted to one. Kings certainly had more than
one and probably great men also, and there were besides
concubines and slaves. Prostitution was in effect organized in the service of religion.[7]

In the *Precepts of Ptah-hotep*, which date from about
2600 B.C., it is said: "If thou wouldst be wise, rule thy
house and love thy wife wholly and constantly. Fill
her stomach and clothe her body, for these are her personal necessities. Love her tenderly and fulfill all her
desires as long as thou hast thy life, for she is an estate
which conferreth great reward upon her lord. Be not
harsh to her, for she will be more easily moved by per-
suasion than by force. Take thou heed to that which

[1] Erman, A.: Ægypten, etc., 224.
[2] *Ibid.*, 87.
[3] Maspero: *l.c.*, III, 172.
[4] Herodotus: II, 142.
[5] *Ibid.*, I, 80.   [6] II, 92.
[7] Maspero: *l.c.*, II, 536.

she wisheth and to that to which her desire runneth, and to that upon which she fixeth her mind [and obtain it for her], for thereby shalt thou make her to stay in thy house. If thou resistest her will, it is ruin to thee. Speak to her heart and show her thy love." [1] The extremest "friend of woman" in any age might admit that these precepts are excessive; if they ever were approximately in the mores, the derision of the Greeks did not lack justification. A later writer of unspecified date warns against the "strange woman" like the writer of Proverbs [2]: "Beware of a strange woman who is not known where she is. Do not look at her when she comes and do not know her. She is like a current of deep water, the whirling force of which one does not know. The woman whose husband is absent writes to thee every day. If there is no witness near her, she rises and spreads her net! O crime worthy of death when one hears of it." Have nothing to do with her and take a wife in thy youth, because "the best thing is one's own house," and because "a wife will give thee a son like thyself." [3]

In Egypt in the class of nobles every woman "brought some land to her husband as dower, but daughters took it away again, so that the fortunes of a family depended on the proportion of females born in it. [4] Each wife had her own house, given to her by her parents or her husband; thus there was no conjugal domicile and the man was not "head of the family," but a guest in his wife's house. The wife administered her own property and received a stipend from her husband; if she contributed to the expenses, she did so voluntarily. In a marriage contract of the time of Ptolemy III (247–221 B.C.) the man promises not to claim the authority of a husband,

[1] Budge, E. A. W.: A History of Egypt, etc., II, 150.　　[2] 6 : 24.
[3] Erman, A.: Ægypten, etc., 223.　　[4] Maspero: l.c., I, 300.

to give to the woman slaves who are named, and to let her dispose of them without interference from him; he recognizes as hers all debts due to her and makes them collectible by her agent; if the husband collects any of them, he promises to pay the proceeds to her and to pay her a penalty besides. In a corresponding document, by a woman, she acknowledges the receipt of the marriage gift and of her share of the goods, and promises to return the same if she is unfaithful.[1] This last stipulation is an exact inversion of the case where the man, by custom or contract, receives a dower which he must repay if he repudiates the woman. Erman[2] thinks that conjugal relations were happy and affectionate. A widower, who had been told by a magician that his second wife had caused an illness from which he suffered, wrote and put in her tomb a letter of remonstrance, in which he rehearsed his attentions and devotion to her.

The Egyptian mores must be accounted for by the extreme traditionalism of that people which caused survivals of old customs to persist by the side of new ones. Contact with Assyrians, Babylonians, Persians, and Greeks produced change but very slowly, although Egyptian men must have been instigated to borrow foreign customs by all motives of selfish interest and vanity. Paturet[3] thinks that he can discern a change in the marriage system after about 500 B.C.; from a free and equal relation it became more servile on the part of the woman and the Semitic notion that there could be no full marriage without a property pledge was accepted in Egypt. Later the woman, without selling herself entirely, made a contract of limited duty. She was lower

---

[1] Paturet, G.: La Condition juridique de la femme dans ancienne Égypte, 42, 50, 54, 72.

[2] Ægypten, etc., I, 217.   [3] 14 to 20.

than if she had sold herself permanently or given herself away. "Nothing in his home experience had prepared a Greek to see a respectable woman come and go in liberty, without veil and without escort, carrying a burden on her shoulder instead of on her head, like a man, running about the market, keeping shop, while her husband or father was shut up at home, weaving fabrics, mixing potter's clay, and turning the potter's wheel or working at his trade. It was an easy inference that the man was a slave and the wife mistress of the family." [1] Accordingly, as soon as a Greek dynasty was seated on the throne, we find that Ptolemy IV (221–205 B.C.) made an ordinance which restrained Egyptian married women by Greek law; gifts and contracts between man and wife ceased, and the wife needed the authorization of her husband for her acts.[2] Under Mohammedanism in Egypt we find the mores completely reversed. The Roman conquest and christianization acted to remold Egyptian mores as to the status of women, a change which may have been brought about before Mohammedanism came in. All the conquerors were antagonistic to the Egyptian mores in regard to this matter, and they favored the change, which was in the interest of men.

In Homer the relations of young unmarried persons is free and unconventional, although there is a code of propriety. Wives were bought and the bargain is very purely commercial in motive; fathers were also moved by political and dynastic motives. The purchase contract and the formal ceremony distinguished the status-wife from the concubine; and there were also slaves and captives who were at their lords' mercy. The concubine or slave, who had no status, was chosen for love. "When the chief wife was also the loved wife, affection was very

---

[1] Maspero; *l.c.*, III, 797.   [2] Paturet; *l.c.*, 42.

strong and true"; the best example is that of Hector and Andromache. Wives were held to fidelity: Penelope was a heroine; Clytemnestra "led to bitter words against all women." The fidelity of women is a duty on account of the rights which their masters have acquired in them by capture or purchase; if they violate it the paramour must pay a fine. No divorce occurs in Homer. The gods and goddesses present a picture of another community marked throughout by disreputable conduct as compared with the human community.[1] The quarrels of Zeus and Hera give us a picture of conjugal life which is more distasteful than any presented as of men. The pair are vain, frivolous, and jealous, and give cause for jealousy; their love-making is not dignified; they live like a couple in a French novel, who have decided to get on by not demanding too much of each other. It is a mistake to think that the custom of "purchase" degraded women; we find that, in barbarism, purchase is explained as a remuneration to the father for the expense of rearing the girl — she is not "bought" like a slave. Purchase also runs down through all grades of ceremony and survival. Then, too, the woman's father gave her a dowry-like gift, a transaction which shows that the purchase idea no longer characterizes the relation of the parties, but is a survival by the side of a new conception of marriage. From a pecuniary point of view the two gifts were incongruous, but as regards the sentiments which determined their meaning, they could well continue together.[2] The wooing in Homer is simple and natural, open and straightforward, though the language is often naïve and to our usage unrefined. The mores are not clearly defined because of the military and heroic plane on which the poems move.

[1] Keller, A. G.: Homeric Society, chap. V.   [2] Od. I, 277; II, 53.

The women attend the heroes in the bath, a custom which to us seems inconsistent with the other sex mores but it illustrates well the power of the mores to extend approval, for the sake of an interest, to an incongruous usage. The gods give wives, so that marriages are made in heaven; they bless the marriage of a man who pleases them,[1] and they give children.[2] "Nothing is stronger and nobler than when man and wife, united in harmony of mind, rule their house in wisdom." [3] Achilles says: "Every brave and sensible man loves his consort." [4] Cases occur in which a man renounces a slave woman out of respect to his wife,[5] but there are others in which he declares that he prefers the slave woman.[6] The case of Penelope was complicated: it was not sure that her husband was dead; her son was a boy, but he grew to manhood and became her guardian as she had been his. She was clever and wise and managed well a difficult situation the phases of which changed as time went on, but always presented new difficulties. Telemachus declared to her with rude plainness that he was master [7]; he told her to go to the women's quarters and attend to the housework and to leave deliberation to men. Thus he defined her "sphere." Hesiod, as quoted in the *Anthology* of Stobæus,[8] says: "If a man has had the luck to get a wife who suits him, that is the acme of good fortune; if he has a bad one it is the worst disaster." Menander is also quoted: "If we rightly judge the matter, marriage is indeed an evil, but necessity imposes this evil on us."

Augustine [9] has preserved from Varro a myth of early

---

[1] Od., XV, 26; IV, 208.

[2] *Ibid.*, IV, 12; XVI, 117.   [3] *Ibid.*, VI, 182–184; Il., VI, 407.

[4] Il., IX, 341–342; Friedreich, J. B.: Die Realien in der Iliade und Odyssee, 197–200; especially 199 on the sex mores.

[5] Od., I, 431; Il., IX, 132; XIX, 261.   [6] Il., I, 112.

[7] Od., I, 356.   [8] 69.   [9] De Civitate Dei, XVIII, 9.

Attica. In the time of Cecrops an olive tree suddenly appeared at one place and water burst forth at another. The oracle explained the portent to mean that the people must choose between Minerva (the olive tree) and Neptune (the spring) as patron of their new city, Athens. Cecrops summoned all the people, male and female, for women then voted, to make their choice. The men voted for Neptune and the women for Minerva, and the latter triumphed by a majority of one; at this Neptune was angry and inundated Attica. The Athenians punished the women by taking from them the right to vote, by abolishing the usage that children took their names from the mother, and by depriving them of the name of Athenian women. This story seems to be a myth embodying a tradition of the mother-family and accounting for the change from it to the father-family, with a decline in the societal position of women. There are two obscure but very interesting Greek myths in which women rebel against marriage. The daughters of Prœtus treated with contempt the temple of Hera, patroness of marriage. Aphrodite punished them with madness, but after wandering about they were cured in the temple of Artemis. Their example led Argive women to forsake their husbands and slay their children; similarly the women on Lemnos despised Aphrodite and slew their husbands.[1] The myths suggest that the marriage institution was such that women revolted against it.

In the seventh and sixth centuries a series of lyric poets (Sappho, Anacreon) developed a strong erotic conception of love which was passionate and, according to later standards, vicious.[2] Such a sentiment the Greeks always understood by "love." They felt a great joy in

[1] Farnell, L. R.: The Cults of the Greek States, II, 448.
[2] Beloch, J.: Griechische Geschichte, I, 258.

living, were gay and light-hearted, but heartless and superficial. "The systematic repression of a natural appetite was totally foreign to Greek modes of thought"; "the Greek conception of excellence was the full and perfect development of humanity in all its organs and functions."[1] To such a scheme of life women were essential, but it offered them little honor. Simonides of Amorgos (seventh century B.C.) classified women, saying that God made of earth the lazy ones, of the sea the fickle ones. Other classes Simonides distinguished by the animals whom they resembled in character; for instance, the bee class was those who were industrious, thrifty, faithful — healthy mothers with grace and high virtues.[2] Aristotle says that in former times all Greeks bought each other's wives.[3] Lykurgus in Sparta and Solon in Athens[4] adopted very low and different policies about the discipline and relations of the sexes; their standpoint was that of man or the state, and woman was used for purposes assumed to be good, and in ways assumed to be expedient and practicable. Whether any good resulted to the male sex or the state under either plan is very doubtful, but the women were degraded in each case. At Athens, in order to have children of full civil standing, it was necessary that a man should marry the daughter of a citizen, but the women of this class were so secluded in the women's apartments, and lived such a remote life, that young men could not know young women. Therefore the wife of full rank was a status-wife. In the fifth century very many Athenians married foreign wives, in spite of the disabilities which their children would incur; it seems evident that they became acquainted

[1] Lecky, W. E. H.: History of European Morals, etc., II, 291; Mahaffy, J. P.: Social Life in Greece, etc., 104, 117.

[2] Bergk, T.: Griechische Literaturgeschichte, II, 197.

[3] Politics, II, 5, 11.   [4] Athenæus: Deipnos, 25.

with these women and formed attachments, which it was impossible to do with Athenian women. By the side of the legitimate order there came into existence a class of courtesans, who exercised, by education, beauty, wit, grace, and coquetry, the influence over man which belonged to woman, and to which Greeks were especially susceptible. If Athenæus may be believed, this class was very numerous. He gives a collection of the *bons mots* attributed to them and specifies the ones who were in more or less enduring relations with all the well-known men of Athens. While the status-wives were shut up at home, keeping house and nursing children, these love-wives enjoyed the society of the men and influenced the state; and some of them became famous in more ways than one. Aspasia made a trade of educating courtesans; Socrates refers to her a man whom he sought to indoctrinate with higher doctrines of conjugal duty.[1] Cicero[2] tells a story in which she appears as the instructress of Xenophon and his wife, showing them by the Socratic method that every man wants the best wife and every woman the best husband possibly to be had; therefore, to satisfy each other, each should strive to be as good as possible. She was, it appears, the competent teacher of the art of matrimony, and is credited with a share in the great movement to emancipate women. Aristophanes[3] attributes the Peloponnesian war to the anger of Pericles, on her account, against Megareans who had stolen two of her courtesans. Socrates[4] says that she was skilled in rhetoric and had taught many orators, including Pericles. Such were the mores by the end of the fifth century; wives at home like servants, intellectual recrea-

[1] Xenophon: Economicus, 3, 14.
[2] De Inventione Rhetorica, I, 31 (51).
[3] Acharnians, 524.   [4] Menexenos, 236.

tion sought in conversation, sexual passion gratified in dissipation with courtesans. This ran through the society according to wealth. In an oration against Neæra it is said: "We have courtesans for pleasure, concubines for daily companions, wives for mothers of legitimate children and for housekeepers." [1] This expressed exactly the mores of that time. In discussing the reasons for the headlong descent of the Greeks in the third and second centuries, it is to be remembered that they were breeding out their nationality by begetting children with foreigners and slaves, and by family and social mores which selected against the women of full blood.

The Greeks thought that a wise man would never confide entirely in his wife; therefore he never had complete community of interest with her. The reason was the same which would keep him from community of interest with children. He looked to women for the joy of life in all its higher and lower forms.

In the tragedies of the fifth century general statements about women often occur. They are almost always disparaging. In Æschylus's *Suppliants* the king says: "A woman's fears are ever uncontrolled," and the female chorus answers: "A woman by herself is nothing worth." In the *Agamemnon* Ægisthus says: "Guile is the woman's function." Women have no judgment, but are persuaded before the facts are known. In the *Seven against Thebes* Eteocles declares women to be a nuisance in trouble and prosperity. They are arrogant when they have power, while in war-time they get frightened and flutter about doing no good, but helping the enemy. Let them be kept out of affairs. "Oh, Zeus, what a tribe thou gavest us in women!" In the *Ajax* Tecmessa, a captive, says to her lord: "Since the hour that made me thine I live

[1] Quoted by Athenæus, XIII, 31.

for thee." In the *Eumenides* Apollo asserts that woman
does not beget; she is only nurse; the mother only cher-
ishes the germ. He uses Pallas as a proof that one could
be born without a mother, but not without a father. In
Sophocles's *Trachinian Maidens* Deianeira, the heroine,
"the most real woman's soul that the Athenian drama-
tists ever put upon the stage,"[1] says that love is invincible; she feels it herself, and so it would be madness for
her to blame her husband and his new love, if they too
have fallen under it — "No shame to them and it does
not harm me." Antigone says: "We must remember
that we are only women and cannot strive with men.
We are under authority."

In the Periclean age Athens had become a great city,
and it was hard for women to move about in it freely,
for they were in need of escort and protection. Hence
they became secluded, especially in the higher classes;
in the country they had more important functions, contributed more, and therefore were more free.[2] Thucydi-
des[3] attributes to Pericles the saying that women are
best when men never mention them, either to praise
or blame. Pericles himself, in his relation to Aspasia,
"lightly broke the barriers of the conventional morals
of the time"; "according to the spirit of that age, the
natural right of love must prevail over the right of marriage which human ordinances had created. Deliverance
from every constraint was the effort of that age, and it was
most nearly realized at Athens."[4] The current view was
that marriage was a necessary evil, a business arrangement, part of the arrangement of an establishment, an
arrangement as unsentimental as a contract to buy or
hire a house. Property interests might make a marriage

[1] Rohde, E.: Psyche, II, 237.
[2] Mahaffy, 133.
[3] II, 45.
[4] Beloch, J.: *l.c.*, I, 474.

between near relatives advantageous, and half-brother and sister by the same father (not mother) might marry. Marriages of persons brought together by affection occurred, but were very rare. Women were married young and their will or choice did not enter into the matter. There was no purchase after the sixth century, but the woman received a dowry from her family, sometimes with a promise to double it if she bore children. If such a dowry was not given, the union was regarded as hardly more than concubinage, because the man could so easily divorce the wife if he had no dowry to restore; hence the dowry was a security for the woman against his caprice.[1] The change from the custom that the suitor pays the father to the custom that the father pays the suitor is undoubtedly due to the fact that suitors became rarer than marriageable girls; for the variations in customs about marriage gifts are always significant of the conjuncture of the interests of the parties. Women who disposed of themselves were those who had no dowry, when the custom was to bring a dowry in marriage. The marriage in Greece was preceded by a formal betrothal. The wedding consisted in the delivery of the bride to the bridegroom by her *kurios*, the man who had authority over her. No officer of church or state had any function, for the proceeding was entirely domestic and belonged to the family; religious sacrifices were made some days before the wedding, but were incidental, and were made for good fortune.[2]

The distresses of the Peloponnesian war compelled the Athenians to admit to citizenship the *nothoi*, or children of Athenian men by non-Athenian mothers. There is

[1] Blümner, H.: Griechische Privatalterthümer, 260–264.

[2] Müller, O.: Untersuchungen zur Geschichte des attischen Bürger- und Eherechts, 746.

some evidence that they allowed men to take two wives each (*e.g.*, Socrates and Euripides).[1]   Possibly the public necessities also forced them to think of emancipating women,[2] for secluded wives could hardly take the initiative in such a movement.   Very strangely the initiative has been ascribed to the courtesans.   That there was such a movement is best proved by the ridicule which Aristophanes poured out on it in his *Lysistrata;* either somebody went so far as to propose community of women or Aristophanes meant to affirm that emancipation would lead to that.   In his *Woman's Parliament* he developed the farcical element in such a plan; evidently he regarded everything as mere suggestion for his fun-making. In his *Thesmophoria-festival* he took up the defense of women against utterances in Euripides's *Hippolytus.* Hippolytus is a woman-hater and celibate, but Hera, enraged at such rebellion against love, inspires a passion for him in his stepmother, Phædra.   The chorus develops the idea that love is a mighty catastrophe for joy or ill, and that Hera allows no contempt for it; love maddens the hearts and deludes the senses of all whom it attacks. The conception is that of an erotic passion.   The relationship of the two does not enter into the tragedy at all, but only that a wife may fall into such a passion and be torn between it and fidelity to her husband.   The result is torment for Hippolytus, and he vents his rage on women.   Why did Zeus ever create them to man's sorrow on earth?   They are a curse.   If more men were wanted they should have been bought.   The father gives his daughter a dowry to get rid of her, and then she costs her husband heavily for dress, etc.   He puts up with her

---

[1] Müller, O.: Untersuchungen zur Geschichte des attischen Bürger- und Eherechts, 795–797.

[2] Bruns, I: Frauenemancipation in Athen, 19 ff.

if he gains anything by marriage; if not, he makes the
best of it. If she is a simpleton, that is best. "Deliver
me from a clever one!" They plot wickedness with servants. He hates them all. Let some one prove them
chaste.

In the tragedies of Euripides the characters often discuss women — evidently the woman question had been
rising through the century. In the *Hekuba* Agamemnon
remarks: "I have a contemptuous opinion of the female
sex." Iphigenia says, in *Iphigenia amongst the Taurians:*
"A man is a great loss to his family, but a woman is not
of much account." Women sympathize with each other
and keep each other's secrets loyally. Orestes says that
women are clever at inventing tricks, and again, that
they have the gift of winning sympathy. In *Iphigenia
at Aulis* the heroine declares that the life of one man is
worth that of ten thousand women. In the *Hippolytus*
Phædra says: "I found out thoroughly that I was only
a woman, a thing which the world dislikes." In the
Andromache Andromache speaks to her maid: "Thou art
a woman. Thou canst invent a hundred ways," and
again, "No cure has been found for a woman's venom,
worse than that of reptiles. We are a curse to man."
"Men of sense should never let gossiping women visit
their wives, for they work mischief." In the *Phœnician
Maidens* one passage states: "It is the nature of women
to love scandal and gossip." In the *Medea* Medea in
soliloquy says to herself: "Thou hast cunning. Women,
though by nature little fit for deeds of valor, are expert
in mischief," and she exhorts Jason, who is a scoundrel,
"Thou shouldst not sink to the level of us poor women,
nor meet us with our own childishness." He says that
women are weak and given to tears, and that it is natural
for a woman to rave against her husband when he is

planning another marriage (as he is); that she could bear
his second marriage if she had self-control. He says that
women think all is well if married life is smooth, but that
men should have been able to get children some other
way without the existence of any women. Medea appeals
to Jason's oaths and promises to her which he pledged
with his right hand; she would not complain if she were
childless, but they have children. The sneak answers
that he is going to marry the king's daughter for the
good of the family. Medea says: "He who was all the
world to me — my own husband — has turned out a villain.
Women are unfortunate. They buy a husband at the
high price and get a tyrant. It is always a great question whether they make a good choice. Divorce is dis-
creditable to women. If we are clever enough to manage
a husband, it is well; otherwise we may better die. The
husband can go out, if vexed; the wife must stay at
home. Better go through battle three times than through
childbirth once." She is led to discuss the status of
woman: "The dawn of respect to women is breaking.
They shall be basely slandered no more. The ancient
poets wrote much about their faithlessness. This shall
cease. If Apollo had given us the gift of versifying I
would have answered them. History shows up their sex
as much as ours." In the *Bacchantes* the question is
raised whether chastity is native to women; if it is,
they will not fall when assailed in the mysteries of Dio-
nysus. In the *Andromache* the heroine says that a wife
must learn the ways of her husband's country and his
own, and not try to impose the ways in which she was
brought up. Her lord also has taken a wife who mal-
treats Andromache, the bond-maid. The wife says to
her: "Do not bring amongst us barbaric customs which
we think crimes. It is a shame here for a man to have

two wives. All men who care to live honorable lives are content to devote themselves to one lawful love." Andromache says that for Hector she would have borne a rival, if Hera had charmed him with another woman, and that she often nursed his illegitimate children to spare him annoyance. The chorus affirms that a husband should be content with one wife and not give her rights to another. In the *Electra* Clytemnæstra says that she killed her husband because he brought home a captive concubine. Women are fools, but if a man humiliates his wife, let her retaliate; she is then blamed and not he. Electra answers that if a woman has sense, she will always submit to her husband; it is not befitting for her to insist on rights. In the *Trojan Women* Hekuba tells how she behaved in wedlock in order to describe an ideal wife. She stayed at home and did not gossip. Going abroad gives a bad reputation. She was modest and silent before her husband, and knew when to rule him and when to yield to him.

Athenæus quotes a great many writers, of whom we otherwise know nothing, in regard to love, marriage, and women. They are nearly all contemptuous, sarcastic, or hostile, except where they speak of women as a means of pleasure. In no case is conjugal affection described; there is no evidence of knowledge or appreciation of it.

Aristophanes devoted three comedies to the woman question. In the *Lysistrata* the women determine to bring peace, and at the end Lysistrata, having brought together representatives of Athens and Sparta, reconciles them by arguments which any modern historian would say covered the common sense of the situation and do credit to the statesmanship of Aristophanes. If it was conceivable that women could see and urge such a solution of the case, great honor was done them, and it was most unfortunate for Greece that they were excluded from diplomacy.   In the *Thesmophoria-festival* the female chorus leader asks why, if women are a curse, men woo them, pursue, guard, and watch them, and follow them when they go away.   She tells the men that they rob the public treasury and that some of them threw away their arms in battle and ran.   Bruns[1] takes the comedies of Aristophanes as proof that there had been earlier a discussion of woman's right and status which is not in the literature, and that in this discussion it had been proposed to admit them to political functions and military service.

Thus it appears that at the end of the fifth century there was some agitation of the question of woman's status and function in society.   The philosophers of the fourth century took part in the discussion.   The first document is the dialogue in Xenophon's *Economicus*. Ischomachus, supposed to be Xenophon, gives a rhetorical and artificial statement.   It is, however, very remarkable that, even in the way of fiction, any man of that time could imagine a man making such an attempt to get upon a basis of affectionate confidence and cooperation with his wife, for the story stands entirely by itself in the literature.   The other participants in the dialogue hear with astonishment his story of his method with his wife, and what he tells of the response of the young woman shows that she had had no education to enable her to understand it; that is to say, it was entirely outside of the mores of the society.   Plato thought that the question was real, because one-half of the state was losing its effective force and happiness; he wanted women educated better, but he thought of Spartan ways with favor, even those which seemed devised to eradicate feminine

[1] Frauenemancipation in Athen, 21.

modesty and sex propriety. In this way his discussion became a Utopian speculation which had no value.[1] In the *Republic* he advances to a more sweeping theory,[2] denying that any fundamental difference of capacities or capabilities goes with the sex difference. He lays stress on the difference of muscular strength only. From these dogmatic assumptions he argues that women should have the same education as men and share all social and political functions with them.

Aristotle also thought that women should be better educated, though he regarded them as, by nature, inferior to men, and therefore created to obey. In the *Problemata* he asks why it is considered more direful to kill a woman than a man, although any male is better than any female.[3] In the *History of Animals* he says that a woman is more compassionate, tearful, envious, complaining, fond of slander, quarrelsome, despondent, imprudent, unveracious, confiding, vindictive, watchful, less active, and requires less food. In this time the bankruptcy of the Spartan system was known to all the world; the Spartan women were useless and in the way in war, and the population had fallen off so that the state was ruined by a single lost battle. Women held the property,[4] and were free, bold, intemperate, and luxurious.[5] Aristotle ended by putting women back just where they were according to the existing mores. Their powers were limited; they had a sphere which was suitable for them; let them do their duty in it.[6]

If we may judge of the views of Menander by the fragments,[7] he held very adverse judgments about women and marriage. Jerome, in his first tract against

---

[1] Laws, 781, 805, 806.
[2] Fifth and following books.
[3] Prob., XXIX, 11.
[7] In Stobæus LXX.

[4] Politics, II, 9, 2.
[5] *Ibid.*, IV, 8, 23; 15, 13.
[6] *Ibid.*, I, 5, 7; I, 13, 3 and 9; III, 4, 7.

Jovinianus, quotes Theophrastus,[1] where the question is: "Ought a wise man to marry?" The preliminary answer is: "Yes, if the woman is pretty, of good morals and breeding, and of honest parents, and if the man is in good health and rich. These conditions are rarely all fulfilled. Hence the wise man will not marry." The author proceeds to justify this opinion by very derogatory assertions about women: "Whatever defect she has, you do not know it until after the marriage. Nothing else do you buy without a trial. A wife is not shown until she is given to you, lest she may not suit you." "Women are frivolous, vicious, intriguing, exacting, and selfish. None of the reasons given for marriage will bear examination." None of these philosophers had any influence to make the sex mores better; they had no criticism of the existing mores, no conception of the evils, no plan of reform. At most the contrast with Sparta suggested some reflections.

We may gather together the features of these mores into a distinct picture as follows. Women were valued to procreate children for their husbands and the state; also to serve the pleasure of men. They were "by nature" inferior. They had no schools and their education depended on chances at home, while they lacked the stimulus of social intercourse with men. Wives and courtesans were both injured by their juxtaposition and competition and by pæderasty, which was not recognized as a vice.[2] Beloch says that it is an unfounded prejudice that Greek women, in the classical period, had an unworthy position, or that their status had fallen since the Homeric period; but he lays too much stress on purchase in Homer.[3] He further argues that the *hetæræ* gave back to Greek women

---

[1] Friedländer, L.: Sittengeschichte Roms, I, 276, refers this tract to Seneca, and it is given amongst the fragments (*de nuptiis*) at the end of Seneca's works, ed. Haase.

[2] Beloch, J.: *l.c.*, I, 232.   [3] *Ibid.*, 471.

in the Hellenistic period equality with men, and with that their rôle was played out.[1] The lot of wives was endurance, submission, and sacrifice to the egoism of men, although there were some noble exceptions, due to the personal character either of the man or the woman. Culture bore on only one-half of the nation. The "virtues" of a woman were in the main the same as those of a slave; the parallel in our time would be found in servants. Although there was no harem, the women's apartments were retired and secluded. The women and the men would meet in the house more or less, and the men might be satisfied with the women and like them. The latter were supposed to be where they belonged, performing the functions which were incumbent on them. They could go out only rarely and for especial reasons. Religious festivals gave them their only important opportunity to go abroad and see public activity. The purchase of supplies and visiting were also recognized occasions, and one or two passages are cited which recognize walking exercise as a reason for going out. The laws of Solon helped to establish the tendency of the mores in this direction.[2] No woman could go out unless she had passed her youth. The turtle was the symbol of woman; seclusion and silence. It is still an open question whether Athenian status-wives went to the theatre to see the tragedies, but it is believed that they never were present at the comedies. In this matter also the *hetœræ* were free. In the *Woman's Parliament* of Aristophanes [3] there is reference to a law requiring that men and women sit separately. It must be taken as a very significant symptom of the mores of a community if some comedies of Aristophanes ever could have been presented before a public audience even of men only; much more if any

[1] Beloch, J.: *l.c.*, 473.   [2] Plutarch: Solon.   [3] Line 21.

women were present; and if the latter were *hetæræ* the
case might be worse. We miss the evidence of the refined
taste and æsthetic sense of limits with which the Greeks
have been credited. Every woman had a "lord" and was
under tutelage. No respectable woman would appear
at table with men, even with her husband's guests in
his own home, and it was a great breach of propriety
for a man to enter another man's house when the women
were there and the man away. There were strict rules
of propriety of conduct and language in the presence of
women, but the motive was respect for the men to whom
they belonged, not for themselves. In spite of all this,
adultery of wives is spoken of as a familiar fact; also
women often ruled. In Sparta they were said to do so
commonly; but this was in part because the system concentrated land and other property in their hands.[1]   In
the fourth century there were some women who were
distinguished for the kind of learning which was current
in the period. One woman of good birth at Athens,
about 320 B.C., married a cynic for love and followed
him into his "beggar-life"; her parents disapproved but
did not forbid. There were also some women in that
period who wrote poetry.[2]   After the conquest of Alexander there is nothing more to be said about the sex mores
of Greece, for in the general relaxation of all mores, all
social energy, and all national traditions, the family fell
into the general form which prevailed throughout the
Hellenistic world. The facts which we have found show
that the Greek family would easily undergo modification
toward the Oriental form.

[1] Plutarch: Agis and Lykurgus; Becker-Hermann: Charikles, last chapter.
[2] Beloch, J.: *l.c.*, II, 442.

WITCHCRAFT

IV

WITCHCRAFT

[1909]

IN the first half of the fifteenth century, when the Church considered its victory over heresy complete, the doctrine of witchcraft was perfected. Complaint was made in 1340 that Thomas Aquinas had not stated when witchcraft was heresy. The Inquisition undertook the solution of this question, using the results of the scholastics to sustain the different notions and ward off the objections of common sense until the juristic notion of the witch was developed, which led directly to epidemic persecution.[1] Mediæval philosophy never felt the necessity of modifying a position on account of a concession which it had been obliged to make. It left the inconsistent statements side by side until they became familiar and current together. About 1430, from the confessions of witches, a comprehensive statement was made up of the tenets of the "new sect," as witches were called: the sabbath, the flight on a broomstick, the renunciation of God, the scorn of the eucharist and the cross, the worship of the devil, and the sex-crime with him, the homage to him, the murder and eating of infants, the various kinds of witchcraft; in short, the entire inventory of witch-traits, which remained the standards of witch-persecutions for three hundred years.[2]

The old tradition was that witchcraft was especially

[1] Hansen, J.: Zauberwahn, Inquisition und Hexenprozess, etc., 211.
[2] Ibid., 416.

an art of women. When the notion of sex-commerce between demons and women was invented and made commonplace, the whole tradition was directed against women as basely seductive, passionate, and licentious by nature. Then the Inquisition made processes of detection and trial by torture, and these were applied against witches. The cruelest punishment known, burning alive, was applied to them. The inquisitors Institoris and Sprenger prepared a book, the *Malleus Maleficarum* (Hammer of Witches). A Roman Catholic historian maintains that their purpose was to silence the priests who denied that there were any witches.[1] The two inquisitors mentioned had already been at work for five years in Constance, and had caused forty-eight confessed witches to be executed by the civil authority.[2] The *Malleus* "is to be reckoned amongst the most mischievous productions in all the literature of the world"[3]; "it was the most portentous monument of superstition which the world has produced."[4] Between 1487 (the date of first publication) and 1669 twenty-five editions of it were published: sixteen in Germany, seven in France, and two in Italy; none elsewhere. A forged approval by the theological faculty of Cologne was published with it. This won its way for it everywhere.[5] The writers profess a venomous and malignant hostility to women; they present women as extravagantly sensual and libidinous, and so as dangerous to men, and subject to seduction by demons.[6] This is their major premise, which they perhaps exaggerated on account of the deductions to be built on it. It is now not believed that women are more

[1] Janssen, J.: Geschichte des deutschen Volkes, etc., VIII, 510, 511, n. 2.
[2] *Ibid.*, 517.   [3] Hansen, J.: *l.c.*, 473.
[4] Lea, H. C.: A History of the Inquisition of the Middle Ages, III, 543.
[5] Hansen, J.: *l.c.*, 475.
[6] Malleus, 76 (ed. 1576; Venice); Hansen, J.: *l.c.*, 482–485.

sensual than men, but decidedly the contrary. Chrysostom on Matt. 19 is quoted in the *Malleus* as if it was he who said: "It is not expedient to marry," and then a diatribe against women is added, which seems, partly on account of the typographical arrangement, to be also quoted from Chrysostom, although it cannot be found in his works. It is added that a woman is superstitious and credulous, and that she has a *lubricam linguam*, so that she must tell everything to another woman. That women are deceitful is proved by Delilah. This view of women had been growing for centuries, especially while asceticism was in fashion. The *Malleus* was intended to be a text-book for judges of secular courts, who were charged to conduct witch-trials.[1] In Germany it met with opposition, and the witch-persecutors were forced to go back to Rome for a ratification of their authority. This led to the publication of a bull by the Pope, Innocent VIII, in 1484,[2] in which he referred to the great amount of sorcery reported from Germany — which may show that persecution was going on there at that time.[3] This bull, with the *Malleus*, formed a new point of departure in the witch-delusion in 1485, for in the bull Innocent gave the witch-prosecutors full authority in the premises and ordered the Bishop of Strassburg to support and help them, and to call in the secular arm, if necessary. After that, to question the reality of witchcraft was to question the utterance of the Vicar of Christ, and to aid anyone accused was to impede the Inquisition.[4]

For three hundred years, in all countries of Christendom, the *Malleus* was the codex used by jurists and ecclesiastics, Protestants and Catholics. It was a codification

[1] Hansen, J.: *l.c.*, 495.

[2] Text in Hoensbroech, Graf von: Das Papstthum in seiner sozial-kulturellen Wirksamkeit, etc., I, 384.

[3] Janssen, J.: *l.c.*, VIII, 508, n.   [4] Lea, H. C.: *l.c.*, III, 540.

of the whole mass of fables and myths, with ridiculous and obscene attachments, which had come down through the whole course of history.   It is amazing that the male half of the human race should have thus calumniated the female half of it.   There may have been some reaction against the equally senseless adoration of women in the twelfth and thirteenth centuries, but the *Malleus* supported its denunciation of women by scholastic methods and theological arguments.   "It caused on this domain an immeasurable harm to the human race." [1] All the material in the *Malleus* is heaped together without criticism.   From the second half of the thirteenth century popular tales and superstitions had been taken up by the Church and incorporated in Christian theology, and as a consequence sex-commerce between demons and women had been made a crime.   Jurists were now charged to detect and punish it.[2]   Innocent VIII, in his bull of 1484, asserts the reality of such commerce in the most positive manner.   "The only result of the school theology of the Middle Ages had been to give to the popular delusions a learned drapery and to incorporate them in the Christian world-philosophy. This made them capable of dangerous application in the administration of justice.   The notion of sex-commerce between demons and women had ceased to be a popular delusion.   It was a part of learned theology.[3]   "The reaction on each other of theological thinking and of omnipotence, without any appeal, in the administration of justice led to the combination of Church faith and popular delusion and produced the witch-mania.   Under the cloak of religion and in the name of justice, that mania became a senseless rage against supposed witch-persons." [4]

[1] Hansen, J.: *l.c.*, 490.   [3] *Ibid.*, 187.
[2] *Ibid.*, 187.   [4] *Ibid.*, 176.

"There is nothing fouler in all literature than the stories and illustrative examples by which these theories were supported."[1] Many persons accused of witchcraft were vicious, immoral, criminals, or justly unpopular; but inasmuch as there is no such thing as a witch, or witchcraft, they suffered, although innocent of the charge. The total suffering endured under this charge it is impossible to conceive.

The jurists accepted the charge to detect and exterminate witches, and fulfilled it, as it appears, heartily. The witch-trials were worse than the heresy trials by the Inquisition; there was less chance for the accused.[2] The system of trial, preceded by imprisonment and petty torture of mind, which wore out the courage and nerve-resistance of the accused, consisted in torture which led the victim to assent to anything in order to get a speedy death. Mediæval dungeons are now shown to tourists, who can judge how long an old woman could bear imprisonment there in cold; darkness, and dampness, in contact with rats and vermin. They "confessed" anything. They often said that the devil first appeared to them as a handsome young cavalier, with a poetical name, who seduced them. Scherr interprets these instances as cases in which shameless mothers sold their daughters to men for pleasure.[3] "He who studies the witch-trials believes himself transferred into the midst of a race which has smothered all its own nobler human instincts — reason, justice, shame, benevolence, and sympathy — in order to cultivate devilish instincts. Out of that domain which seems to men the most precious and most elevated in life, that of religion, a Medusa-head grins at the spectator and arrests his blood in his veins. Amongst

[1] Lea, H. C.: *l.c.*, III, 385.   [2] *Ibid.*, 515.
[3] Scherr, J.: Deutsche Kultur- und Sittengeschichte, 372.

Christian people, in the bosom of a culture one thousand years old, judicial murder is made a permanent institution, hundreds of thousands of innocent persons, after refined torture of the body and nameless mental sufferings, are executed in the most cruel manner. These facts are so monstrous that all other aberrations of the human race are small in comparison."[1]

It is a pleasant task to gather such cases as can be found of resistance by ecclesiastics to the prevalent mania. In 1279, at Ruffach, in Alsatia, a Dominican nun was accused of baptizing a wax image, either to destroy an enemy or to win a lover. The peasants carried her to a field and would have burned her, but she was rescued by the friars.[2] The Bishop of Brixen, in the Tyrol, in 1485, met the inquisitor Institoris, when he came to begin the persecution, and forced him to leave the country.[3] At Arras and Amiens, in 1460, the ecclesiastics suppressed a witch-persecution at its beginning.[4] At Innsbrück the bishop's representative arrested the work of Institoris as not conformable to the rules of legal practice; the questions about sex-practice were suppressed as irrelevant, and a protest was made against the superficial proceedings of the inquisitor.[5] The state of Venice resisted witch-persecutions more successfully than it resisted heresy, although it never satisfied the Church authorities; the self-centered and suspicious republic had mores of its own which withstood outside interference. - In 1518 the Senate was officially informed that the inquisitor had burned seventy witches in Valcamonica; that he had as many more in prison, and that those suspected or accused numbered five thousand, or one-fourth of the population

[1] Hoensbroech, *l.c.*, I, 382, citing from Riezler, Hexenproz. in Baiern, 1.
[2] Lea, H. C.: *l.c.*, III, 434.   [3] Hoensbroech: *l.c.*, I, 516.
[4] Lea, H. C.: *l.c.*, III, 533.
[5] Flade, P.: Das römische Inquisitionsverfahren in Deutschland, etc., 102.

of the valleys. The Signoria stopped all proceedings, but Leo X ordered the inquisitor to use excommunication and interdict if he was interfered with.[1]

If it be asked what can explain the phenomena of aberration both of thought and feeling which underlay the witch-mania, perhaps the suggestion of Scherr [2] is the best explanation. The German ecclesiastics were won by the increase of power which the delusion offered to the hierarchy. The civil authorities were won by the chance of pecuniary gain, for the fortunes of witches were confiscated. Two-thirds were given to the territorial sovereign, while the other third was divided between judges, magistrates, minor ecclesiastics, spies, delators, and executioners, by a ratio adjusted to their rank. During the Thirty Years' War, when everybody else in Germany underwent impoverishment, witch-judges grew rich. Therefore half the witch-murders may well be accredited to greed for money, while the other half must be charged to fanaticism and credulous simplicity.[3]

"Epidemic witch-persecution never appeared except in the dominions of the Church of Rome. It never broke out in the lands of the Greek Church, although in them also the ancient notions about magic were widely held, and the environment contained the same circumstances and forces." "In Servia and Bulgaria there is not even any legend of witch-burning, which is a proof that the Turks did not allow any such usage to come into existence."[4] Nevertheless, the Balkan peoples had inherited the whole tradition of antiquity and barbarism quite as directly as the peoples of the Romish Church.

The Protestant reformers broke with the Church on

[1] Lea, H. C.: l.c., III, 546.   [2] L.c., 374.
[3] Janssen, J.: l.c., VIII, 539, 633.
[4] Krauss, F. S.: Volksglaube und religiöser Brauch der Südslaven, 123.

one or another point of dogma and morals, but they accepted all the traditions which did not involve the dogmas which seemed to them false. They laid great stress on the authority of Scripture, and therefore thought the existence of demons and witches quite beyond question. They accepted and used the *Malleus* as the codex of witchcraft, and they outstripped the Inquisition in cruelty and wrong-headedness. The witchcraft notion had now been formulated and given back to the popular classes with ecclesiastical sanction, and for two centuries it was a part of the mores of Christendom in which all churches and sects agreed. In fact it was after the reformation-schism took place that witch-persecutions became a great mania throughout Christendom, and especially in Germany.[1] Under Calvin, at Geneva, in 1542, many witches were executed.[2] In Italy witchcraft was confined, for the most part, to mountain regions. In other provinces it was confounded with crimes of poisoning, abortion, or the fomentation of conspiracies in private families.[3] Luther was distinguished for his faith in the devil; Satan was to him quite as real as God, and far more familiar; he saw satanic agency in whatever annoyed him.[4] Sin and Satan were conjoined; the one presupposed the other. Luther explained a cretin as the offspring of a demon and a woman, and on his own responsibility[5] ordered that it be drowned.

Early in the sixteenth century the secular authorities of Protestant and Catholic countries employed the utmost severity in the extirpation of witches, of whose existence and horrible activity everybody was convinced. The cumulative notion of witches was no longer a spe-

[1] Scherr, J.: *l.c.*, 369, 372. [2] Janssen, J.: *l.c.*, VIII, 546.
[3] Symonds, J. A.: The Catholic Reaction, I, 455.
[4] Lecky, W. E. H.: History of the Rise and Influence of the Spirit of Rationalism in Europe, I, 82. [5] Scherr, J.: *l.c.*, 375.

cial possession of inquisitors, but it had penetrated all cultivated and uncultivated classes, and was embodied in a great literature. The fine arts, in their most popular forms, combined with printing, seized on the fantastic notions of witchcraft which the witches' flight and witches' sabbath offered. These were represented in copper and wood engravings.[1] About 1490 or 1500 Molitoris published a *Dialogus de pythonicis mulieribus*, the conclusions of which are thus summed up: (1) Satan cannot of his own power do evil deeds, but God sometimes lets him do them, to a limited extent; (2) he cannot exceed the limit; (3) by permission of God he presents illusions of men transformed into beasts; (4) witch-flights and sabbath are illusions; (5) incubes and succubes cannot procreate; (6) the devil can only conjecture and use his knowledge of stars; (7) nevertheless, witches by worshiping Satan are real heretics and apostates; (8) therefore they ought to be burned.

One of the earliest literary expressions of opposition to the witch-doctrine was by Jehan de Meung in the *Romaunt de la Rose*.[2] De Meung has been called the Rabelais and the Voltaire of the thirteenth century. He was a critic and skeptic and ridiculed the notions in the current demonism, the witch-flights and "straying with Dame Habundia,"[3] as well as the devils with claws and tails. He says that some attribute nature's war, storms, etc., to demons, but "such tales are not worth two sticks, being but vain imagining." He refers the notions of the devil's action on men to sleep-walking and dreams. He believed in astrology and hallucinations, which he thought explained the alleged witch-phenomena. But he distrusted and hated women as much as Institoris

[1] Hansen, J.: *l.c.*, 520.   [2] Pt. II.
[3] Verses, 18, 565; 19, 110; 19, 302.

or Sprenger. In the fourteenth and fifteenth centuries some theologians expressed doubt about witches and witchcraft [1]: in 1505 Samuel de Cassinis, a Minorite, published a tract against witch-flights as untrue, although he said that evil by sorcery and witch-adulteries with demons were true; this is said to have been the first systematic attempt to oppose the witch-mania.[2]   Janssen is able to affirm that the writers for and against witchcraft and witches are equal in all sects and professions.[3]   Bodin, one of the leaders of the sixteenth century, especially in political philosophy, political economy, and the doctrine of money,[4] wrote a book [5] in which he described witch-doings as if upon his own knowledge of facts, when he was, like the popes, only rehearsing the popular stories.   He believed that the early death of Charles IX was due to the fact that he spared the life of a sorcerer on condition that he would inform on his colleagues. Kepler, the astronomer, believed in witches and had great difficulty in saving his mother, who was a shrew,[6] from execution as one. Opposition to the mania was dangerous, for it was a proof that the objector was a sorcerer. At Treves, in 1592, several Jesuits, a Carthusian, a Carmelite, and some magistrates were accused; one magistrate, who had himself condemned many, was accused and executed, and another died under the seventh torture.[7]   Laymann, Tanner, and Von Spee are three Jesuits who, in the first part of the seventeenth century, resisted the delusion, although in vain.[8]   Von Spee wrote his *Cautio Criminalis*

---

[1] Lecky, W. E. H.: Rationalism, I, 103.   [2] Hansen, J.: *l.c.*, 510.

[3] *L.c.*, VIII, 585. See a list of them, Lecky, W. E. H.: Rationalism, I, 105, and Janssen, J.: *l.c.*, VIII, 551.

[4] Baudrillart, H. : J. Bodin et son Temps, 167, 183, 494; Lecky, W. E. H.: Rationalism, I, 88, 107.

[5] De Magorum Daimonomania.   [7] *Ibid.*, 637–639.

[6] Janssen, J.: *l.c.*, VIII, 667.   [8] *Ibid.*, 654.

because he was especially outraged by the fact that the judges dared not acquit and free anyone whom they had tortured, because to do so would publish the fact that they had acted hastily and erroneously. In spite of the frightful treatment to which they were subjected, some women held out through the torture and were entitled to acquittal; in the logic of the times this proved that the devil helped them.[1] Von Spee was born in 1591, wrote his book in 1627, when he was a professor at Würzburg, and published it anonymously. He had been confessor to condemned witches, and was led to remonstrate against the irrationality of the proceedings. "Treat the heads of the Church," said he, "treat the judges, or treat me, as you treat these unhappy persons — subject us to the same tortures, and you will find wizards in us all." [2] Montaigne had more success: in 1588 he led the reaction in France, treating the delusion with scorn. Hobbes, in England, followed him, but Sir Matthew Hale, a distinguished judge, and Sir Thomas Browne, a prominent physician, held the proofs of the reality of witchcraft to be indisputable.[3] The former wrote a book to defend the doctrine of witches.[4] The whole Puritan party was carried into great excess in this matter, apparently by their fanatical doctrine of the Scriptures. Witch persecution reached the highest point of cruelty and inhumanity in Scotland, as it seems, and the invention of instruments of torture seems there to have reached its

[1] Hoensbroech: l.c., I, 551.
[2] Ebner, T.: Friedrich von Spee und die Hexenprocesse seiner Zeit; Hansen, J.: l.c., 445.
[3] Lecky, W. E. H.: Rationalism, I, 128.
[4] Witchcraft. A Collection of Modern Relations of Matter of Fact Concerning Witches and Witchcraft Upon the Persons of People. To which is prefixed a Meditation Concerning the Mercy of God in Preserving Us from the Malice and Power of Evil Angels. Written in 1661. 12mo, pp. 64. It is very rare and is insignificant.

highest point. An iron frame was locked on the head of a witch, upon which there were four large prongs, which were put in her mouth. The frame was fastened to the wall of the dungeon so that she could neither sit nor stand nor lie. A man on each side of her prevented her from sleeping for four or five nights in succession. In 1596 Alison Balfour withdrew a confession which she had made, explaining it by saying that when she made it she had been tortured several times in the caspieclaws (iron frame for the legs heated from time to time over a brazier), from which she had been taken several times dead and "without remembrance of good or evil." Her husband had been in the stocks and her son tortured in the boots, and her daughter in the thumb-screws, so that they had all been so tormented that, partly to escape greater torture, and upon promise of her life, she had made confession "falsely against her soul and conscience, and not otherwise." [1]   Stoll [2] quotes part of a poem by Nicolas Remy, a witch-judge, in which he described a woman under trial who saw devils in the room. The last execution for witchcraft in Scotland occurred in 1722, at Dornoch; this witch had ridden on her own daughter, transformed into a pony and shod by the devil, which made the girl lame in hands and feet. [3]

The witch-persecutions were at their height in Germany about 1600. They were popular; the crowd enjoyed the executions, and they clung to the notion of witchcraft to account especially for calamities which affected only a few. Hailstorms and whirlwinds, which are of great evil effect on a narrow area, were attributed to witches. Barrenness of beasts and women was attributed to witches.

[1] Sharpe, C. K.: A Historical Account of the Belief in Witchcraft in Scotland, 86.

[2] Suggestion und Hypnotismus in der Völkerpsychologie, 429.

[3] Sharpe, C. K.: l.c., 199.

If a man got a good crop by careful farming, he was
accused of transferring his neighbor's crops to his own
ground. Passionate love and hate were thought to be
due to witchcraft,—in fact, the whole life-philosophy as
to the aleatory element was built upon this belief. The
crowd treated the executions as a spectacle and hooted
at the victims.[1] Old women, witches, accused young
women whom they named of bearing infants from their
necks of the size of a finger.[2] In 1816 witches confessed,
under torture, that they had, by witchcraft, introduced
fifty-seven bushels of fleas into Vienna.[3] That such assertions obtained a hearing and belief shows that "the
minds of men were imbued with an order of ideas which
had no connection with experience."[4] It also shows that
pure skepticism, instead of being wrong, is a necessary
protection against folly. Sidonie von Bork was a beautiful girl whom the Duke of Stettin wanted to marry,
though she was of lower rank than he. His family
objected to the match and she was put in a convent. In
1618, at the age of eighty, she was burned as a witch,
women having named her, under torture, as one of their
companions at a witches' sabbath. At Wolfenbüttel, in
1591, a woman one hundred and six years old was burned
after being dragged over the ground for a time.[5] The
trials and torture were attended by degrading and insult-
ing treatment of the accused.[6] The devil was supposed to
help his own; therefore, if an accused woman endured the
torture, it was not inferred that she was innocent, but
that the devil was helping her, and new and more hideous
torture was necessary to solve the doubt. Shearing was
introduced by the inquisitors, about 1460, in France

[1] Janssen, J.: l.c., VIII, 532.   [3] Ibid., 620.

[2] Ibid., 687.   [4] Lecky, W. E. H.: Rationalism, I, 102.

[5] Janssen, J.: l.c., VIII, 677.

[6] Hansen, J.: l.c., 463; Janssen, J.: l.c., VIII, 517.

and Italy.[1] The German writers say that it was too
hostile to German mores to be allowed in Germany. In
1679, in the Tyrol, a woman was tortured until she
accused her own children of witchcraft. After her execution her son, fourteen years old, and her daughter, twelve
years old, were beheaded and their bodies were burned,
while another son, nine years old, and a daughter, six
years old, were flogged and forced to witness the execution of their older brother and sister.[2]

Scherr[3] says that it is not an exaggerated estimate,
but a very moderate one, that the witch-persecutions cost
one hundred thousand lives in Germany. Remigius,
a witch-judge, boasted that, between 1580 and 1595, in
Lothringia, he had executed eight hundred witches.[4]
"Paramo boasts that, in a century and a half from the
commencement of the sect in 1404, the Holy Office had
burned at least thirty thousand witches who, if they
had been left unpunished, would easily have brought the
whole world to destruction"; Lea inquires, most reasonably, "Could any Manichean offer more practical evidence that Satan was lord of the visible universe?"[5]
This figure is far more trustworthy than those which are
in the books about the number of persons executed for
heresy.[6] The witch-persecutions covered two centuries,
from 1450 to 1650, so the above estimate would mean
that, on an average, five hundred were executed in a
year. The executions often included a great number at
once — such was especially the case during the century
of greatest activity, from 1580 on.[7] The last mass burning in Germany was in 1678, when ninety-seven persons

[1] Hansen, J.: l.c., 463.　　　　　　　　[2] Hoensbroech: l.c., I, 515.
[3] Geschichte der deutschen Frauenwelt, II, 167.
[4] Scherr, J.: Deutsche Kultur- und Sittengeschichte, 379.
[5] Lea, H. C.: l.c., III, 549.　　　　　　[6] Flade, P.: l.c. 90
[7] Scherr, J.: l.c., 381.

were burned together.[1] There were notorious cases in
which witches under torture had confessed things which
the whole neighborhood knew to be false. For instance,
a woman confessed that she had put her husband to death
by witchcraft, when it was a matter of public notoriety
that he was run over by a heavily laden wagon.[2] It must
be supposed that such cases gradually affected popular faith about witch-doctrines, although that faith was
never directly affected by anything. The belief in witches
was due to hysteria and suggestion. The books, dramas
and preaching of the later Middle Ages and the sixteenth
century were full of it, and they fed the daimonistic
notions which are at the basis of all popular religion.[3]
Witchcraft became the popular philosophy for the whole
aleatory element in life. This put it into the heads of a
class of people to be witches if they could [4]; hysterical
women, for instance, courted the notoriety and power
and loved the consciousness of causing fear, in spite of
the risk. Many perfectly sound-minded and innocent
women could not be sure that they were not witches.
They had had dreams suggested by the popular notions,
or had suffered from nervous affections which fell in with
the popular superstitions. The whole subject and the
mode of treatment of witchcraft is thoroughly popular,
and the suggestion in it is clear. Western Europe was
overrun by persons who offered cures for all the ills of
life, and the cures were always magical or partly magical. No one would have believed in any other. People
of both sexes of the criminal, vicious, and vagabond
classes enacted, sometimes in costume, what they had
heard about witch-orgies.[5] Many herbs were in com-

[1] Scherr, J.: l.c., 382.   [4] Ibid., 529.
[2] Janssen, J.: l.c., VIII, 633.   [5] Ibid., 533.
[3] Ibid., 531.

mon use to produce sleep, or visions, or nerve excitement, or abortion, or to cure sterility and impotence.
The notion that any desired result could be reached by
swallowing something, especially if it was nasty, had
scarcely any limits. Somnambulists were often supposed
to be caught on their way to the witches' sabbath. Fried-
mann testifies, from his own experience as a physician,
that hallucinations by night, but waking, occur in the
case of elderly persons, especially females; they are
nervous excitements due to slight decrease of mental
power, such as a layman would hardly notice, and grotesque figures or black men are the most common forms
of these frightful illusions.[1] "Witchcraft depended on
general causes and represented the prevailing modes of
religious thought."[2] "Witch-persecution is a problem
in the history of civilization which, although it may now
be regarded as settled, yet has closer connection with our
time than one might think upon only superficial consideration. The elementary notions on which the delusion was based are even yet continued in the doctrines of
almost all the accepted religious systems."[3] Witchcraft
issued out of the most ancient and fundamental popular
faiths, and it seized on all which the religion offered and
appropriated it. Then it produced such imitations as
the perverted mass idea, and the notion that Satan begot
Merlin, the magician in the Arthur legend, with a virgin
woman.[4] The interlacing of witchcraft with popular
world-philosophy and life-policy is evident at every step,
and the contributions of suggestion are easily seen. Its
combination with criminal purposes and acts must never
be overlooked, for private malice and enmity, the desire
to extort money, and various political and personal

[1] Ueber Wahnideen im Völkerleben, 249.
[2] Lecky, W. E. H.: Rationalism, I, 123.
[3] Hansen, J.: l.c., vii.
[4] Scherr, J.: l.c., 359.

projects made use of the witch-delusion. One of the most
striking cases is that of Erich II of Braunschweig-Kalen-
berg, who, being heavily indebted, turned Catholic, in
1572, in order to enter the Spanish service. He accused
his wife and four of her ladies of bewitching him to punish
him for his apostasy; his wife ran away to her family
home, but the ladies were repeatedly tortured to the
extremest limit. As they knew nothing and could say
nothing, they were held to have proved their innocence.[1]

No argument ever made any way against this delusion.
Lecky [2] thinks that "its decline presented a spectacle,
not of argument or conflict, but of silent evanescence and
decay." The credit of putting an end to it belonged to a
series of great skeptics and free thinkers from Montaigne
to Voltaire, who killed it with scorn and contempt. In
England this view of it got strong help from the skeptical
reaction against Puritanism, after the restoration of the
Stuarts. The great men led the intelligent classes to this
view, and they led the masses to understand that that was
the proper view, just as now all intelligent people treat
spiritualism. The Evangelical and Puritan parties kept
up the faith in witchcraft: Richard Baxter wrote against
witchcraft, but John Wesley reaffirmed the faith in it [3];
King James I presided at the torture of Doctor Fian
(John Cunningham) for causing a storm which hindered
the king from returning from Denmark. The victim
never confessed, but was burned. Agnes Sampson is
otherwise said to have done the harm; she, it appears,
went to sea in a sieve.[4] In 1720 F. Hutchinson's *Witchcraft* was published, in which the author tries to explain
the texts of the Bible about witches, and interprets the
witches as impostors; he tells a story of an Anglican

[1] Janssen, J.: *l.c.*, VIII, 646.   [3] *Ibid.*, 140.
[2] Rationalism, I, 115.   [4] *Ibid.*, 123; Sharpe, C. K.: *l.c.*, 64.

clergyman, eighty years old, who was executed for witch-craft.

In the reign of Queen Anne the rural population still believed in witchcraft. Addison .tells how he and Sir Roger de Coverley visited Moll White and found a broomstick and a cat. Sir Roger said that Moll had often been brought before him for making children spit pins and giving maids the nightmare, and "that the country people would be tossing her into a pond and trying experiments with her every day if it was not for him and his chaplain." Several witches were executed during the reign of Anne, but capital punishment for witchcraft was abolished in 1736.[1] Gibbon says that "the French and English lawyers of the present age allow the theory and deny the practice of witchcraft." [2]

Witchcraft was a recognized crime in the laws of the New England colonies. There were several isolated cases in Massachusetts before the Salem outbreak, some of them very sad and outrageous.[3] The persecutions all had a popular character and all showed the passion and cruelty of which a village democracy is capable against an unpopular person. Cotton Mather stands personally responsible for using his great personal influence, in connection with the Glover case (1688), to spread faith in witchcraft. Increase Mather published, in 1693, *An Account of the Tryals of the New England witches, with cases of conscience concerning witchcrafts and Evil Spirits personating Men*. A doctrine which he formulated and which destroyed some excellent people who were accused at Salem was that Satan could just as well appear in the person of a pious man or woman as in that of a wicked

[1] Ashton, J.: Social Life in the Reign of Queen Anne, 93.
[2] Decline and Fall, Chap. XXV, n. x.
[3] Upham, C. W.: Salem Witchcraft, I.

one, to work his harm; therefore the character of the
accused went for nothing. Cotton Mather was befooled by
a clever girl, who played on his vanity. While the mania
raged no one could oppose it, and those who tried to do
so became victims of it. The notion of sex-intercourse
between Satan and women came out again at Salem, and
Glanvil and Sir Matthew Hale were treated as great
authorities. The ministers were warned to be careful,
but they could not deny the reality of witchcraft.[1] The
New England case is especially important because it
shows how limited in space and time an outburst of a
popular mania may be.

The fundamental notion of this delusion is that men,
with the help of demons whom they invoke for that
purpose, can do harm, and that the attempts to invoke
the demons are now actually made. This notion belongs
to-day to the acknowledged doctrine of the Catholic
Church, and has its place in all the authoritative Catholic
books on ethics. Perhaps it has adherents amongst
Protestants.[2] Leo XIII ordered every priest to read
aloud a prayer on the steps of the altar after every mass
in which occurs the petition: "Holy Archangel Michael,
throw Satan and all other spirits of hell, who roam in the
world to destroy men, back into hell." [3]

In 1749 Mia Renata, a nun seventy years old, who had
entered the convent at the age of nineteen, was beheaded
and her body was burned as a witch at Würzburg, under
the authority of the prince-bishop of that place. She
was accused of trying to seduce the nuns and bewitching
them with gout and neuralgia,[4] and all the old witch-

[1] Hutchinson, T.: The Witchcraft Delusion of 1692, I, in New England
Historical and Genealogical Register, XXIV, 381.
[2] Hansen, J.: l.c., 6; on page 88 authorities are quoted from the Catholic
writers on ethics.
[3] Hoensbroech: l.c., I, 358.   [4] Scherr, J.: l.c., 384 and Appendix.

doctrines are in the twelve findings of the court. In 1756 a fourteen-year-old girl was beheaded as a witch at Landshut, in Bavaria, because she had made a wager with the devil. In 1782, at Glarus, in Switzerland, a maid-servant was executed for witchcraft; she had given pin-seed to a child, which germinated in its stomach so that it spat pins. The last witch execution in Germany was in 1775, a woman charged with carnal intercourse with Satan.[1] In Poland and Hungary witch-persecutions continued until the end of the eighteenth century.[2] In 1672 Colbert directed the judges in France to receive no accusation of sorcery against anyone,[3] but in 1718 the Parliament of Rouen burned a man for that crime.[4] In 1781 the Inquisition burned a witch at Seville for making a pact with Satan and practicing fornication with him.[5] "Incredible to relate, on the 22d of April, 1751, a rabble of about five thousand persons beset the workhouse at Tring, in Hertfordshire, where, seizing Luke Osborne and his wife, two persons suspected of witchcraft, they ducked them in a pond till the old woman died; after which her corpse was put to bed to her husband by the mob, of whom only one person was hanged for this detestable outrage."[6] The last law about witchcraft in the British Islands was an Irish statute, which was not repealed until 1821.[7] In 1823 a court in the island of Martinique condemned a man to the galleys for life for "vehement suspicion" of sorcery.[8] In 1863 an old man was put to death by a mob, as a wizard, at Essex, England.[9] In 1873 a witch was burned in Spanish South America.[10] In 1874, in Mexico, several persons were

[1] Hoensbroech: l.c., I, 551.
[2] Scherr, J.: l.c., 387.
[3] Lecky, W. E. H.: Rationalism, I, 117.
[4] Ibid., 118.
[5] Hansen, J.: l. c., 532.
[6] Sharpe, C. K.: l.c., 176.
[7] Lecky, W. E. H.: Rationalism, I, 70.
[8] Lea, H. C.: l.c., I, 561.
[9] Lecky, W. E. H.: Rationalism, I, 139.
[10] Umschau, VII, 241.

publicly burned as sorcerers. In 1885 Christian negroes
in Hayti practiced the old rites of sorcery, killing and
eating children.¹ In the early history of Illinois some
negroes were hanged at Cahokia for witchcraft.² In 1895
a woman was tortured to death, as a witch, by her relatives
in Tipperary, Ireland.³ An Associated Press dispatch of
July 11, 1897, described the act of two men, in Mexico,
who dragged a woman eighty years old to death, tied to
their horses by the feet, for bewitching the sister of one of
them. In Lyme, Connecticut, in October, 1897, a band
of religious fanatics attempted to drive the devil out
of a rheumatic old woman by bruising and immersing
her.⁴ In a cablegram in the New York *Times*, December 14, 1900, it was stated that an Italian in London
burned a pin-studded wax image of President McKinley
on the steps of the American Embassy. In 1903 a moun-
taineer in North Carolina, whose wife could not make
the butter come, thought that a neighboring woman had
bewitched the milk. He pinned up a portrait of her on
the wall and shot a silver bullet through it.⁵

These cases show that belief in witchcraft is not dead.
It is latent and may burst forth anew at any moment.
"The difference [from age to age] is not so much in the
amount of credulity as in the direction it takes." ⁶ At
the present day it is in politics. Lecky thought that
the cause of persecution was the intensity of dogmatic
opinion⁷; that may be a cause, for no man is tolerant
about anything about which he cares very much and

¹ Globus, XLVII, 252, 264.
² Reynolds, J.: History of Illinois, 51; date of the execution not given.
Many modern cases are collected in the Popular Science Monthly, XLVII, 73.
³ New York Times, March 31 and April 7, 1895.
⁴ *Ibid.*, October 26, 1897.
⁵ Harper's Magazine, No. 637.
⁶ Lecky, W. E. H.: Rationalism, I, 101.   ⁷ Rationalism, II, 39.

in regard to which he thinks that he has "the truth." Struggles for political power, however, cause even intenser rage, and it is political faction which, in the future, may return to violent repression of dissent. In the history of city after city we meet with intensest rancor between classes and factions, and we find this rancor producing extremes of beastly cruelty, when interest seems to call for it. Socialism is, in its spirit and programme, well capable of producing new phenomena of despotism and persecution in order to get or retain social power. Anarchists who are fanatical enough to throw bombs into theaters or restaurants, or to murder kings and presidents just because they are such, are capable of anything which witch-judges or inquisitors have done, if they should think that party success called for it. If bad times should come again upon the civilized world, through overpopulation and an unfavorable economic conjuncture, popular education would decline and classes would be more widely separated. It must then be expected that the old demonism would burst forth again and would reproduce the old phenomena.

RELIGION AND THE MORES

V

RELIGION AND THE MORES
[1910]

MOHAMMEDANISM, Romanism, and Protestantism contain systems of world-philosophy which have been deduced from religious dogmas. The world-philosophy is in each case removed by several steps of deduction from the religious postulates. In each case customs have grown up from the unavoidable compromise between metaphysical dogmas and life interests, and these customs, so far as they inhere in essential traits of human nature or in fundamental conditions of human life, or as far as they have taken on the sanctity of wide and ancient authority, so that they seem to be above discussion, are the mores. Does a Roman Catholic, or a Mohammedan, or a Protestant child begin by learning the dogmas of his religion and then build a life-code on them? Not at all. He begins by living in and according to the mores of his family and societal environment. The vast mass of men in each case never do anything else but thus imbibe a character from the environment. If they learn the religious dogmas at all, it is superficially, negligently, erroneously. They are trained in the ritual, habituated to the usages, imbued with the notions of the societal environment. They hear and repeat the proverbs, sayings, and maxims which are current in it. They perceive what is admired, ridiculed, abominated, desired by the people about them. They learn the code of conduct — what is considered stupid, smart, stylish, clever, or

foolish, and they form themselves on these ideas.   They
get their standards from the standards of their environment.   Behind this, but far behind it for all but the
scholars, are the history and logic by which the mores
are connected with the religious facts or dogmas, and
when the scholars investigate the history and logic they
find that the supposed history is a tissue of myths and
legends and that the logic is like a thread broken at a
hundred points, twisted into myriad windings, and snarled
into innumerable knots.

But now it follows that the mores are affected all the
time by changes in environmental conditions and societal
growth and by changes in the arts, and they follow these
influences without regard to religious institutions or doctrines; or at most, compromises are continually made
between inherited institutions and notions on one side
and interests on the other.   The religion has to follow
the mores.   In its nature, no religion ever changes; for
every religion is absolute and eternal truth.   It never
contains any provision for its own amendment or "evolution."   It would stultify itself if it should say: I am
temporarily or contingently true, and I shall give way to
something truer.   I am a working hypothesis only.   I
am a constitution which may be amended whenever you
please.   "The faith once delivered to the saints" must
claim to be perfect, and the formula itself means that the
faith is changeless.   A scientific or developing religion is
an absurdity.   But then again nothing is absolutely and
eternally true.   Everything must change, and religion
is no exception.   Therefore every religion is a resisting
inertia which is being overcome by moving forces.   Interests are the forces, because they respond, in men, to
hunger, love, vanity, and fear, and the actual mores of
a time are the resultant of the force of interests and the

inertia of religion. The leaders of a period enlist on the side either of the interests or the resistance, and the mass of men float on the resultant current of the mores.

Religion is tradition. It is a product of history and it is embodied in ritual, institutions, and officials, which are historical. From time to time it is observed that the religious generalizations do not hold true; experience does not verify them. At last skepticism arises and new efforts of philosophy are required to reestablish the religious dogmas or to make new compromises. Philosophy appears as a force of revision and revolution. In the New Testament we see a new philosophy undermining and overthrowing rabbinical Judaism. This operation may be found in the history of any religion; and it is often repeated. The institutional and traditional religion stands like an inherited and established product; the philosophy appears like a new and destructive element which claims to be reformatory, and may turn out to be such, but which begins by destruction.

We may see one of these operations in the ecclesiastical schism of the sixteenth century. The mediæval system broke down in the fifteenth century; it was not able to support the weight thrown on it by the great changes of that period. New devices were charged with the great societal duties; for instance, the State was created and charged with duties which the Church had claimed to perform. The State thus got control of marriage, divorce, legitimacy, property, education, etc. These things were in the mores, and the mores changed. The masses accepted the changes and readjusted their ideas accordingly. They turned to the State instead of the Church for the defense and control of great interests, and the schism in the Church was a result. Those who still kept faith in sacramental religion have clung to institutions, ritual, and dogmas which are consistent with sacramental religion; those who rejected sacramental dogmas have made new usages and institutions to fit their religious needs and experience. The latter school have drawn new deductions and inferences from the great principles of their creed and faith. The deductions thus made, when turned into injunctions or inhibitions, impose certain duties which are imperative and arbitrary. For instance, we are told that we must do a thing because the Bible says so, not because there is any rational relation between that act and self-realization. Nobody has ever done what the Bible says. What men have always done, if they tried to do right, was to conform to the mores of the group and the time. Monastic and Puritan sects have tried over and over again in the history of the Church to obey the Gospel injunctions. They begin by a protest against the worldliness of the Church. They always have to segregate themselves. Why? They must get out of the current mores of society and create an environment of their own where they can nurse a new body of mores within which the acts they desire to practice will be possible. They have always especially desired to create a society with the mores which they approved, and to do this they needed to control coming generations through their children or successors. No such effort has ever succeeded. All the churches and nearly all the Christian denominations have, until within a few years, resisted investigation of the truth of history and nature. They have yielded this position in part but not altogether; within a year we have heard of a movement in the Church of Rome to test and verify traditions about history and nature. So far it has been suppressed. In the mores of to-day of all the intelligent classes the investigation of truth is a leading feature, and with justice, since the welfare of mankind primarily depends on correct knowledge of the world in which we live, and of human nature. It is a very heinous fault of the ecclesiastical organizations that they resist investigation or endeavor to control its results, for it alienates them from the mores of the time and destroys their usefulness. The mores will control the religion as they have done hitherto, and as they do now. They have forced an abandonment of ritual and dogma.

However, the case which is really important and which always presents itself in the second stage is that logical inferences as to what men ought to do are constructed upon the world-philosophy. In the New Testament the scribes and Pharisees were denounced because they had bound heavy burdens and laid them on men's shoulders. This referred to the rabbinical constructive duties of ritual and behavior — an elaborate system of duties in which energy was expended with no gain in self-realization. The mediæval Church fell under the dominion of the same tendency, and by construction and inference multiplied restrictions and arbitrary duties which had the same effect. We now hear constructive arguments made to prove from Scripture that there should be no divorce, and that no man should be allowed to marry his deceased wife's sister, although there is no authority at all in Scripture for such prohibitions.

It appears probable that all religious reformations have been due to changes in the mores. Moses led the Israelites out of Egypt in order to get them out of the collision between their mores and those of the Egyptians. The contrast between the mores of the Israelites and Canaanites is emphasized throughout the Old Testament.

It is against the mores of the Jews of the time of Jesus that the New Testament is a revolt; the denunciations of woe on the scribes and Pharisees are an expression of it.   Christianity failed among the Jews because the revolution in the mores which it called for was too great; it was, in reality, a Hellenistic world-philosophy and a treason inside Judaism.   Mohammed's action was based on innovations in the mores of the Arabs which had partially prevailed, and which he adopted and urged with supernatural sanctions against the old mores.   It is probable that Zoroaster and Buddha made themselves exponents of a revolution in the mores of their peoples. Zoroaster's work and the hostility between the Iranians and their kindred of India has made the history of the Persians and of the other peoples of the Euphrates Valley and its neighborhood.

These examples not only show us that the influence of the religion on the mores is not to be denied, but they show us what this influence is and what it is not.   Out of the experience arises the world-philosophy including religion.   Thus there is a constant alternation of action or experience and thought.   So far well, but then the deductions from the world-philosophy begin, and they are metaphysical.   They turn into dogmas which are logical or speculative or fantastic.   There is not a sequence of experience, reflection, action but the sequence is experience, reflection, deduction — perhaps repeated logical deduction, resulting in dogmas as an arbitrary injunction — and then new action.   The ecclesiastics or philosophers get a chance to introduce selfish elements for their own aggrandizement.   Next these dogmatic products are brought back to the world of experience and action as imperative rules of conduct.   They may win outward respect and pretended obedience, but they are evaded. The moral product is chicane and hypocrisy, and this is what enters into the mores.   At the same time, if the

religion offers any bribes or concessions to human passion
or weakness, the mores seize upon these and swell them
into the vices of an age. If the Church sets rigid and
arbitrary rules, it has to sell dispensations; why, then,
should not the age become venal? If people revel in
descriptions of torture and agony, they will be callous
to it. If the religion presents sensual indulgence as a
reward of good conduct, then sensuality is an ideal; it
is licensed, not restricted. In primitive society all customs were sanctioned by ghosts. Hence all customs are
ritual; hence abortion, infanticide, killing the old, cannibalism, and so on, were all ritual acts and not only were
they proper, but within the prescribed conditions they were
duties. When Christendom declared sex-renunciation to
be the ideal of perfection for one-half of civilized men,
and Mohammedanism presented sex-pleasure as the ideal
for the other, a striking picture was presented of the two
poles of excess and ill between which men are placed with
respect to this great dominant interest of the race. All
religions are creations of fantasy. They come out of the
realm of metaphysics. They come down into this world
of sense with authority. The moral ideas come out of
the mores, which move, and they are used to criticise the
religious traditions, which remain stereotyped. Religions
enjoin acts which have become abominable in the mores,
such as cannibalism, human sacrifice, child-sacrifice,
prostitution, intoxication. They aim ·to supersede experience, knowledge, and reason by labors and injunctions.
Galton says [1]: "The religious instructor, in every creed,
is one who makes it his profession to saturate his pupils
with prejudice." Some obey, but the great mass of the
society do, day by day, what will satisfy their interests
according to the best knowledge they have or can get

[1] Inquiries into Human Faculty and its Development, 210.

from the usages of the people around them. These acts
and the thoughts, codes, and standards which go with
them are the mores. Every people, therefore, takes out
of its religion or out of the religion which is brought to
it just what suits its tastes and its ways.

No religion of those which we call world-religions, and
which have a complete system, is ever put in practice
as a whole; the people always take out of it what suits
their tastes and ideas, and that means especially their
mores. Buddhism has run out into quite independent
forms in Ceylon, Tibet, and China and has died out in
Hindustan. Its excessive ritual, its contemplativeness,
its futile learning, the phantasmagoria of supernatural
beings which take the place of a god, its spells and charms
and prayer-wheels bear witness to antecedent traits in the
people who adopted it and which it has never overcome.
The mores follow these traits, not the religious dogmas.
All the elaborate (*i.e.*, civilized) religions impose duties
which are irksome, especially if they are interferences
with interest or with human passions and appetites.
The duties are neglected, and then comes fear of the anger
of the deity. At this point ritual enters in as expia-
tion, and atonement, especially in the forms of self-discipline, sacrifice, self-mutilation, scourging, fines, fasting,
pilgrimages, church-going, etc. Consequently, when
religion is ritual and its methods of reconciling man
and God are ritualistic, all the methods of self-discipline
enter deeply into the mores. Mediæval Christianity and
Mohammedanism illustrate this by the importance ascribed
to fasting, which, as it is employed, is an active agent.
The English ritualists of the last sixty years have introduced ritual as an engine to teach the old doctrine of
religion and to bring the interest of men back to the
mediæval views that the greatest interest of man is the

apparatus and operation (sacraments) by which his fate in the other world may be decided. Zoroastrianism may very probably be due, in the main, to one man, for it seems to be an invented system, but it came out of a body of magi who had long existed and it contains a system made by them and for them. The old demonism of Babylonia overpowered it. For the practical life of persons who were not magi it was realistic and matter of fact. It inculcated industry and thrift and its ideals of virtue were industrial, consisting in good work, in subduing the earth and making it productive; so it fell in with the mores of the people of the Euphrates Valley and strengthened them. Mohammedanism has been a conquering religion; it has been imposed on some people who were heathen. For them it has great influence because its creed is simple and its ritual is simple, but at the same time strict and incessant. It has split into great sects on account of the transformations imposed on it by more civilized people who have adopted it. Its fatalism, lack of civil ideas, spirit of plunder and conquest, fanaticism, and scientific ignorance have entered into the mores of all the people over whom it has gained domination. Hence the mores of Mohammedan nations present a great variety, and often very grotesque combinations. Christianity has taken very different forms among Greeks, Slavs, Latins, and Teutons. It inculcates meekness, but few Christians have ever been meek. It has absorbed all kinds of elements where it has met with native and national habitudes which it could not displace; that is as much as to say that it has had to yield to the mores. We hear a great deal about its victories over heathenism. They were all compromises, and when we get to know the old heathenism we find it again in what we thought were the most

distinctive features of Christianity. The religion of
Odin was a religion of warriors and for warriors. It took
its tone from them and gave back the warrior spirit with
a new sanction and an intensified ideal in this world and
the other. Ferocity, bloodshed, and indifference to death
were antecedents and consequents of the religion..

Sects of religion form upon a single idea or doctrine,
which they always exaggerate. Then the dogma gets
power over the whole life. This is the case in which the
religion rises superior to the mores and molds them, as
in the case of the Quakers. Some sects of India (the
Jains) have put the prohibition against killing anything
whatsoever which has life before everything else, and have
drawn the extremest inferences from it as to what one
ought to do and not do lest he kill anything. Their whole
mode of life and code of duty is a consequence.

Within fifty years in the United States the mores have
very powerfully influenced religion, and the effect is open
to our view. The dogmatic side of religion has been
laid aside by all the Protestant denominations. Many
instances may be shown in which the mores have modified the religion. The attitude toward religion is in the
mores; in recent mores open attacks on religion are
frowned upon as bad manners and religion is treated
with respect. The deism of the eighteenth century was
an attack on religion, but the agnosticism of the nineteenth century, although irreligious, sought no war with
religion. At the same time the interest in religion has
very greatly diminished, and it is a symptom of indifference when men do not care to carry on controversies
about it. The clergy has ceased to preach "theology."
They and their congregations care for theology no longer;
they look upon "morality" as the business of the clergy
and the pulpit. The pulpit, as an institution, no longer

speaks with authority; it tries to persuade, and to do this it has to aim at popularity. It wants to attract attention like newspapers, books, the theater, the lecture-platform, and it has to have recourse, like them, to sensational methods. If it cannot command authority, it must try to recommend itself by the power of reason. The current fashion is social endeavor, especially under the forms of charity; thus are set the lines along which the churches and denominations vie with each other for the approval of the public. A church, therefore, turns into a congeries of institutions for various forms of social amelioration, and the pulpit exercises consist in discussions of public topics, especially social topics, "from an ethical standpoint"; that is, by the application of the ethical, or quasi-cthical, notions which are at present current in our mores. What is that but a remodeling of the ecclesiastical institutions which we have inherited, according to the notions, standards, and faiths which are in the mores of our time? Religion, properly speaking, simply falls away. It is not as strong a motive as humanitarianism, and it is in nowise necessary to the work of social amelioration; often it is a hindrance, as when it diverts energy and capital from social work to ecclesiastical expenditures. When theologians declare that they accept the evolution philosophy because, however the world came to be, God was behind it, this is a fatal concession for religion or theology. When religion withdraws into this position, it has abandoned the whole field of human interest. It may be safe from attack, but it is also powerless and a matter of indifference. Theologians also say now that the miracles of Christ are proved by the character of Christ, not his character by the miracles.[1] This is another apologetic effort which

[1] Robbins: A Christian Apologetic.

is a fatal concession. In the record the miracles are plainly put forward to authenticate the person; if they are construed in the other way they are, in an age whose mores are penetrated by instinctive scorn of magic and miracles, a dead weight on the system. The apology therefore wins nobody, but interposes a repelling force. An apology is always a matter of policy, and it would be far better to drop miracles with witches, hell, personal devil, flood, tower of Babel, and creation in six days, in silence. The various attempts of the eighteenth century (Butler, Paley) to sustain religion or theology by analogies, design, and so on, are entirely outside of our mores. The philosophical or logical methods no longer have any force on the minds of any class in our society. When a church is only a slightly integrated association for ethical discussion and united social effort, religion ceases to be, and when religion withdraws entirely into the domain of metaphysical speculation, it is of no account. In the middle of the nineteenth century those Protestants who wanted to maintain religion for itself, or as an end in itself, did what the situation called for; they made religion once more ritual and tried to revive the "Catholic faith" without the Pope. That would be a revival, to a great extent, of mediæval ecclesiasticism and mores. We are therefore witnesses of a struggle to stem the tide of the mores by concerted action and tactics in the interest of mediæval religion. At the same time the mores of modern civilization are sapping the foundations, not only of mediæval and Greek Christianity, but also of Mohammedanism and Buddhism. The high-church or ritualistic movement is therefore a rally in the battle which has been going on for five hundred years between mediæval Christianity and the improved mores.

In the fifteenth century the great inventions, the geographical discoveries, the extension of commerce, the growth of capital, the rise of the middle class, the revival of learning, the growth of great dynastic states, destroyed the ideals of poverty, obedience, and chastity. The idea of Catholicity died just as the idea of the Crusades did: it was recognized as a chimæra. The Church was not doing the work it stood for in the world. These were fatal facts and courage was found to face them. It was the mores which shifted — moreover, all the bad as well as the good of the mores entered into the change.

The mores are a vast and complex mass of acts and thoughts — not some good and some bad, but all mixed in quality. All the elements are there always. The sects deride and denounce each other and they always select material for their jibes from what they allege to be the facts about each other's influence on the mores.

The Christian Church disapproved of luxury and ornament and repressed them in the mores of Christendom until the fourteenth century. The Renaissance brought in pagan ideas of beauty, art, ornament, pleasure, and joy in life, from which luxury arose. In the present mores of all civilized peoples the love of luxury is strong. It is increasing and is spreading to all classes; those who cannot enjoy it think themselves wronged by the social order. This sentiment is one of the very strongest in the masses; it characterizes the age and is one of those forces which change the face of institutions and produce social war.

The change of interest, in the sixteenth century, to the philosophy and the paganism of the classics included a great reduction in the other-worldliness of the Middle Ages. The point of interest was in this world and this

life, without denial of the truth of a future life; terror of
the future world and anxiety to know how to provide for
it, with eager seizure of the sacramental and sacerdotal
means which the Church provided, all declined. The
Renaissance tried to renew the Greek joy in life with art,
pleasure, music, grace, social enjoyment, freedom, and
luxury, instead of asceticism, ritual, ecclesiasticism, rigid
authority, distrust, and gloom. The religious wars
greatly interfered with the programme of the Renaissance. They partly dispelled gayety and grace. It was
in the mores that the changes occurred. Churches fell
to decay; monasteries disappeared; chantries were suppressed; clergymen abandoned their calling; pilgrimages, processions, retreats — all were neglected. Some
lamented and protested; others applauded; the greatest
number were indifferent. The attitude depended on the
place and circumstances, above all upon commercial and
industrial interests and upon intellectual attainments.
The great fact was that faith in sacramentarianism as a
philosophy of this life and the other was broken, and the
mores which had been the outcome of that faith fell
into neglect. The Counter-reformation arose from supposed effects of the Church schism on the mores. The
removal of the other world to a remoter place in human
interest was a great change in religion; at its best, modern religion became a guide of life here, not a preparation for another life. Modern thought has been realistic
and naturalistic, and the mores have all conformed to
this world-philosophy. The other-worldliness has been
ethical. It has been at war with the materialism of this
world, a war which is in the mores, for we are largely
under the dominion of those secondary or remoter dogmas
deduced from grand conceptions of world-philosophy and
inculcated as absolute authority. Our mores at the same

time instinctively tend toward realistic and naturalistic
views of life for which a new world-philosophy is growing
up. Here we have the explanation of the gulf which
is constantly widening between the "modern spirit"
and the traditional religion. Some cling to the traditional religion in one or another of its forms, which, after
all, represent only the grades of departure from the
mediæval form toward complete harmony with the
modern mores. What the mores always represent is
the struggle to live as well as possible under the conditions. Traditions, so far as they come out of other
conditions and are accepted as independent authorities
in the present conditions, are felt as hindrances. It is
because our religious traditions now do not assume
authority, but seek to persuade, that active war against
them has ceased and that they are treated with more
respect at present than in the eighteenth and nineteenth
centuries.

Other-worldliness — that is, care about the life after
death and anxiety to secure bliss there by proper action
here — occupied a large share of the interest of mediæval
men. Another element was feudalism, a form of society
which arises under given conditions, as we see from the
numerous cases of it in history. Mediæval society shows
us a great population caught up in the drift of these two
currents, one of world-philosophy and the other of societal environment, and working out all social customs and
institutions into conformity with them. The force of
this philosophy and the energy of the men are astounding.
In the civil world there was disintegration, but in the
moral world there was coherence and comprehensiveness
in the choice of ideals and in the pursuit of them. In
the thirteenth century there was a culmination in which
the vigorous expansion of all the elements reached a

degree of development which is amazing. The men of the time fell into the modes of feudalism as if it had been the order of nature; they accepted it as such. They accepted the leadership of the Church with full satisfaction. Preaching and ritual, with popular poetry aided by symbolism in art, were the only ways of acting on the minds of the mass; there was no tendency to reflection and criticism any more than among barbarians. The mores were the simple, direct, and naïve expression of the prevailing interests of the period; that is why they are so strong and their interaction is so vigorous. The sanction of excommunication was frightful in its effect on beliefs and acts. The canon law is an astonishing product of the time; it is really a codification of the mores modified somewhat, especially in the later additions, by the bias which the Church wanted to impress on the mores. It is because the canon law is fictitious in its pretended historical authority, and because the citations in it from the Fathers are selected and interpreted for a purpose, that it really expressed just the mores of the time. "The Decretals were invented to furnish what was entirely lacking; that is, a documentary authority, running back to Apostolic times, for the divine institution of the primacy of the Pope and of the teaching office of bishops." [1] The period entirely lacked historical sense and critical method; what it had received from the last preceding generation was and must have been always. But that was the mores. Horror of heretics, witches, Mohammedans, Jews was in them, and so were all the other intense faiths, loves, desires, hates, and efforts of the period. In the lack of reading, travel, and discussion there was very little skepticism. Life went on from day

[1] Eicken, H. von: Geschichte und System der mittelalterlichen Weltanschauung, 656.

to day by repetition along grooves of usage and habit. Such life makes strong mores, but also rigid and mechanical ones. In modern times the thirst for reality has developed criticism and skepticism; everything is discussed and questioned. There are few certainties in our knowledge. Our mores are flexible, elastic, and to some extent unstable, but they have strong guarantees. They are to a great extent rational, because if they are not rational they perish; they are open and intelligent, because they are supported by literature and wide discussion; they are also tough, and rather organic than mechanical.

All modern students of the mediæval world have noted the contradictions and inconsistencies of living and thinking. Of these the most important is the contradiction between renunciation of the world and ruling the world; a Gregory VII or an Innocent III goes from one to the other of these without a sense of moral jar, and the modern students who fix their minds on one or the other have two different conceptions of the Middle Ages. Phantasms and ideals have no consistency. A man who deals with them instead of dealing with realities may have a kaleidoscopic relation between his ideas, which relation may be symmetrical and poetically beautiful; but he will have no nexus of thought between his ideas, and therefore no productive combination of them. The mediæval people had a great number of ideals, and they went from one to the other by abrupt transitions without any difficulty. They had intense feelings and enthusiasm for their ideals, but when an intense feeling instead of deep knowledge is the basis of conviction there is no mental or moral consistency.

I have maintained that the religion comes out of the mores and is controlled by them. The religion, however, sums up the most general and philosophic elements in the mores and inculcates them as religious dogmas. It also forms precepts on them. For an example we may note how the humanitarianism of modern mores has colored and warped Christianity. Humanitarianism grew out of economic power developed by commerce, inventions, steam, and electricity. Humanitarianism led to opposition to slavery, and to the emancipation of women. These are not doctrines of the Bible or of Middle-Age Christianity. They were imposed on modern religion by the mores. Then they came from the religion to the modern world as religious ideas and duties, with religious and ecclesiastical sanctions. This is the usual interplay of the mores and religion.

THE MORES OF THE PRESENT AND THE FUTURE

VI

THE MORES OF THE PRESENT AND THE FUTURE

[1909]

THE great utility of studying the origin and history of the mores would be to form judgments about their present status and future tendency. The future tendency can never be discussed beyond the immediate future without running into predictions which would always be vague and in a high degree uncertain. For instance, there is now more or less discussion about divorce, and it will unquestionably affect the mores about marriage. Whether the discussion properly reflects any movement of popular interest is an important question with regard to the present status and tendency. Also, if we could reach results with regard to the present drift of things, we might become convinced of the probable changes in the marriage institution, but more definite or far-reaching predictions about marriage would be unwise.

It will be well to begin with a restatement of the definition of the mores. When a number of men living in neighborhood have the same needs, each one of them attempts to satisfy his need as well as he can whenever it recurs. They notice each other's efforts and select the attempt which satisfies the need best with the least pain or exertion. A selection results by which one way becomes customary for all — a habit for each and a custom for the society. This way is a folkway. It has the power of a habit and custom, and is carried on by tradition. It has the character originally of an experiment. It is established by selection and approved by experience. Here then we have some reflection and some judgment: the reflection is caused by pleasure or pain, which the lowest savages experience and use for criticism; and the judgments are the most simple, consisting only in comparison of effort and satisfaction. From the reflection and judgment there arises at last an opinion as to the relation of the mode of satisfying needs to welfare. This is a moral opinion; namely, an opinion that a usage is favorable to welfare. When a folkway has this moral and reflective judgment added to it, it becomes a part of the mores. The moral inferences become wider and vaguer as they go on, but they constitute, when taken together, the best thinking men can do on human life and wisdom in it. The mores are the customs in which life is held when taken together with the moral judgments as to the bearing of the same on welfare.

The mores, in their origin, were immediately connected with ghost fear and religion, because they came down by tradition from ancestors. This gave them the sanction of a high and vague authority from the other world and created the first notion of duty. Together these elements made up the mental life of men for ages, when they were laying the foundations of all our mental operations and forming our first mental outfit.

I use the word "folkways" for ways of doing things which have little or no moral element. The greatest and best example is language. Language is habit and custom; its formation is made by acts of judgment, although the consideration is slight, the judgment is vague and unconscious, and the authority of tradition prevails. Uneducated people make or destroy a language, in their life, satisfying their interests and needs; expe-

diency seems to be the highest motive.   Abortion and
infanticide are folkways which simply satisfy the desire
to avoid care and toil.   Children are a great trouble
and adults try to shirk the burden;   they adopt direct
means to get rid of it.   Religion sanctifies the acts and
they become customary;   then they are a law and beyond
argument.   In time, however, conditions change.   If,
for example, warriors are needed, then abortion and
infanticide do not seem wise beyond question; the means
of getting food may be easier, and affection has a
chance to grow.   Then these folkways are subjected to
reflection again and a new judgment is formed, with the
result that the customs are set aside by doubt and revolt.
While they last they are mores, not folkways.   The murder
of children had a moral judgment of wisdom and right
policy in it while it was practiced, and the same may be
said of the custom of killing the old.

What now are some of the leading features in the mores
of civilized society at the present time?   Undoubtedly
they are monogamy, anti-slavery, and democracy.   All
people now are more nervous than anybody used to be.
Social ambition is great and is prevalent in all classes.
The idea of class is unpopular and is not understood.
There is a superstitious yearning for equality.   There is
a decided preference for a city life, and a stream of population from the country into big cities.   These are facts
of the mores of the time, and our societies are almost
unanimous in their response if there is any question
raised on these matters.

It is very difficult to discuss the mores; we can hardly
criticise them, for they are our law of right.   We are all
in them, born in them, and made by them.   How can
we rise above them to pass judgment on them?   Our
mores are very different from those of the Middle Ages.

Mediæval people conceived of society under forms of status as generally as we think of it under forms of individual liberty. The mores of the Orient and the Occident differ from each other now as they apparently always have differed: the Orient is a region where time, faith, tradition, and patience rule, while the Occident forms ideals and plans and spends energy and enterprise to make new things with thoughts of progress. All details of life follow the leading ways of thought of each group. We can compare and judge ours and theirs, but independent judgment of our own, without comparison with other times or other places, is possible only within narrow limits.

Let us first take up the nervous desire and exertion which mark the men of our time in the Western civilized societies. There is a wide popular belief in what is called progress. The masses in all civilized states strain toward success in some adopted line. Struggling and striving are passionate tendencies which take possession of groups from time to time. The newspapers, the popular literature, and the popular speakers show this current and popular tendency. This is what makes the mores. A select minority may judge otherwise, and in time their judgment may be accepted and ratified and may make the mores of another age; but the mores are always the ways of the great masses at a time and place. The French were formerly thought to be mercurial, the English sober, and the Germans phlegmatic. The Germans have become nervous; they struggle feverishly for success and preeminence; the war of 1871 and the foundation of the German Empire have made them nationally proud, and made them feel on a level with any other state. Such a change was sure to produce great changes in the mores within two or three generations.

Germany now has ambition for the first place among nations; she is sensitive and suspicious, and often seems quarrelsome. The English, in the Boer War, went through crises of excitement of which it was supposed they were insusceptible. The French, burdened by debt and taxes, feel some sense of losing ground in the rank of nations, and the national party is a product of this feeling. It seems to believe that a truculent and ferocious behavior will win adherents. Perhaps it is right, in view of the nervous temper of the age — certainly the old love of moderation and sobriety in politics seems to be diminishing. The United States is stimulated by its growth and prosperity to unlimited hope and ambition. Professor Giddings [1] thinks that he has proved statistically that the "mental 'mode' of the American people as a whole is ideo-emotional to dogmatical-emotional," and that the market for books confirms this. The market for books could prove only the mental mode of that part of the public which reads books. What fraction is that? It would be most interesting and important to know. Of the books published, Professor Giddings finds that fifty per cent. aim to please, and appeal to emotion or sentiment; forty per cent. aim to convert, and appeal to belief, ethical emotion, or self-interest; eight per cent. are critical and aim to instruct — they appeal to reason. This means that our literature is almost entirely addressed to the appetite for day-dreaming, romantic longings, and sentimentalism, to theoretical interest in crime, adventure, marital infelicity, family tragedies, and the pleasure of emotional excitement, while a large part of it turns upon ethical emotion and ignorant zeal in social matters. This literature reflects the mores and at the same time strengthens them. The people who are

[1] Psychological Review, VIII, 337.

educated on it are trained either to Philistinism or to become the victims of suggestion. No question produced by the fall of silver could possibly be a proper political question. When it was proposed, in the United States, to make the adoption of the single silver standard a party issue and to take a vote on it, consequences were produced which were interesting for the mores. In the first place, there were interests at stake — those of the silver miners and the debtors. Interests dominate modern politics, but always more or less secretly, because it is not admitted in the mores to be right that they should dominate. Hence another pretext must be put forward to cover the interest. The best pretext is always an abstruse doctrine in the theory of public welfare. A protective tariff is never advocated because it will enable some citizens to win wealth by taxing others; it is always advocated as a prosperity policy for the country. Henry C. Carey elevated a protective tariff to a philosophy of society. When the New York courts held a law to be valid which forbade a saloon to be licensed within two hundred feet of a schoolhouse, the saloon-keepers attacked the schools as a nuisance detrimental to property.[1] The advocates of a single silver standard put forward their proposition as a prosperity policy, and they elaborated a philosophy to serve as a major premise to it. Their ultimate philosophy was that gold is a mischief-maker to mankind, while silver is an agent of good. Obviously this is mythology, and is not capable of discussion. The silver question as a political issue was, therefore, a recent and very striking proof of the persistence in the mores of a great modern civilized state of the methods of mythology which have come down to us from prehistoric man. Mythology is in the popular mores.

[1] Riis, J. A.: The Battle with the Slum, 336.

There are mores corresponding to each of the great stages of the industrial organization — hunting, herding, and agricultural. When two groups which are on different stages are neighbors, or when one part of a group advances to another stage, while the remainder still practices the old form, conflicts arise. The Indian and Iranian branches of the Aryans separated under intense enmity and mutual contempt when the Iranians became tillers. All the ways of one people which conform to its industrial pursuits are an abomination to the other. The best explanation yet suggested of the statements of Cæsar and Tacitus about the Germans is that the Germans were, at that period, between nomadism and settled agriculture. There is a deep contrast of mores between town and country, agriculture on the one side and manufactures, commerce, banking, etc., on the other, and this contrast may, at any time, rise to an antagonism. The antagonism is kept down if the two classes meet often; it is developed if they become strictly separated. The town looks upon the country as rustic and uncultivated; the country looks upon the town as vicious and corrupt. The industrial interests of the two are antagonistic, and one may be subjected to the other, as is always the case under a protective tariff, for the protective system never can do anything but make the stronger form of industry carry the weaker. It is a characteristic of our time that in all civilized countries the population is moving from the country to the towns. This movement is not due to the same forces in all countries. Wherever agriculture is burdened by taxes to favor manufacturing, the legislation causes, or intensifies, the movement. It is not probable that the love of luxury, excitement, social intercourse, and amusement is any greater now than it always has been, but popular literature has spread the hunger for it to classes of people who never felt it formerly. The hunger enters into the mores and becomes a characteristic of the age.

The people in the slums and tenement houses will not give up the enjoyment of the streets for any amount of rural comfort. Other classes try to help them, assuming that, to them, crowds, noise, filth, contagious diseases, and narrow quarters, must be painful. The evidence is that they like the life, and are indifferent to what others consider its evils and discomforts. They like it because it satisfies the strongest desires in the mores of our time. The people in the slums feel the same desires as those other people who have clubs, balls, visitors, the park, opera, theater, and all the other means of excitement, gossip, and entertainment which make up fashionable city life.

In Germany it is said that the country population still increases rapidly by a high birth rate.[1] When the land is all taken up this means that there is a surplus in the rural population which goes into the wages class, and a part of it seeks the towns to become unskilled laborers or handicraftsmen. It was formerly believed that great cities consume population; that there is a waste which would produce diminution if it were not for the influx from the country. City life exercises a selection on this immigration from the country; a part of it is consumed by vice and misery and disappears; another part advances to greater social power in two or three generations; another part settles into the tenement houses and recruits the city proletariat. Nowhere in the world, perhaps, are the effects of this migration from the country to the city so strikingly apparent as in New

[1] Ammon, O.: Die Gesellschaftsordnung und ihre natürlichen Grundlagen, 94.

England, for here we see farms abandoned, houses torn
down, and land returning to a state of nature.   Cities,
however, now have a number of institutions of rescue
and protection, which are believed to redeem the old
destruction, so that cities do not, nowadays, consume
population.   The migration affects the mores of both
the rural and the urban population.   Their ideas, standards, ways of looking at things, ambitions, appetites,
concepts of right and wrong, and their judgments on
all the policy of life are affected by the efflux and reflux
between town and country.

One of the most noteworthy and far-reaching features
in modern mores is the unwillingness to recognize a
vow or to enforce a vow by any civil or ecclesiastical
process, although vows have the full authority of Scripture.[1]   It is by the mores that vows have been judged
wrong, and if they are made, neglect to fulfill them is
regarded with indifference.   In modern mores it is allowed
that a man may change his mind as long as he lives.
This view is produced by the doctrine of liberty.   At
the most he may incur liability for damages, if his vow
causes damage to somebody else.   The marriage vow is
the only one which remains in our mores, and no doubt
the leniency of divorce has been largely due to the
unwillingness to enforce a vow by which it may appear
later that one's life career has been injured.   It does not
at all lie in the mores to give the vow prominence as the
aspect of marriage which determines what it is.   On
the contrary, the wedding ceremony is a striking case of
ritual, since people attach importance to the ceremony,
not to the rational sense of what is said and done.

The mores of the latter half of the nineteenth century
were marked by the decline of the dominion of the clas-

[1] Deut. xxiii, 21.

sical culture which had prevailed since the Renaissance. In art this was marked by a return to nature as the only model and an abandonment of the classical models. In architecture it was marked by a revival of Gothic and Renaissance forms, but with a wide eclecticism, the outcome of which is not yet reached. In religion two tendencies were developed, one to mediævalism, the other to agnosticism. What was most important for the mores was the toleration of each other, with which these opposite tendencies in religion existed side by side. Militant infidelity, or religion, was regarded as bad form, and heresy hunting became ridiculous. The popular philosophy became realistic, and the tests of value which were accepted were more and more frankly commercial; "ideal good" lost esteem and "material good" controlled. This was nothing new in the history of mankind, but the opportunities of wealth, comfort, and luxury never before were offered to the whole of a society in any such manner and degree, and the utilities of wealth for all purposes of mankind never were so obvious and immediate. The classical culture and the religious philosophy had offered ideals which were no longer highly valued, and the way was clear for the dominion of materialistic standards and ideals. They spread everywhere, in spite of all protests and denials. The state won greatly in importance, and political institutions extended their operations over the field of the mores. Political institutions took the place of ecclesiastical institutions as adjuncts of the economic struggle for existence. The eighteenth century had bequeathed to the nineteenth a great mass of abstract notions about rights and about the ultimate notions of political philosophy, and in the nineteenth century many of these notions were reduced to actuality in constitutions, laws, and judicial rulings.

The masses in all civilized nations were led to believe that their welfare could be obtained by dogmatic propositions if such propositions were enacted into constitutions and laws. This faith has entered into the mores of all civilized men and now rules their discussion of social questions. Rights, justice, liberty, and equality are the watchwords instead of the church, faith, heaven, and hell. The amount of superstition is not much changed, but it now attaches to politics, not to religion.

The grand controlling fact in modern society is that the earth is underpopulated on the existing stage of the arts. As a consequence men are in demand. The human race is going through a period of enlargement with ease and comfort; accordingly a philosophy of optimism prevails, and the world-beatifiers reign in philosophy. Since, as a fact, the struggle for existence and competition of life are not severe, the philosophy prevails that so they always ought to be. An ethical ideal is carried into nature. It is a fact that the great masses of the human race get on very well with a minimum of education, for the conditions favor most, proportionately, those who are worst off — the unskilled laborers. Hence we find it preached as a doctrine that men, if in crowds, know the truth, feel virtuously, and act wisely by intuition, without education or training.

All modern economic developments have tended to level classes and ranks, and therefore to create democracy, and to throw political power into the hands of the most numerous class; the courtiers of power, therefore, turn to the masses with the same flattery and servility which they used to pay to kings, prelates, and nobles. At every boundary line at which the interests of individuals or groups meet in the competition of life, there is strife and friction, and at all such points there are rights

which are in the mores or the laws and which have been
produced by the need to solve the collisions of power
and interest in peace. There is, therefore, always another
resource for the party which has been defeated in the
competition of life; they can appeal to rights and fight
over again, on the political domain, what they have lost
on the economic domain. Inasmuch as the masses
cannot win on the economic domain because their opponents, though few in number, have talent, knowledge,
craft, and capital, and inasmuch as the masses have
political power, this appeal from the field of economic
effort to that of politics is characteristic of the age. It
now gives form and color to both the economic and political effort, and it is dominating all the mores which have to
do with either. The master of industry dare not neglect
political power; the statesman cannot maintain an
independent footing against capitalistic interest. Primarily, we see a war between plutocracy and democracy.
Secondarily, we see a combination of the two loom up in
the future — the apostles of socialism, state socialism,
municipalization, etc., are all working for it. In the combination the strongest element will rule, and the strongest
element is capital. The defeat and decline of the Democratic political party in the United States within forty
years, its incompetence as an opposition party, its chase
after any captivating issue, its evolution into populism,
coupled with administrative folly, the fear and distrust
which it has consequently inspired in all who have anything, so that they turn to the ruling party for security
at the sacrifice of everything else, the more and more
complete surrender, at the same time, of the Republican
party to the character of a conspiracy to hold power
and use it for plutocratic ends, are phenomena already
observable of the coming consolidation of political and

monetary power. The more industrial and pecuniary functions are confided to the State or city, the more rapidly will this result be brought about. The place to watch to see whether the result will be arrested or not is in the mores. Do the people show strong political sense? Do they show real insight into their own institutions and the spirit of the same, so that they cannot be deceived by political fallacies? Do they resist the allurements of glory and cling to the genuine forces which make for national health and strength? Are they cynical about political corruption, or honestly outraged by it? Is their world-philosophy ignoble? Do they resist a steal because it is a steal or because they are not in it? Are they captivated by appeals to national vanity or do they turn aside from such appeals with contempt? These are the questions which decide the trend of institutions and the destiny of states, and the answer to them must be sought in the mores.

Parties formed on interests invent dogmas which will serve as major premises for the especial inferences which will suit their purpose. These are the "great principles" of history which are always preached as eternal and immutable. John of Salisbury, the friend of Thomas à Becket, taking part in the quarrel of the prelate with the king, which really was a quarrel of the Roman law concept of the State with the Church, developed, in his *Polycraticus*, notions of the sovereignty of the people and of republican self-government. Guelphs argued the sovereignty of the people to get the alliance of the middle class against the emperor, in Italy; while Ghibellines used the same argument to get the alliance of the middle class against the popes, in Germany.[1] St. Augustine thought

[1] Betzold, F. von: Die Lehre von der Volkssouveränetät während des Mittel-Alters, in Sybel's Zeitschrift, XXXVI, 313.

that the State was due to sin, while Gregory VII said
that it was the work of the devil. This was in order to
exalt the Church. The "two sword" doctrine [1] furnished
a dogmatic basis for mediæval society: Pope and Emperor
side by side, with the Pope above. The Church was
due to God, the State was a human invention. Hence
arose the doctrine that the State was based on a contract
between ruler and ruled, and the inference that tyrannicide
was justifiable, an inference which was so frequently
put into practice in the sixteenth century that its fallacy
was demonstrated. Any ruler of whose acts anybody
disapproved was a tyrant. Then the doctrine of contract was changed into the later "social compact" of
the democratic republican form with natural rights, which
ran from Grotius to Rousseau. This doctrine was used
by Mariana and other Jesuits against the absolute kings
(at first, of Spain); it was thoroughly destructive of the
mediæval doctrines of political authority and of rights.

When the Americans, in 1776, revolted against the
colonial policy of England, they found a great number of
principles afloat, and had great trouble to select the one
which would suit their purpose without suggesting other
inferences which would be unwelcome. The first paragraph of the Declaration of Independence contains a
number of these great principles which were supposed
to be axioms of political philosophy. In 1898, when we
forced our rule on the Philippine Islands, some of these
principles were very inconvenient. In time we shall
have to drop others of them. There are no dogmatic
propositions of political philosophy which are universally
and always true; there are views which prevail, at a
time, for a while, and then fade away and give place to
other views. Each set of views colors the mores of a

[1] Luke 22: 38.

period. The eighteenth century notions about equality, natural rights, classes, etc., produced nineteenth century states and legislation, all strongly humanitarian in faith and temper; at the present time the eighteenth century notions are disappearing, and the mores of the twentieth century will not be tinged by humanitarianism as those of the last hundred years have been. If the State should act on ideas of every man's duty, instead of on notions of natural rights, evidently institutions and usages would undergo a great transformation.

While the views of rights are thus afloat on the tide of interest and carry with them, in the ebb and flow, a great mass of corollaries, it does not appear that the doctrine and institutions of constitutional government are being more thoroughly understood or more firmly established. Yet constitutional government is the guarantee of interests and welfare. It is a product of experience; it contains institutions by which collisions of interest can be adjusted and rights can be secured. Yet it does not offer many definitions or dogmatic statements about rights and interests. If men turn from the institutions and put faith in abstract propositions, evidently the chances of welfare will be greatly changed. At the present time constitutional institutions are the great reliance for rights and justice and the great ground of hope and confidence in the future. Nevertheless, constitutional government can never overcome the mores. We have plenty of cases of experiment to prove that constitutional institutions of the best type fall into corruption and decay unless the virtues of political self-control exist in high vigor and purity in the mores of the society.

We see, then, in the status and outlook of the present time, these facts: underpopulation of the globe and increasing control of natural forces give easier conditions for the struggle for existence. This means the most to those who have inherited the least. It is, however, obviously a temporary advantage, for the human race will, in a few generations, find itself face to face with overpopulation and harder conditions. In the meantime philosophies and notions win general acceptance which are relatively true in the exceptional period. They are broadly stated and confidently accepted in the mores and in legislation. Rights are changed in popular opinion and in constitutions, and the location of political power is shifted, especially as between classes; notions about property, marriage, family, inheritance, and so on, change to suit facts and faiths about the struggle for existence. Then groups and parties will form and war will occur between them. Great dogmas will be put forth at all stages of these movements and appropriate watchwords will never be wanting.

SOCIOLOGY

VII

SOCIOLOGY

[1881]

EACH of the sciences which, by giving to man greater knowledge of the laws of nature, has enabled him to cope more intelligently with the ills of life, has had to fight for its independence of metaphysics. We have still lectures on metaphysical biology in some of our colleges and in some of our public courses, but biology has substantially won its independence. Anthropology is more likely to give laws to metaphysics than to accept laws from that authority. Sociology, however, the latest of this series of sciences, is rather entering upon the struggle than emerging from it. Sociology threatens to withdraw an immense range of subjects of the first importance from the dominion of *a priori* speculation and arbitrary dogmatism, and the struggle will be severe in proportion to the dignity and importance of the subject. The struggle, however, is best carried forward indirectly, by simply defining the scope of sociology and by vindicating its position amongst the sciences, while leaving its relations to the other sciences and other pursuits of men to adjust themselves according to the facts. I know of nothing more amusing in these days than to see an old-fashioned metaphysician applying his tests to the results of scientific investigation, and screaming with rage because men of scientific training do not care whether the results satisfy those tests or not.

Sociology is the science of life in society. It investigates the forces which come into action wherever a human society exists. It studies the structure and functions of the organs of human society, and its aim is to find out the laws in subordination to which human society takes its various forms and social institutions grow and change. Its practical utility consists in deriving the rules of right social living from the facts and laws which prevail by nature in the constitution and functions of society. It must, without doubt, come into collision with all other theories of right living which are founded on authority, tradition, arbitrary invention, or poetic imagination.

Sociology is perhaps the most complicated of all the sciences, yet there is no domain of human interest the details of which are treated ordinarily with greater facility. Various religions have various theories of social living, which they offer as authoritative and final. It has never, so far as I know, been asserted by anybody that a man of religious faith, in any religion, could not study sociology or recognize the existence of any such science; but it is incontestably plain that a man who accepts the dogmas about social living which are imposed by the authority of any religion must regard the subject of right social living as settled and closed, and he cannot enter on any investigation the first groundwork of which would be doubt of the authority which he recognizes as final. Hence social problems and social phenomena present no difficulty to him who has only to cite an authority or obey a prescription.

Then again the novelists set forth "views" about social matters. To write and read novels is perhaps the most royal road to teaching and learning which has ever been devised. The proceeding of the novelists is kaleidoscopic. They turn the same old bits of colored glass over and over again into new combinations. There is no limit, no sequence, no bond of consistency. The romance-writing social philosopher always proves his case, just as a man always wins who plays chess with himself.

Then again the utopians and socialists make easy work of the complicated phenomena with which sociology has to deal. These persons, vexed with the intricacies of social problems and revolting against the facts of the social order, take upon themselves the task of inventing a new and better world. They brush away all which troubles us men and create a world free from annoying limitations and conditions — in their imagination. In ancient times, and now in half-civilized countries, these persons have been founders of religions. Something of that type always lingers around them still and among us, and is to be seen amongst the reformers and philanthropists, who never contribute much to the improvement of society in any actual detail, but find a key principle for making the world anew and regenerating society. I have even seen faint signs of the same mysticism in social matters in some of the green-backers who have "thought out" in bed, as they relate, a scheme of wealth by paper money, as Mahomet would have received a surah or Joe Smith a revelation about polygamy. Still there are limits to this resemblance, because in our nineteenth century American life a sense of humor, even if defective, answers some of the purposes of common sense.

Then again all the whimsical people who have hobbies of one sort or another come forward with projects which are the result of a strong impression, an individual misfortune, or an unregulated benevolent desire, and which are therefore the product of a facile emotion, not of a laborious investigation.

Then again the *dilettanti* make light work of social questions. Everyone, by the fact of living in society, gathers some observations of social phenomena. The belief grows up, as it was expressed some time ago by a professor of mathematics, that everybody knows about the topics of sociology. Those topics have a broad and generous character. They lend themselves easily to generalizations. There are as yet no sharp tests formulated. Above all, and worst lack of all as yet, we have no competent criticism. Hence it is easy for the aspirant after culture to venture on this field without great danger of being brought to account, as he would be if he attempted geology, or physics, or biology. Even a scientific man of high attainments in some other science, in which he well understands what special care, skill, and training are required, will not hesitate to dogmatize about a topic of sociology. A group of half-educated men may be relied upon to attack a social question and to hammer it dead in a few minutes with a couple of commonplaces and a sweeping *a priori* assumption. Above all other topics, social topics lend themselves to the purposes of the diner-out.

Two facts, however, in regard to social phenomena need only be mentioned to be recognized as true. (1) Social phenomena always present themselves to us in very complex combinations, and (2) it is by no means easy to interpret the phenomena. The phenomena are often at three or four removes from their causes. Tradition, prejudice, fashion, habit, and other similar obstacles continually warp and deflect the social forces, and they constitute interferences whose magnitude is to be ascertained separately for each case. It is also impossible for us to set up a social experiment. To do that we should need to dispose of the time and liberty of a certain number of men. It follows that sociology requires a special method, and that probably no science requires such peculiar skill and sagacity in the observer and interpreter of the phenomena which are to be studied. One peculiarity may be especially noted because it shows a very common error of students of social science. A sociologist needs to arrange his facts before he has obtained them; that is to say, he must make a previous classification so as to take up the facts in a certain order. If he does not do this he may be overwhelmed in the mass of his material so that he never can master it. How shall anyone know how to classify until the science itself has made some progress? Statistics furnish us the best illustration at the present time of the difficulty here referred to.

When, now, we take into account these difficulties and requirements, it is evident that the task of sociology is one which will call for especial and long training, and that it will probably be a long time yet before we can train up any body of special students who will be so well trained in the theory and science of society as to be able to form valuable opinions on points of social disease and social remedy. But it is a fact of familiar observation that all popular discussions of social questions seize directly upon points of social disease and social remedies. The diagnosis of some asserted social ill and the prescription of the remedy are undertaken offhand by the first comer, and without reflecting that the diagnosis of a social disease is many times harder than that of a disease in an individual, and that to prescribe for a society is to prescribe for an organism which is immortal. To err in prescribing for a man is at worst to kill him; to err in prescribing for a society is to set in operation injurious forces which extend, ramify, and multiply their effects in ever new combinations throughout an indefinite future. It may pay to experiment with an individual, because he cannot wait for medical science to be perfected; it cannot pay to experiment with a society, because the society does not die and can afford to wait.

If we have to consider the need of sociology, innumerable reasons for studying it present themselves. In spite of all our acquisitions in natural science, the conception of a natural law—which is the most important good to be won from studying natural science — is yet exceedingly vague in the minds of ordinary intelligent people, and is very imperfect even amongst the educated. That conception is hardly yet applied by anybody to social facts and problems.   Social questions force themselves upon us in multitudes every year as our civilization advances and our society becomes complex.   When such questions arise they are wrangled over and tossed about without any orderly discussion, but as if they were only the sport of arbitrary whims.   Is it not then necessary that we enable ourselves, by study of the facts and laws of society, to take up such questions from the correct point of view, and to proceed with the examination of them in such order and method that we can reach solid results, and thus obtain command of an increasing mass of knowledge about social phenomena?   The assumption which underlies almost all discussion of social topics is that we men need only to make up our minds what kind of a society we want to have, and that then we can devise means for calling that society into existence.   It is assumed that we can decide to live on one spot of the earth's surface or another, and to pursue there one industry or another, and then that we can, by our devices, make that industry as productive as any other could be in that place.   People believe that we have only to choose

whether we will have aristocratic institutions or democratic institutions. It is believed that statesmen can, if
they will, put a people in the way of material prosperity.
It is believed that rent on land can be abolished if it is
not thought expedient to have it. It is assumed that
peasant proprietors can be brought into existence anywhere where it is thought that it would be an advantage
to have them. These illustrations might be multiplied
indefinitely. They show the need of sociology, and if
we should go on to notice the general conceptions of
society, its ills and their remedies, which are held by
various religious, political, and social sects, we should
find ample further evidence of this need.

Let us then endeavor to define the field of sociology.
Life in society is the life of a human society on this
earth. Its elementary conditions are set by the nature
of human beings and the nature of the earth. We have
already become familiar, in biology, with the transcendent importance of the fact that life on earth must be
maintained by a struggle against nature, and also by
a competition with other forms of life. In the latter
fact biology and sociology touch. Sociology is a science
which deals with one range of phenomena produced by
the struggle for existence, while biology deals with another. The forces are the same, acting on different fields
and under different conditions. The sciences are truly
cognate. Nature contains certain materials which are
capable of satisfying human needs, but those materials
must, with rare and mean exceptions, be won by labor,
and must be fitted to human use by more labor. As
soon as any number of human beings are struggling each
to win from nature the material goods necessary to support life, and are carrying on this struggle side by side,
certain social forces come into operation. The prime

condition of this society will lie in the ratio of its numbers to the supply of materials within its reach. For the supply at any moment attainable is an exact quantity, and the number of persons who can be supplied is arithmetically limited. If the actual number present is very much less than the number who might be supported, the condition of all must be ample and easy. Freedom and facility mark all social relations under such a state of things. If the number is larger than that which can be supplied, the condition of all must be one of want and distress, or else a few must be well provided, the others being proportionately still worse off. Constraint, anxiety, possibly tyranny and repression, mark social relations. It is when the social pressure due to an unfavorable ratio of population to land becomes intense that the social forces develop increased activity. Division of labor, exchange, higher social organization, emigration, advance in the arts, spring from the necessity of contending against the harsher conditions of existence which are continually reproduced as the population surpasses the means of existence on any given status.

The society with which we have to deal does not consist of any number of men. An army is not a society. A man with his wife and his children constitutes a society, for its essential parts are all present, and the number more or less is immaterial. A certain division of labor between the sexes is imposed by nature. The family as a whole maintains itself better under an organization with division of labor than it could if the functions were shared so far as possible. From this germ the development of society goes on by the regular steps of advancement to higher organization, accompanied and sustained by improvements in the arts. The increase of population goes on according to biological laws which are capable of multiplying the species beyond any assignable limits, so that the number to be provided for steadily advances and the status of ease and abundance gives way to a status of want and constraint. Emigration is the first and simplest remedy. By winning more land the ratio of population to land is once more rendered favorable. It is to be noticed, however, that emigration is painful to all men. To the uncivilized man, to emigrate means to abandon a mass of experiences and traditions which have been won by suffering, and to go out to confront new hardships and perils. To the civilized man migration means cutting off old ties of kin and country. The earth has been peopled by man at the cost of this suffering.

On the side of the land also stands the law of the diminishing return as a limitation. More labor gets more from the land, but not proportionately more. Hence, if more men are to be supported, there is need not of a proportionate increase of labor, but of a disproportionate increase of labor. The law of population, therefore, combined with the law of the diminishing returns, constitutes the great underlying condition of society. Emigration, improvements in the arts, in morals, in education, in political organization, are only stages in the struggle of man to meet these conditions, to break their force for a time, and to win room under them for ease and enlargement. Ease and enlargement mean either power to support more men on a given stage of comfort or power to advance the comfort of a given number of men. Progress is a word which has no meaning save in view of the laws of population and the diminishing return, and it is quite natural that anyone who fails to understand those laws should fall into doubt which way progress points, whether towards wealth or poverty. The laws of population and the diminshing return, in their combination, are the iron spur which has driven the race on to all which it has ever achieved, and the fact that population ever advances, yet advances against a barrier which resists more stubbornly at every step of advance, unless it is removed to a new distance by some conquest of man over nature, is the guarantee that the task of civilization will never be ended, but that the need for more energy, more intelligence, and more virtue will never cease while the race lasts. If it were possible for an increasing population to be sustained by proportionate increments of labor, we should all still be living in the original home of the race on the spontaneous products of the earth. Let him, therefore, who desires to study social phenomena first learn the transcendent importance for the whole social organization, industrial, political, and civil, of the ratio of population to land.

We have noticed that the relations involved in the struggle for existence are twofold. There is first the struggle of individuals to win the means of subsistence from nature, and secondly there is the competition of man with man in the effort to win a limited supply. The radical error of the socialists and sentimentalists is that they never distinguish these two relations from each other. They bring forward complaints which are really to be made, if at all, against the author of the universe for the hardships which man has to endure in his struggle with nature. The complaints are addressed, however, to society; that is, to other men under the same hardships. The only social element, however, is the competition of life, and when society is blamed for the ills which belong to the human lot, it is only burdening those who have successfully contended with those ills with the further task of conquering the same ills over again for somebody else. Hence liberty perishes in all socialistic schemes, and the tendency of such schemes is to the deterioration of society by burdening the good members and relieving the bad ones. The law of the survival of the fittest was not made by man and cannot be abrogated by man. We can only, by interfering with it, produce the survival of the unfittest. If a man comes forward with any grievance against the order of society so far as this is shaped by human agency, he must have patient hearing and full redress; but if he addresses a demand to society for relief from the hardships of life, he asks simply that somebody else should get his living for him. In that case he ought to be left to find out his error from hard experience.

The sentimental philosophy starts from the first principle that nothing is true which is disagreeable, and that we must not believe anything which is "shocking," no matter what the evidence may be. There are various stages of this philosophy. It touches on one side the intuitional philosophy which proves that certain things must exist by proving that man needs them, and it touches on the other side the vulgar socialism which affirms that the individual has a right to whatever he needs, and that this right is good against his fellow men. To this philosophy in all its grades the laws of population and the diminishing return have always been very distasteful. The laws which entail upon mankind an inheritance of labor cannot be acceptable to any philosophy which maintains that man comes into the world endowed with natural rights and an inheritor of freedom. It is a death-blow to any intuitional philosophy to find out, as an historical fact, what diverse thoughts, beliefs, and actions man has manifested, and it requires but little actual knowledge of human history to show that the human race has never had any ease which it did not earn, or any freedom which it did not conquer. Sociology, therefore, by the investigations which it pursues, dispels illusions about what society is or may be, and gives instead knowledge of facts which are the basis of intelligent effort by man to make the best of his circumstances on earth. Sociology, therefore, which can never accomplish anything more than to enable us to make the best of our situation, will never be able to reconcile itself with those philosophies which are trying to find out how we may arrange things so as to satisfy any ideal of society.

The competition of life has taken the form, historically, of a struggle for the possession of the soil. In the simpler states of society the possession of the soil is tribal, and the struggles take place between groups, producing the wars and feuds which constitute almost the whole of early history. On the agricultural stage the tribal or communal possession of land exists as a survival, but it gives way to private property in land whenever the community advances and the institutions are free to mold themselves. The agricultural stage breaks up tribal relations and encourages individualization. This is one of the reasons why it is such an immeasurable advance over the lower forms of civilization. It sets free individual energy, and while the social bond gains in scope and variety, it also gains in elasticity, for the solidarity of the group is broken up and the individual may work out his own ends by his own means, subject only to the social ties which lie in the natural conditions of human life. It is only on the agricultural stage that liberty as civilized men understand it exists at all. The poets and sentimentalists, untaught to recognize the grand and world-wide cooperation which is secured by the free play of individual energy under the great laws of the social order, bewail the decay of early communal relations and exalt the liberty of the primitive stages of civilization. These notions all perish at the first touch of actual investigation. The whole retrospect of human history runs downwards towards beast-like misery and slavery to the destructive forces of nature. The whole history has been one series of toilsome, painful, and bloody struggles, first to find out where we were and what were the conditions of greater ease, and then to devise means to get relief. Most of the way the motives of advance have been experience of suffering and instinct. It is only in the most recent years that science has undertaken to teach without and in advance of suffering, and as yet science has to fight so hard against tradition that its authority is only slowly winning recognition. The institutions whose growth constitutes the advance of civilization have their guarantee in the very fact that they grew and became established. They suited man's purpose better than what went before. They are all imperfect, and all carry with them incidental ills, but each came to be because it was better than what went before, and each of which has perished, perished because a better one supplanted it.

It follows once and for all that to turn back to any defunct institution or organization because existing institutions are imperfect is to turn away from advance and is to retrograde. The path of improvement lies forwards. Private property in land, for instance, is an institution which has been developed in the most direct and legitimate manner. It may give way at a future time to some other institution which will grow up by imperceptible stages out of the efforts of men to contend successfully with existing evils, but the grounds for private property in land are easily perceived, and it is safe to say that no *a priori* scheme of state ownership

or other tenure invented *en bloc* by any philosopher and
adopted by legislative act will ever supplant it.   To talk
of any such thing is to manifest a total misconception of
the facts and laws which it is the province of sociology to
investigate.   The case is less in magnitude but scarcely
less out of joint with all correct principle when it is
proposed to adopt a unique tax on land, in a country
where the rent of land is so low that any important
tax on land exceeds it, and therefore becomes indirect,
and where also political power is in the hands of small
landowners, who hold, without ever having formulated
it, a doctrine of absolute property in the soil such as is
not held by any other landowners in the world.

Sociology must exert a most important influence on
political economy.   Political economy is the science
which investigates the laws of the material welfare of
human societies.   It is not its province to teach individuals how to get rich.   It is a social science.   It was
the first branch of sociology which was pursued by man
as a science.   It is not strange that when the industrial
organization of society was studied apart from the organism of which it forms a part it was largely dominated
over by arbitrary dogmatism, and that it should have
fallen into disrepute as a mere field of opinion, and of
endless wrangling about opinions for which no guarantees
could be given.   The rise of a school of "historical"
economists is itself a sign of a struggle towards a positive
and scientific study of political economy, in its due relations to other social sciences, and this sign loses none of
its significance in spite of the crudeness and extravagance
of the opinions of the historical economists, and in spite
of their very marked tendency to fall into dogmatism and
hobby-riding.   Political economy is thrown overboard
by all groups and persons whenever it becomes trouble-

some. When it got in the way of Mr. Gladstone's land-
bill he relegated it, by implication, to the planet Saturn,
to the great delight of all the fair-traders, protectionists, soft-money men, and others who had found it in
the way of their devices. What political economy needs
in order to emerge from the tangle in which it is now
involved, and to win a dignified and orderly development,
is to find its field and its relations to other sciences fairly
defined within the wider scope of sociology. Its laws
will then take their place not as arbitrary or broken fragments, but in due relation to other laws. Those laws
will win proof and establishment from this relation.

For instance, we have plenty of books, some of them
by able writers, in which the old-fashioned Malthusian
doctrine of population and the Ricardian law of rent are
disputed because emigration, advance in the arts, etc.,
can offset the action of those laws or because those laws
are not seen in action in the United States. Obviously
no such objections ever could have been raised if the
laws in question had been understood or had been put
in their proper bearings. The Malthusian law of population and the Ricardian law of rent are cases in which
by rare and most admirable acumen powerful thinkers
perceived two great laws in particular phases of their
action. With wider information it now appears that the
law of population breaks the barriers of Malthus'
narrower formulæ and appears as a great law of biology.
The Ricardian law of rent is only a particular application
of one of the great conditions of production. We have
before us not special dogmas of political economy, but
facts of the widest significance for the whole social development of the race. To object that these facts may be
set aside by migration or advance in the arts is nothing
to the purpose, for this is only altering the constants in

the equation, which does not alter the form of the curve, but only its position relatively to some standard line. Furthermore, the laws themselves indicate that they have a maximum point for any society, or any given stage of the arts, and a condition of under-population, or of an extractive industry below its maximum, is just as consistent with the law as a condition of over-population and increasing distress. Hence inferences as to the law of population drawn from the status of an under-populated country are sure to be fallacious. In like manner arguments drawn from American phenomena in regard to rent and wages, when rent and wages are as yet only very imperfectly developed here, lead to erroneous conclusions. It only illustrates the unsatisfactory condition of political economy, and the want of strong criticism in it, that such arguments can find admission to its discussions and disturb its growth.

It is to the pursuit of sociology and the study of the industrial organization in combination with the other organizations of society that we must look for the more fruitful development of political economy. We are already in such a position with sociology that a person who has gained what we now possess of that science will bring to bear upon economic problems a sounder judgment and a more correct conception of all social relations than a person who may have read a library of the existing treatises on political economy. The essential elements of political economy are only corollaries or special cases of sociological principles. One who has command of the law of the conservation of energy as it manifests itself in society is armed at once against socialism, protectionism, paper money, and a score of other economic fallacies. The sociological view of political economy also includes whatever is sound in the dogmas of the "historical school" and furnishes what that school is apparently groping after.

As an illustration of the light which sociology throws on a great number of political and social phenomena which are constantly misconstrued, we may notice the differences in the industrial, political, and civil organizations which are produced all along at different stages of the ratio of population to land.

When a country is under-populated newcomers are not competitors, but assistants. If more come they may produce not only new quotas, but a surplus besides, to be divided between themselves and all who were present before. In such a state of things land is abundant and cheap. The possession of it confers no power or privilege. No one will work for another for wages when he can take up new land and be his own master. Hence it will pay no one to own more land than he can cultivate by his own labor, or with such aid as his own family supplies. Hence, again, land bears little or no rent; there will be no landlords living on rent and no laborers living on wages, but only a middle class of yeoman farmers. All are substantially on an equality, and democracy becomes the political form, because this is the only state of society in which the dogmatic assumption of equality, on which democracy is based, is realized as a fact. The same effects are powerfully reenforced by other facts. In a new and under-populated country the industries which are most profitable are the extractive industries. The characteristic of these, with the exception of some kinds of mining, is that they call for only a low organization of labor and small amount of capital. Hence they allow the workman to become speedily his own master, and they educate him to freedom, independence, and self-reliance. At the same time, the social groups being only vaguely marked off from each other, it is easy to pass from one class of occupations, and consequently from one social grade, to another. Finally, under the same circumstances education, skill, and superior training have but inferior value compared with what they have in densely populated countries. The advantages lie, in an under-populated country, with the coarser, unskilled, manual occupations, and not with the highest developments of science, literature, and art.

If now we turn for comparison to cases of over-population we see that the struggle for existence and the competition of life are intense where the pressure of population is great. This competition draws out the highest achievements. It makes the advantages of capital, education, talent, skill, and training tell to the utmost. It draws out the social scale upwards and downwards to great extremes and produces aristocratic social organizations in spite of all dogmas of equality. Landlords, tenants (i.e., capitalist employers), and laborers are the three primary divisions of any aristocratic order, and they are sure to be developed whenever land bears rent and whenever tillage requires the application of large capital. At the same time liberty has to undergo curtailment. A man who has a square mile to himself can easily do as he likes, but a man who walks Broadway at noon or lives in a tenement-house finds his power to do as he likes limited by scores of considerations for the rights and feelings of his fellowmen. Furthermore, organization with subordination and discipline is essential in order that the society as a whole may win a support from the land. In an over-populated country the extremes of wealth and luxury are presented side by side with the extremes of poverty and distress. They are equally the products of an intense social pressure. The achievements of power are highest, the rewards of prudence, energy, enterprise, foresight, sagacity, and all other industrial virtues is greatest; on the other hand, the penalties of folly, weakness, error, and vice are most terrible. Pauperism, prostitution, and crime are the attendants of a state of society in which science, art, and literature reach their highest developments. Now it is evident that over-population and under-population are only relative terms. Hence as time goes on any under-populated nation is surely moving forward towards the other status, and is speedily losing its natural advantages which are absolute, and also that relative advantage which belongs to it if it is in neighborly relations with nations of dense population and high civilization; *viz.*, the chance to borrow and assimilate from them the products, in arts and science, of high civilization without enduring the penalties of intense social pressure.

We have seen that if we should try by any measures of arbitrary interference and assistance to relieve the victims of social pressure from the calamity of their position we should only offer premiums to folly and vice and extend them further. We have also seen that we must go forward and meet our problems. We cannot escape them by running away. If then it be asked what the wit and effort of man can do to struggle with the problems offered by social pressure, the answer is that he can do only what his instinct has correctly and surely led him to do without any artificial social organization of any kind, and that is, by improvements in the arts, in science, in morals, in political institutions, to widen and strengthen the power of man over nature. The task of dealing with social ills is not a new task. People set about it and discuss it as if the human race had hitherto neglected it, and as if the solution of the problem was to

be something new in form and substance, different from
the solution of all problems which have hitherto engaged
human effort. In truth, the human race has never done
anything else but struggle with the problem of social
welfare. That struggle constitutes history, or the life
of the human race on earth. That struggle embraces
all minor problems which occupy attention here, save
those of religion, which reaches beyond this world and
finds its objects beyond this life. Every successful effort
to widen the power of man over nature is a real victory
over poverty, vice, and misery, taking things in general
and in the long run. It would be hard to find a single
instance of a direct assault by positive effort upon poverty,
vice, and misery which has not either failed or, if it has
not failed directly and entirely, has not entailed other
evils greater than the one which it removed. The only
two things which really tell on the welfare of man on
earth are hard work and self-denial (in technical language,
labor and capital), and these tell most when they are
brought to bear directly upon the effort to earn an honest
living, to accumulate capital, and to bring up a family
of children to be industrious and self-denying in their
turn. I repeat that this is the way to work for the welfare of man on earth; and what I mean to say is that the
common notion that when we are going to work for the
social welfare of man we must adopt a great dogma,
organize for the realization of some great scheme, have
before us an abstract ideal, or otherwise do anything but
live honest and industrious lives, is a great mistake.
From the standpoint of the sociologist pessimism and
optimism are alike impertinent. To be an optimist one
must forget the frightful sanctions which are attached
to the laws of right living. To be a pessimist one must
overlook the education and growth which are the product

of effort and self-denial. In either case one is passing judgment on what is inevitably fixed, and on which the approval or condemnation of man can produce no effect. The facts and laws are, once and for all, so, and for us men that is the end of the matter. The only persons for whom there would be any sense in the question whether life is worth living are primarily the yet unborn children, and secondarily the persons who are proposing to found families. For these latter the question would take a somewhat modified form: Will life be worth living for children born of me? This question is, unfortunately, not put to themselves by the appropriate persons as it would be if they had been taught sociology. The sociologist is often asked if he wants to kill off certain classes of troublesome and burdensome persons. No such inference follows from any sound sociological doctrine, but it is allowed to infer, as to a great many persons and classes, that it would have been better for society, and would have involved no pain to them, if they had never been born.

In further illustration of the interpretation which sociology offers of phenomena which are often obscure, we may note the world-wide effects of the advances in the arts and sciences which have been made during the last hundred years. These improvements have especially affected transportation and communication; that is, they have lessened the obstacles of time and space which separate the groups of mankind from each other and have tended to make the whole human race a single unit. The distinction between over-populated and under-populated countries loses its sharpness, and all are brought to an average. Every person who migrates from Europe to America affects the comparative status of the two continents. He lessens the pressure in the country he leaves and increases it in the country to which he goes. If he goes to Minnesota and raises wheat there, which is carried back to the country he left as cheap food for those who have not emigrated, it is evident that the bearing upon social pressure is twofold. It is evident, also, that the problem of social pressure can no longer be correctly studied if the view is confined either to the country of immigration or the country of emigration, but that it must embrace both. It is easy to see, therefore, that the ratio of population to land with which we have to deal is only in peculiar and limited cases that ratio as it exists in England, Germany, or the United States. It is the ratio as it exists in the civilized world, and every year that passes, as our improved arts break down the barriers between different parts of the earth, brings us nearer to the state of things where all the population of Europe, America, Australasia, and South Africa must be considered in relation to all the land of the same territories, for all that territory will be available for all that population, no matter what the proportion may be in which the population is distributed over the various portions of the territory. The British Islands may become one great manufacturing city. Minnesota, Texas, and Australia may not have five persons to the square mile. Yet all will eat the meat of Texas and the wheat of Minnesota and wear the wool of Australia manufactured on the looms of England. That all will enjoy the maximum of food and raiment under that state of things is as clear as anything possibly can be which is not yet an accomplished fact. We are working towards it by all our instincts of profit and improvement. The greatest obstacles are those which come from prejudices, traditions, and dogmas, which are held independently of any observation of facts or any correct reasoning, and which set the right hand working against the left. For instance, the Mississippi Valley was, a century ago, as unavailable to support the population of France and Germany as if it had been in the moon. The Mississippi Valley is now nearer to France and Germany than the British Islands were a century ago, reckoning distance by the only true standard; *viz.*, difficulty of communication. It is a fair way of stating it to say that the improvements in transportation of the last fifty years have added to France and Germany respectively a tract of land of the very highest fertility, equal in area to the territory of those states, and available for the support of their population. The public men of those countries are now declaring that this is a calamity, and are devising means to counteract it.

The social and political effects of the improvements which have been made must be very great. It follows from what we have said about the effects of intense social pressure and high competition that the effect of thus bringing to bear on the great centers of population the new land of outlying countries must be to relieve the pressure in the oldest countries and at the densest centers. Then the extremes of wealth and poverty, culture and brutality, will be contracted and there will follow a general tendency towards an average equality which, however, must be understood only within very broad limits. Such is no doubt the meaning of the general tendency towards equality, the decline of aristocratic institutions, the rise of the proletariat, and the ambitious expansion, in short, which is characteristic of modern civilized society. It would lead me too far to follow out this line of speculation as to the future, but two things ought to be noticed in passing. (1) There are important offsets to the brilliant promise which there

190 ESSAYS OF WILLIAM GRAHAM SUMNER

is for mankind in a period during which, for the whole civilized world, there will be a wide margin of ease between the existing population and the supporting power of the available land. These offsets consist in the effects of ignorance, error, and folly — the same forces which have always robbed mankind of half what they might have enjoyed on earth. Extravagant governments, abuses of public credit, wasteful taxation, legislative monopolies and special privileges, juggling with currency, restrictions on trade, wasteful armaments on land and sea, and other follies in economy and statecraft, are capable of wasting and nullifying all the gains of civilization. (2) The old classical civilization fell under an irruption of barbarians from without. It is possible that our new civilization may perish by an explosion from within. The sentimentalists have been preaching for a century notions of rights and equality, of the dignity, wisdom, and power of the proletariat, which have filled the minds of ignorant men with impossible dreams. The thirst for luxurious enjoyment has taken possession of us all. It is the dark side of the power to foresee a possible future good with such distinctness as to make it a motive of energy and persevering industry — a power which is distinctly modern. Now the thirst for luxurious enjoyment, when brought into connection with the notions of rights, of power, and of equality, and dissociated from the notions of industry and economy, produces the notion that a man is robbed of his rights if he has not everything that he wants, and that he is deprived of equality if he sees anyone have more than he has, and that he is a fool if, having the power of the State in his hands, he allows this state of things to last. Then we have socialism, communism, and nihilism; and the fairest conquests of civilization, with all their promise of solid good to man, on the sole conditions of virtue and wisdom, may be scattered to the winds in a war of classes, or trampled underfoot by a mob which can only hate what it cannot enjoy.

It must be confessed that sociology is yet in a tentative and inchoate state. All that we can affirm with certainty is that social phenomena are subject to law, and that the natural laws of the social order are in their entire character like the laws of physics. We can draw in grand outline the field of sociology and foresee the shape that it will take and the relations it will bear to other sciences. We can also already find the standpoint which it will occupy, and, if a figure may be allowed, although we still look over a wide landscape largely enveloped in mist, we can see where the mist lies and define the general features of the landscape, subject to further corrections. To deride or contemn a science in this state would certainly be a most unscientific proceeding. We confess, however, that so soon as we go beyond the broadest principles of the science we have not yet succeeded in discovering social laws, so as to be able to formulate them. A great amount of labor yet remains to be done in the stages of preparation. There are, however, not more than two or three other sciences which are making as rapid progress as sociology, and there is no other which is as full of promise for the welfare of man. That sociology has an immense department of human interests to control is beyond dispute. Hitherto this department has been included in moral science, and it has not only been confused and entangled by dogmas no two of which are consistent with each other, but also it has been without any growth, so that at this moment our knowledge of social science is behind the demands which existing social questions make upon us. We are face to face with an issue no less grand than this: Shall we, in our general social policy, pursue the effort to realize more completely that constitutional liberty for which we have been struggling throughout modern history, or shall we return to the mediæval device of functionaries to regulate procedure and to adjust interests?   Shall we try to connect with liberty an equal and appropriate responsibility as its essential complement and corrective, so that a man who gets his own way shall accept his own consequences, or shall we yield to the sentimentalism which, after preaching an unlimited liberty, robs those who have been wise out of pity for those who have been foolish?   Shall we accept the inequalities which follow upon free competition as the definition of justice, or shall we suppress free competition in the interest of equality and to satisfy a baseless dogma of justice?   Shall we try to solve the social entanglements which arise in a society where social ties are constantly becoming more numerous and more subtle, and where contract has only partly superseded custom and status, by returning to the latter, only hastening a more complete development of the former?   These certainly are practical questions, and their scope is such that they embrace a great number of minor questions which are before us and which are coming up. It is to the science of society, which will derive true conceptions of society from the facts and laws of the social order,[1] studied without prejudice or bias of any sort, that we must look for the correct answer to these questions. By this observation the field of sociology and the work which it is to do for society are sufficiently defined.

[1] It has been objected that no proof is offered that social laws exist in the order of nature.   By what demonstration could any such proof be given *a priori?*   If a man of scientific training finds his attention arrested, in some group of phenomena, by these sequences, relations, and recurrences which he has learned to note as signs of action of law, he seeks to discover the law. If it exists, he finds it.   What other proof of its existences could there be?

THE ABSURD EFFORT TO MAKE THE WORLD OVER

VIII

THE ABSURD EFFORT TO MAKE THE WORLD OVER

[1894]

IT will not probably be denied that the burden of proof is on those who affirm that our social condition is utterly diseased and in need of radical regeneration. My task at present, therefore, is entirely negative and critical: to examine the allegations of fact and the doctrines which are put forward to prove the correctness of the diagnosis and to warrant the use of the remedies proposed.

The propositions put forward by social reformers nowadays are chiefly of two kinds. There are assertions in historical form, chiefly in regard to the comparison of existing with earlier social states, which are plainly based on defective historical knowledge, or at most on current stock historical dicta which are uncritical and incorrect. Writers very often assert that something never existed before because they do not know that it ever existed before, or that something is worse than ever before because they are not possessed of detailed information about what has existed before. The other class of propositions consists of dogmatic statements which, whether true or not, are unverifiable. This class of propositions is the pest and bane of current economic and social discussion. Upon a more or less superficial view of some phenomenon a suggestion arises which is embodied in a philosophical proposition and promulgated as a truth. From the form and nature of such propositions they can always be brought under the head of "ethics." This word at least gives them an air of elevated sentiment and purpose, which is the only warrant they possess. It is impossible to test or verify them by any investigation or logical process whatsoever. It is therefore very difficult for anyone who feels a high responsibility for historical statements, and who absolutely rejects any statement which is unverifiable, to find a common platform for discussion or to join issue satisfactorily in taking the negative.

When anyone asserts that the class of skilled and unskilled manual laborers of the United States is worse off now in respect to diet, clothing, lodgings, furniture, fuel, and lights; in respect to the age at which they can marry; the number of children they can provide for; the start in life which they can give to their children, and their chances of accumulating capital, than they ever have been at any former time, he makes a reckless assertion for which no facts have been offered in proof. Upon an appeal to facts, the contrary of this assertion would be clearly established. It suffices, therefore, to challenge those who are responsible for the assertion to make it good.

If it is said that the employed class are under much more stringent discipline than they were thirty years ago or earlier, it is true. It is not true that there has been any qualitative change in this respect within thirty years, but it is true that a movement which began at the first settlement of the country has been advancing with constant acceleration and has become a noticeable feature within our time. This movement is the advance in the industrial organization. The first settlement was made by agriculturists, and for a long time there was scarcely any organization. There were scattered farmers, each working for himself, and some small towns with only

rudimentary commerce and handicrafts. As the country
has filled up, the arts and professions have been differen-
tiated and the industrial organization has been advancing.
This fact and its significance has hardly been noticed at
all; but the stage of the industrial organization existing
at any time, and the rate of advance in its development,
are the absolutely controlling social facts. Nine-tenths
of the socialistic and semi-socialistic, and sentimental or
ethical, suggestions by which we are overwhelmed come
from failure to understand the phenomena of the industrial organization and its expansion. It controls us all
because we are all in it. It creates the conditions of
our existence, sets the limits of our social activity, regu-
lates the bonds of our social relations, determines our
conceptions of good and evil, suggests our life-philosophy,
molds our inherited political institutions, and reforms
the oldest and toughest customs, like marriage and property. I repeat that the turmoil of heterogeneous and
antagonistic social whims and speculations in which we
live is due to the failure to understand what the industrial organization is and its all-pervading control over
human life, while the traditions of our school of philosophy
lead us always to approach the industrial organization,
not from the side of objective study, but from that of
philosophical doctrine. Hence it is that we find that the
method of measuring what we see happening by what are
called ethical standards, and of proposing to attack the
phenomena by methods thence deduced, is so popular.

The advance of a new country from the very simplest
social coordination up to the highest organization is a
most interesting and instructive chance to study the
development of the organization. It has of course been
attended all the way along by stricter subordination and
higher discipline. All organization implies restriction of

liberty. The gain of power is won by narrowing individual range. The methods of business in colonial days were loose and slack to an inconceivable degree. The movement of industry has been all the time toward promptitude, punctuality, and reliability. It has been attended all the way by lamentations about the good old times; about the decline of small industries; about the lost spirit of comradeship between employer and employee; about the narrowing of the interests of the workman; about his conversion into a machine or into a "ware," and about industrial war. These lamentations have all had reference to unquestionable phenomena attendant on advancing organization. In all occupations the same movement is discernible — in the learned professions, in schools, in trade, commerce, and transportation. It is to go on faster than ever, now that the continent is filled up by the first superficial layer of population over its whole extent and the intensification of industry has begun. The great inventions both make the intension of the organization possible and make it inevitable, with all its consequences, whatever they may be. I must expect to be told here, according to the current fashions of thinking, that we ought to control the development of the organization. The first instinct of the modern man is to get a law passed to forbid or prevent what, in his wisdom, he disapproves. A thing which is inevitable, however, is one which we cannot control. We have to make up our minds to it, adjust ourselves to it, and sit down to live with it. Its inevitableness may be disputed, in which case we must re-examine it; but if our analysis is correct, when we reach what is inevitable we reach the end, and our regulations must apply to ourselves, not to the social facts.

Now the intensification of the social organization is

what gives us greater social power. It is to it that we owe our increased comfort and abundance. We are none of us ready to sacrifice this. On the contrary, we want more of it. We would not return to the colonial simplicity and the colonial exiguity if we could. If not, then we must pay the price. Our life is bounded on every side by conditions. We can have this if we will agree to submit to that. In the case of industrial power and product the great condition is combination of force under discipline and strict coordination. Hence the wild language about wage-slavery and capitalistic tyranny.

In any state of society no great achievements can be produced without great force. Formerly great force was attainable only by slavery aggregating the power of great numbers of men. Roman civilization was built on this. Ours has been built on steam. It is to be built on electricity. Then we are all forced into an organization around these natural forces and adapted to the methods or their application; and although we indulge in rhetoric about political liberty, nevertheless we find ourselves bound tight in a new set of conditions, which control the modes of our existence and determine the directions in which alone economic and social liberty can go.

If it is said that there are some persons in our time who have become rapidly and in a great degree rich, it is true; if it is said that large aggregations of wealth in the control of individuals is a social danger, it is not true.

The movement of the industrial organization which has just been described has brought out a great demand for men capable of managing great enterprises. Such have been called "captains of industry." The analogy with military leaders suggested by this name is not misleading. The great leaders in the development of the industrial organization need those talents of executive and administrative skill, power to command, courage, and fortitude, which were formerly called for in military affairs and scarcely anywhere else. The industrial army is also as dependent on its captains as a military body is on its generals. One of the worst features of the existing system is that the employees have a constant risk in their employer. If he is not competent to manage the business with success, they suffer with him. Capital also is dependent on the skill of the captain of industry for the certainty and magnitude of its profits. Under these circumstances there has been a great demand for men having the requisite ability for this function. As the organization has advanced, with more impersonal bonds of coherence and wider scope of operations, the value of this functionary has rapidly increased. The possession of the requisite ability is a natural monopoly. Consequently, all the conditions have concurred to give to those who possessed this monopoly excessive and constantly advancing rates of remuneration.

Another social function of the first importance in an intense organization is the solution of those crises in the operation of it which are called the conjuncture of the market. It is through the market that the lines of relation run which preserve the system in harmonious and rhythmical operation. The conjuncture is the momentary sharper misadjustment of supply and demand which indicates that a redistribution of productive effort is called for. The industrial organization needs to be insured against these conjunctures, which, if neglected, produce a crisis and catastrophe; and it needs that they shall be anticipated and guarded against as far as skill and foresight can do it. The rewards of this function for the bankers and capitalists who perform it are very great. The captains of industry and the capitalists who operate on the conjuncture, therefore, if they are successful, win, in these days, great fortunes in a short time. There are no earnings which are more legitimate or for which greater services are rendered to the whole industrial body. The popular notions about this matter really assume that all the wealth accumulated by these classes of persons would be here just the same if they had not existed. They are supposed to have appropriated it out of the common stock. This is so far from being true that, on the contrary, their own wealth would not be but for themselves; and besides that, millions more of wealth, many-fold greater than their own, scattered in the hands of thousands, would not exist but for them.

Within the last two years I have traveled from end to end of the German Empire several times on all kinds of trains. I reached the conviction, looking at the matter from the passenger's standpoint, that, if the Germans could find a Vanderbilt and put their railroads in his hands for twenty-five years, letting him reorganize the system and make twenty-five million dollars out of it for himself in that period, they would make an excellent bargain.

But it is repeated until it has become a commonplace which people are afraid to question, that there is some social danger in the possession of large amounts of wealth by individuals. I ask, Why? I heard a lecture two years ago by a man who holds perhaps the first chair of political economy in the world. He said, among other things, that there was great danger in our day from great accumulations; that this danger ought to be met by taxation, and he referred to the fortune of the Rothschilds and to the great fortunes made in America to prove his point. He omitted, however, to state in what the danger consisted or to specify what harm has ever been done by the Rothschild fortunes or by the great fortunes accumulated in America. It seemed to me that the assertions he was making, and the measures he was recommending, ex-cathedra, were very serious to be thrown out so recklessly. It is hardly to be expected that novelists, popular magazinists, amateur economists, and politicians will be more responsible. It would be easy, however, to show what good is done by accumulations of capital in a few hands — that is, under close and direct management, permitting prompt and accurate application; also to tell what harm is done by loose and unfounded denunciations of any social component or any social group. In the recent debates on the income tax the assumption that great accumulations of wealth are socially harmful and ought to be broken down by taxation was treated as an axiom, and we had direct proof how dangerous it is to fit out the average politician with such unverified and unverifiable dogmas as his warrant for his modes of handling the direful tool of taxation.

Great figures are set out as to the magnitude of certain fortunes and the proportionate amount of the national wealth held by a fraction of the population, and eloquent exclamation-points are set against them. If the figures were beyond criticism, what would they prove? Where is the rich man who is oppressing anybody? If there was one, the newspapers would ring with it. The facts about the accumulation of wealth do not constitute a plutocracy, as I will show below. Wealth, in itself considered, is only power, like steam, or electricity, or knowledge. The question of its good or ill turns on the question how it will be used. To prove any harm in aggregations of wealth it must be shown that great wealth is, as a rule, in the ordinary course of social affairs, put to a mischievous use. This cannot be shown beyond the very slightest degree, if at all.

Therefore, all the allegations of general mischief, social corruption, wrong, and evil in our society must be referred back to those who make them for particulars and specifications. As they are offered to us we cannot allow them to stand, because we discern in them faulty observation of facts, or incorrect interpretation of facts, or a construction of facts according to some philosophy, or misunderstanding of phenomena and their relations, or incorrect inferences, or crooked deductions.

Assuming, however, that the charges against the existing "capitalistic" — that is, industrial — order of things are established, it is proposed to remedy the ill by reconstructing the industrial system on the principles of democracy. Once more we must untangle the snarl of half ideas and muddled facts.

Democracy is, of course, a word to conjure with. We have a democratic-republican political system, and we like it so well that we are prone to take any new step which can be recommended as "democratic" or which will round out some "principle" of democracy to a fuller fulfillment. Everything connected with this domain of political thought is crusted over with false historical traditions, cheap philosophy, and undefined terms, but it is useless to try to criticize it. The whole drift of the world for five hundred years has been toward democracy. That drift, produced by great discoveries and inventions, and by the discovery of a new continent, has raised the middle class out of the servile class. In alliance with the crown they crushed the feudal classes. They made the crown absolute in order to do it. Then they turned against the crown and, with the aid of the handicraftsmen and peasants, conquered it. Now the next conflict which must inevitably come is that between the middle capitalist class and the proletariat, as the word has come to be used. If a certain construction is put on this conflict, it may be called that between democracy and plutocracy, for it seems that industrialism must be developed into plutocracy by the conflict itself. That is the conflict which stands before civilized society to-day. All the signs of the times indicate its commencement, and it is big with fate to mankind and to civilization.

Although we cannot criticise democracy profitably, it may be said of it, with reference to our present subject, that up to this time democracy never has done anything, either in politics, social affairs, or industry, to prove its power to bless mankind. If we confine our attention to the United States, there are three difficulties with regard to its alleged achievements, and they all have the most serious bearing on the proposed democratization of industry.

1. The time during which democracy has been tried in the United States is too short to warrant any inferences. A century or two is a very short time in the life of political institutions, and if the circumstances change rapidly during the period the experiment is vitiated.

2. The greatest question of all about American democracy is whether it is a cause or a consequence. It is popularly assumed to be a cause, and we ascribe to its beneficent action all the political vitality, all the easiness of social relations, all the industrial activity and enterprise which we experience and which we value and enjoy. I submit, however, that, on a more thorough examination of the matter, we shall find that democracy is a consequence. There are economic and sociological causes for our political vitality and vigor, for the ease and elasticity of our social relations, and for our industrial power

and success. Those causes have also produced democracy, given it success, and have made its faults and errors innocuous. Indeed, in any true philosophy, it must be held that in the economic forces which control the material prosperity of a population lie the real causes of its political institutions, its social class-adjustments, its industrial prosperity, its moral code, and its world-philosophy. If democracy and the industrial system are both products of the economic conditions which exist, it is plainly absurd to set democracy to defeat those conditions in the control of industry. If, however, it is not true that democracy is a consequence, and I am well aware that very few people believe it, then we must go back to the view that democracy is a cause. That being so, it is difficult to see how democracy, which has had a clear field here in America, is not responsible for the ills which Mr. Bellamy and his comrades in opinion see in our present social state, and it is difficult to see the grounds of asking us to intrust it also with industry. The first and chief proof of success of political measures and systems is that, under them, society advances in health and vigor and that industry develops without causing social disease. If this has not been the case in America, American democracy has not succeeded. Neither is it easy to see how the masses, if they have undertaken to rule, can escape the responsibilities of ruling, especially so far as the consequences affect themselves. If, then, they have brought all this distress upon themselves under the present system, what becomes of the argument for extending the system to a direct and complete control of industry?

3. It is by no means certain that democracy in the United States has not, up to this time, been living on a capital inherited from aristocracy and industrialism. We have no pure democracy. Our democracy is limited

at every turn by institutions which were developed in England in connection with industrialism and aristocracy, and these institutions are of the essence of our system. While our people are passionately democratic in temper and will not tolerate a doctrine that one man is not as good as another, they have common sense enough to know that he is not; and it seems that they love and cling to the conservative institutions quite as strongly as they do to the democratic philosophy. They are, therefore, ruled by men who talk philosophy and govern by the institutions. Now it is open to Mr. Bellamy to say that the reason why democracy in America seems to be open to the charge made in the last paragraph, of responsibility for all the ill which he now finds in our society, is because it has been infected with industrialism (capitalism); but in that case he must widen the scope of his proposition and undertake to purify democracy before turning industry over to it. The socialists generally seem to think that they make their undertakings easier when they widen their scope, and make them easiest when they propose to remake everything; but in truth social tasks increase in difficulty in an enormous ratio as they are widened in scope.

The question, therefore, arises, if it is proposed to reorganize the social system on the principles of American democracy, whether the institutions of industrialism are to be retained. If so, all the virus of capitalism will be retained. It is forgotten, in many schemes of social reformation in which it is proposed to mix what we like with what we do not like, in order to extirpate the latter, that each must undergo a reaction from the other, and that what we like may be extirpated by what we do not like. We may find that instead of democratizing capitalism we have capitalized democracy — that is, have brought in plutocracy. Plutocracy is a political system in which the ruling force is wealth. The denunciation of capital which we hear from all the reformers is the most eloquent proof that the greatest power in the world to-day is capital. They know that it is, and confess it most when they deny it most strenuously. At present the power of capital is social and industrial, and only in a small degree political. So far as capital is political, it is on account of political abuses, such as tariffs and special legislation on the one hand and legislative strikes on the other. These conditions exist in the democracy to which it is proposed to transfer the industries. What does that mean except bringing all the power of capital once for all into the political arena and precipitating the conflict of democracy and plutocracy at once? Can any-one imagine that the masterfulness, the overbearing disposition, the greed of gain, and the ruthlessness in methods, which are the faults of the master of industry at his worst, would cease when he was a functionary of the State, which had relieved him of risk and endowed him with authority? Can anyone imagine that politicians would no longer be corruptly fond of money, intriguing, and crafty when they were charged, not only with patronage and government contracts, but also with factories, stores, ships, and railroads? Could we expect anything except that, when the politician and the master of industry were joined in one, we should have the vices of both unchecked by the restraints of either? In any socialistic state there will be one set of positions which will offer chances of wealth beyond the wildest dreams of avarice; viz., on the governing committees. Then there will be rich men whose wealth will indeed be a menace to social interests, and instead of industrial peace there will be such war as no one has dreamed of yet:

the war between the political ins and outs — that is, between those who are on the committee and those who want to get on it.

We must not drop the subject of democracy without one word more. The Greeks already had occasion to notice a most serious distinction between two principles of democracy which lie at its roots. Plutarch says that Solon got the archonship in part by promising equality, which some understood of esteem and dignity, others of measure and number. There is one democratic principle which means that each man should be esteemed for his merit and worth, for just what he is, without regard to birth, wealth, rank, or other adventitious circumstances. The other principle is that each one of us ought to be equal to all the others in what he gets and enjoys. The first principle is only partially realizable, but, so far as it goes, it is elevating and socially progressive and profitable. The second is not capable of an intelligible statement. The first is a principle of industrialism. It proceeds from and is intelligible only in a society built on the industrial virtues, free endeavor, security of property, and repression of the baser vices; that is, in a society whose industrial system is built on labor and exchange. The other is only a rule of division for robbers who have to divide plunder or monks who have to divide gifts. If, therefore, we want to democratize industry in the sense of the first principle, we need only perfect what we have now, especially on its political side. If we try to democratize it in the sense of the other principle, we corrupt politics at one stroke; we enter upon an industrial enterprise which will waste capital and bring us all to poverty, and we set loose greed and envy as ruling social passions.

If this poor old world is as bad as they say, one more

reflection may check the zeal of the headlong reformer. It is at any rate a tough old world. It has taken its trend and curvature and all its twists and tangles from a long course of formation. All its wry and crooked gnarls and knobs are therefore stiff and stubborn. If we puny men by our arts can do anything at all to straighten them, it will only be by modifying the tendencies of some of the forces at work, so that, after a sufficient time, their action may be changed a little and slowly the lines of movement may be modified. This effort, however, can at most be only slight, and it will take a long time. In the meantime spontaneous forces will be at work, compared with which our efforts are like those of a man trying to deflect a river, and these forces will have changed the whole problem before our interferences have time to make themselves felt. The great stream of time and earthly things will sweep on just the same in spite of us. It bears with it now all the errors and follies of the past, the wreckage of all the philosophies, the fragments of all the civilizations, the wisdom of all the abandoned ethical systems, the debris of all the institutions, and the penalties of all the mistakes. It is only in imagination that we stand by and look at and criticize it and plan to change it. Everyone of us is a child of his age and cannot get out of it. He is in the stream and is swept along with it. All his sciences and philosophy come to him out of it. Therefore the tide will not be changed by us. It will swallow up both us and our experiments. It will absorb the efforts at change and take them into itself as new but trivial components, and the great movement of tradition and work will go on unchanged by our fads and schemes. The things which will change it are the great discoveries and inventions, the new reactions inside the social organism, and the changes in the earth itself on account of changes in the cosmical forces. These causes will make of it just what, in fidelity to them, it ought to be. The men will be carried along with it and be made by it. The utmost they can do by their cleverness will be to note and record their course as they are carried along, which is what we do now, and is that which leads us to the vain fancy that we can make or guide the movement. That is why it is the greatest folly of which a man can be capable, to sit down with a slate and pencil to plan out a new social world.

STATE INTERFERENCE

IX

STATE INTERFERENCE

[1887]

I DESIRE, in this paper, to give an explanation and justification of extreme prejudice against State interference, and I wish to begin with a statement from history of the effect upon the individual of various forms of the State.

It appears, from the best evidence we possess, according to the most reasonable interpretation which has been given to it, that the internal organization of society owes its cohesion and intensity to the necessity of meeting pressure from without. A band of persons, bound by ties of neighborhood or kin, clung together in order to maintain their common interests against a similar band of their neighbors. The social bond and the common interest were at war with individual interests. They exerted coercive power to crush individualism, to produce uniformity, to proscribe dissent, to make private judgment a social offense, and to exercise drill and discipline.

In the Roman State the internal discipline gave victory in contests with neighbors. Each member of the Roman community was carried up by the success of the body of which he was a member to the position of a world-conqueror. Then the Roman community split up into factions to quarrel for the spoils of the world, until the only escape from chronic civil war and anarchy was a one-man power, which, however, proved only a mode of disintegration and decay, not a cure for it. It has often been remarked with astonishment how lightly men and women of rank at Rome in the first century of our era held their lives. They seem to have been ready to open their veins at a moment's notice, and to quit life upon trivial occasion. If we can realize what life must have been in such a State we can, perhaps, understand this. The Emperor was the State. He was a mortal who had been freed from all care for the rights of others, and his own passions had all been set free. Any man or woman in the civilized world was at the mercy of his caprices. Anyone who was great enough to attract his attention, especially by the possession of anything which mortals covet, held his life at the utmost peril. Since the Empire was the world, there was no escape save to get out of the world. Many seemed to hold escape cheap at that price.

At first under the Empire the obscure people were safe. They probably had little to complain of, and found the Empire gay and beneficent; but it gradually and steadily absorbed every rank and interest into its pitiless organization. At last industry and commerce as well as all civil and social duties took the form of State functions. The ideal which some of our modern social philosophers are preaching was realized. The State was an ethical person, in the strictest sense of the word, when it was one man and when every duty and interest of life was construed towards him. All relations were regulated according to the ethics of the time, which is, of course, all that ethical regulation ever can amount to. Every duty of life took the form and name of an "obsequium"; that is, of a function in the State organism.

Now the most important relation of the citizen to the State is that of a soldier, and the next is that of a taxpayer, and when the former loses importance the latter becomes the chief. Accordingly the obsequia of the citizens in the later centuries were regulated in such a way that the citizen might contribute most to the fiscus. He was not only made part of a machine, but it was a tax-paying machine, and all his hopes, rights, interests, and human capabilities were merged in this purpose of his existence. Slavery, as we ordinarily understand the term, died out, but it gave way to a servitude of each to all, when each was locked tight in an immense and artificial organization of society. Such must ever be the effect of merging industry in the State. Every attempt of the Roman handicraftsmen to better themselves was a breach of the peace; disobedience was rebellion; resistance was treason; running away was desertion.

Here, then, we have a long history, in which the State power first served the national interest in contest with outside powers, and then itself became a burden and drew all the life out of the subject population.

In the Middle Ages a society which had been resolved into its simple elements had to re-form. The feudal form was imposed upon it by the conditions and elements of the case. It was as impossible for a man to stand alone as it had been on the hunting or pastoral stage of life or on the lower organizations of civilization. There was once more necessity to yield personal liberty in order to get protection against plunder from others, and in order to obtain this protection it was necessary to get into a group and to conform to its organization. Here again the same difficulty soon presented itself. Protection against outside aggression was won, but the protecting power itself became a plunderer.

This oppression brought about guild and other organizations for mutual defense. Sometimes these organizations themselves won civil power; sometimes they were under some political sovereign, but possessed its sanction. The system which grew up was one of complete regulation and control. The guilds were regulated in every function and right. The masters, journeymen, and apprentices were regulated in their relations and in all their rights and duties. The work of supplying a certain community with any of the necessaries of life was regarded as a privilege and was monopolized by a certain number. The mediæval system, however, did not allow this monopoly to be exploited at the expense of consumers, according to the good will of the holders of it. The sovereign interfered constantly, and at all points, wherever its intervention was asked for. It fixed prices, but it also fixed wages, regulated kinds and prices of raw materials, prescribed the relation of one trade to another, forbade touting, advertising, rivalry; regulated buying and selling by merchants; protected consumers by inspection; limited importations, but might force production and force sales.

Here was plainly a complete system, which had a rational motive and a logical method. The object was to keep all the organs of society in their accepted relations to each other and to preserve all in activity in the measure of the social needs. The plan failed entirely. It was an impossible undertaking, even on the narrow arena of a mediæval city. The ordinances of an authority which stood ready to interfere at any time and in any way were necessarily inconsistent and contradictory. Its effect upon those who could not get into the system — that is, upon the vagabondage of the period — has never, so far as I know, been studied carefully, although that is the place to look for its most distinct social effect. The most interesting fact about it, however, is that the privilege of one age became the bondage of the next and that the organization which had grown up for the mutual defense of the artisans lost its original purpose and became a barrier to the rise of the artisan class. The organization was a fetter on individual enterprise and success.

The fact should not be overlooked here that, if we are to have the mediæval system of regulation revived, we want it altogether. That system was not, in intention, unjust. According to its light it aimed at the welfare of all. It was not its motive to give privileges, but a system of partial interference is sure to be a system of favoritism and injustice. It is a system of charters to some to plunder others. A mediæval sovereign would never interfere with railroads on behalf of shippers and stop there. He would fix the interest on bonds and other fixed charges. He would, upon appeal, regulate the wages of employees. He would fix the price of coal and other supplies. He would never admit that he was the guardian of one interest more than another, and he would interfere over and over again as often as stockholders, bondholders, employees, shippers, etc., could persuade him that they had a grievance. He would do mischief over and over again, but he would not do intentional injustice.

After the mediæval system broke up and the great modern States formed, the royal power became the representative and champion of national interests in modern Europe, and it established itself in approximately absolute power by the fact that the interest of the nations to maintain themselves in the rivalry of States seemed the paramount interest. Within a few months we have seen modern Germany discard every other interest in order to respond to the supposed necessity of military defense. Not very long ago, in our Civil War, we refused to take account of anything else until the military task was accomplished.

In all these cases the fact appears that the interest of the individual and the social interest have been at war with each other, while, again, the interests of the individual in and through the society of which he is a member are inseparable from those of the society. Such are the two aspects of the relation of the unit and the whole which go to make the life of the race. The individual has an interest to develop all the personal elements there are in him. He wants to live himself out. He does not want to be planed down to a type or pattern. It is the interest of society that all the original powers it contains should be brought out to their full value. But the social movement is coercive and uniformitarian. Organization and discipline are essential to effective common action, and they crush out individual enterprise and personal variety. There is only one kind of cooperation which escapes this evil, and that is cooperation which is voluntary and automatic, under common impulses and natural laws. State control, however, is always necessary for national action in the family of nations and to prevent plunder by others, and men have never yet succeeded in getting it without falling under the necessity of submitting to plunder at home from those on whom they rely for defense abroad.

Now, at the height of our civilization and with the best light that we can bring to bear on our social relations, the problem is: Can we get from the State security for individuals to pursue happiness in and under it, and yet not have the State itself become a new burden and hindrance only a little better than the evil which it wards off?

It is only in the most recent times, and in such measure as the exigencies of external defense have been diminished by the partial abandonment of motives of plunder and conquest, that there has been a chance for individualism to grow. In the latest times the struggle for a relaxation of political bonds on behalf of individual liberty has taken the form of breaking the royal power and forcing the king to take his hands off. Liberty has hardly yet come to be popularly understood as anything else but republicanism or anti-royalty.

The United States, starting on a new continent, with full chance to select the old-world traditions which they would adopt, have become the representatives and champions in modern times of all the principles of individualism and personal liberty. We have had no neighbors to fear. We have had no necessity for stringent State discipline. Each one of us has been able to pursue happiness in his own way, unhindered by the demands of a State which would have worn out our energies by expenditure simply in order to maintain the State. The State has existed of itself. The one great exception, the Civil War, only illustrates the point more completely *per contra*. The old Jeffersonian party rose to power and held it, because it conformed to the genius of the country and bore along the true destinies of a nation situated as this one was. It is the glory of the United States, and its calling in history, that it shows what the power of personal liberty is — what self-reliance, energy, enterprise, hard sense men can develop when they have room and liberty and when they are emancipated from the burden of traditions and faiths which are nothing but the accumulated follies and blunders of a hundred generations of "statesmen."

It is, therefore, the highest product of political institutions so far that they have come to a point where, under favorable circumstances, individualism is, under their protection, to some extent possible. If political institutions can give security for the pursuit of happiness by each individual, according to his own notion of it, in his own way, and by his own means, they have reached their perfection. This fact, however, has two aspects. If no man can be held to serve another man's happiness, it follows that no man can call on another to serve his happiness. The different views of individualism depend on which of these aspects is under observation. What seems to be desired now is a combination of liberty for all with an obligation of each to all. That is one of the forms in which we are seeking a social philosopher's stone.

The reflex influence which American institutions have had on European institutions is well known. We have had to take as well as give. When the United States put upon their necks the yoke of a navigation and colonial system which they had just revolted against, they showed how little possible it is, after all, for men to rise above the current notions of their time, even when geographical and economic circumstances favor their emancipation. We have been borrowing old-world fashions and traditions all through our history, instead of standing firmly by the political and social philosophy of which we are the standard-bearers.

So long as a nation has not lost faith in itself it is possible for it to remodel its institutions to any extent. If it gives way to sentimentalism, or sensibility, or political mysticism, or adopts an affectation of radicalism, or any other *ism*, or molds its institutions so as to round out to a more complete fulfillment somebody's theory of the universe, it may fall into an era of revolution and political insecurity which will break off the continuity of its national life and make orderly and secure progress impossible. Now that the royal power is limited, and that the old military and police States are in the way of transition to jural States, we are promised a new advance to democracy. What is the disposition of the new State as regards the scope of its power? It unquestionably manifests a disposition to keep and use the whole arsenal of its predecessors. The great engine of political abuse has always been political mysticism. Formerly we were told of the divine origin of the State and the divine authority of rulers. The mystical contents of "sovereignty" have always provided an inexhaustible source of dogma and inference for any extension of State power. The new democracy having inherited the power so long used against it, now shows every disposition to use that power as ruthlessly as any other governing organ ever has used it.

We are told that the State is an ethical person. This is the latest form of political mysticism. Now, it is true that the State is an ethical person in just the same sense as a business firm, a joint stock corporation, or a debating society. It is not a physical person, but it may be a metaphysical or legal person, and as such it has an entity and is an independent subject of rights and duties. Like the other ethical persons, however, the State is just good for what it can do to serve the interests of man, and no more. Such is far from being the meaning and utility of the dogma that the State is an ethical person. The dogma is needed as a source from which can be spun out again contents of phrases and deductions previously stowed away in it. It is only the most modern form of dogmatism devised to sacrifice the man to the institution which is not good for anything except so far as it can serve the man.

One of the newest names for the coming power is the "omnicracy." Mankind has been trying for some thousands of years to find the right -ocracy. None of those which have yet been tried have proved satisfactory. We want a new name on which to pin new hopes, for mankind "never is, but always to be blessed." Omnicracy has this much sense in it, that no one of the great dogmas of the modern political creed is true if it is affirmed of anything less than the whole population, man, woman, child, and baby.   When the propositions are enunciated in this sense they are philosophically grand and true. For instance, all the propositions about the "people" are grand and true if we mean by the people every soul in the community, with all the interests and powers which give them an aggregate will and power, with capacity to suffer or to work; but then, also, the propositions remain grand abstractions beyond the realm of practical utility. On the other hand, those propositions cannot be made practically available unless they are affirmed of some limited section of the population, for instance, a majority of the males over twenty-one; but then they are no longer true in philosophy or in fact.

Consequently, when the old-fashioned theories of State interference are applied to the new democratic State, they turn out to be simply a device for setting separate interests in a struggle against each other inside the society. It is plain on the face of all the great questions which are offered to us as political questions to-day, that they are simply struggles of interests for larger shares of the product of industry.   One mode of dealing with this distribution would be to leave it to free contract under the play of natural laws.   If we do not do this, and if the State interferes with the distribution, how can we stop short of the mediæval plan of reiterated and endless interference, with constant diminution of the total product to be divided?

We have seen above what the tyranny was in the decay of the Roman Empire, when each was in servitude to all; but there is one form of that tyranny which may be still worse.   That tyranny will be realized when the same system of servitudes is established in a democratic state; when a man's neighbors are his masters; when the "ethical power of public opinion" bears down upon him at all hours and as to all matters; when his place is assigned to him and he is held in it, not by an emperor or his satellites, who cannot be everywhere all the time, but by the other members of the "village community" who can.

So long as the struggle for individual liberty took the form of a demand that the king or the privileged classes should take their hands off, it was popular and was believed to carry with it the cause of justice and civilization. Now that the governmental machine is brought within everyone's reach, the seduction of power is just as masterful over a democratic faction as ever it was over king or barons. No governing organ has yet abstained from any function because it acknowledged itself ignorant or incompetent. The new powers in the State show no disposition to do it. Nevertheless, the activity of the State, under the new democratic system, shows itself every year more at the mercy of clamorous factions, and legislators find themselves constantly under greater pressure to act, not by their deliberate judgment of what is expedient, but in such a way as to quell clamor, although against their judgment of public interests. It is rapidly becoming the chief art of the legislator to devise measures which shall sound as if they satisfied clamor while they only cheat it.

There are two things which are often treated as if they were identical, which are as far apart as any two things in the field of political philosophy can be: (1) That everyone should be left to do as he likes, so far as possible, without any other social restraints than such as are unavoidable for the peace and order of society.

(2) That "the people" should be allowed to carry out their will without any restraint from constitutional institutions. The former means that each should have his own way with his own interests; the latter, that any faction which for the time is uppermost should have its own way with all the rest.

One result of all the new State interference is that the State is being superseded in vast domains of its proper work. While it is reaching out on one side to fields of socialistic enterprise, interfering in the interests of parties in the industrial organism, assuming knowledge of economic laws which nobody possesses, taking ground as to dogmatic notions of justice which are absurd, and acting because it does not know what to do, it is losing its power to give peace, order, and security. The extra-legal power and authority of leaders over voluntary organizations of men throughout a community who are banded together in order to press their interests at the expense of other interests, and who go to the utmost verge of the criminal law, if they do not claim immunity from it, while obeying an authority which acts in secret and without responsibility, is a phenomenon which shows the inadequacy of the existing State to guarantee rights and give security. The boycott and the plan of campaign are certainly not industrial instrumentalities, and it is not yet quite certain whether they are violent and criminal instrumentalities, by which some men coerce other men in matters of material interests. If we turn our minds to the victims of these devices, we see that they do not find in the modern State that security for their interests under the competition of life which it is the first and unquestioned duty of the State to provide. The boycotted man is deprived of the peaceful enjoyment of rights which the laws and institutions of his country allow him, and he has no redress. The State has forbidden all private war on the ground that it will give a remedy for wrongs, and that private redress would disturb the peaceful prosecution of their own interests by other members of the community who are not parties to the quarrel; but we have seen an industrial war paralyze a whole section for weeks, and it was treated almost as a right of the parties that they might fight it out, no matter at what cost to bystanders. We have seen representative bodies of various voluntary associations meet and organize by the side of the regular constitutional organs of the State, in order to deliberate on proposed measures and to transmit to the authorized representatives of the people their approval or disapproval of the propositions, and it scarcely caused a comment. The plutocracy invented the lobby, but the democracy here also seems determined to better the instruction. There are various opinions as to what the revolution is which is upon us, and as to what it is which is about to perish. I do not see anything else which is in as great peril as representative institutions or the constitutional State.

I therefore maintain that it is at the present time a matter of patriotism and civic duty to resist the extension of State interference. It is one of the proudest results of political growth that we have reached the point where individualism is possible. Nothing could better show the merit and value of the institutions which we have inherited than the fact that we can afford to play with all these socialistic and semi-socialistic absurdities. They have no great importance until the question arises: Will a generation which can be led away into this sort of frivolity be able to transmit intact institutions which were made only by men of sterling thought and power, and which can be maintained only by men of the same type? I am familiar with the irritation and impatience with which remonstrances on this matter are received. Those who know just how the world ought to be reconstructed are, of course, angry when they are pushed aside as busybodies. A group of people who assail the legislature with a plan for regulating their neighbor's mode of living are enraged at the "dogma" of non-interference. The publicist who has been struck by some of the superficial roughnesses in the collision of interests which must occur in any time of great industrial activity, and who has therefore determined to waive the objections to State interference, if he can see it brought to bear on his pet reform, will object to absolute principles. For my part, I have never seen that public or private principles were good for anything except when there seemed to be a motive for breaking them. Anyone who has studied a question as to which the solution is yet wanting may despair of the power of free contract to solve it. I have examined a great many cases of proposed interference with free contract, and the only alternative to free contract which I can find is "heads I win, tails you lose" in favor of one party or the other. I am familiar with the criticisms which some writers claim to make upon individualism, but the worst individualism I can find in history is that of the Jacobins, and I believe that it is logically sound that the anti-social vices should be most developed whenever the attempt is made to put socialistic theories in practice. The only question at this point is: Which may we better trust, the play of free social forces or legislative and administrative interference? This question is as pertinent for those who expect to win by interference as for others, for whenever we try to get paternalized we only succeed in getting policed.

DO WE WANT INDUSTRIAL PEACE?

X

DO WE WANT INDUSTRIAL PEACE?

[1889]

IT cannot be said that the discussion of the so-called labor question has been productive of any positive results in the way of making us understand the facts and relations of the industrial system any better. The discussion has fallen into certain grooves and has revolved around certain assumptions and pet notions. It has become almost hidden under conventionalities and has bred a series of commonplaces. An actual orthodoxy has arisen in connection with it, dissent from which is regarded with horror. A code of discussion has been elaborated for it and a certain conventional tone of mind has come to be recognized as proper to be assumed before taking part in it. Consequently the future historian will read our labor-bureau literature as a revelation of the mental fashion of our time. There never has been any literature just like it, inasmuch as its chief aim is, while maintaining some of the forms of a scientific investigation, to reach results which shall not brush rudely against the pet notions of any important school of social opinion, or against any one of the strong interests which are in conflict.

The consequence of the discussion is not matter for wonder when we consider how it has been carried on. Very rarely has anyone taken part in it who has been a party to the industrial war. The discussion has been almost entirely in the hands of socialists, social reformers, friends of the people, economists, and prophets of a new social dispensation. If these classes of persons take up the discussion of matters affecting the practical relations of parties in the industrial organization, it is inevitable that the discussion should take exactly the turn which has just been described; that is to say, that it should become conventionalized, should lose actuality, should speedily run down into a repetition of commonplaces, should be controlled by dogmatic assumptions, not of fact, but of ethical relation, and in all this should be, as the saying is, "up in a balloon."

It has been said by those who are in the best position to know, that great inventions take place step by step, and that they advance best by reaching a point where all further progress is arrested by one difficulty which can be sharply and specifically defined. Then effort can be concentrated on this point till it is conquered. It is said that when ocean steamers were first built, their development was arrested by the fact that no means then in use were adequate to forge such masses of iron as were required for the shafts. The problem put to the inventors was to invent a steam hammer capable of forging shafts. The problem, being thus set, was soon solved. Other instances in the recent history of electric lighting, the telephone, etc., suggest themselves. It is evident that the progress is most steady and certain when it goes on with a regularity and system which produce a succession of these narrow, specific, sharply defined questions or problems.

In like manner the life of a society brings to the front a series of social and political problems. It is one of the tests of a real, rational, and practical political question that it likewise is specific, narrow in scope, and capable of simple formulation; and on the other hand, it is a sign of a matter which is crude, unreal, fantastic, and certainly not yet ready for practical solution, that it is grand, vague, ethical, and aims at producing "states of things," and not at realizing a single positive result.

For instance, when a State has suspended specie payment, a proper political and public question is: Shall we resume specie payment? Another question which answers the test is: Shall we abolish the protective taxes? It has always been one difficulty with the reform of the civil service, as a political topic or question, that it is not easy to reduce it to an issue of positive form and that it easily runs out into regrets, complaints, scoldings, or alarmist criticisms, whereupon it dissolves and is lost. The so-called silver question has never yet been reduced to a question. It never will be until it is asked whether $412\frac{1}{2}$ grains of standard silver shall be the American dollar. Last year we had the fisheries question, which never really reached public opinion, because it never was reduced to a question.

The labor question is the most remarkable example that could be brought forward of a topic of public talk which has never been reduced to any definite form. According to the only actual attempt to define it which has ever been made by anybody within my knowledge, the labor question means things in general, and consists in a regret that this world is such a hard place in which to get a living and in an enthusiastic aspiration for greater ease and facility in that respect.

The discussion of all ill-defined questions is sure to run off into whims and useless wrangling. Even a real question, if it is not yet ripe, must undergo a great deal of preliminary thrashing (which ought to be accomplished on the academic arena) before it can be got into the positive form of a public political question or a proposed

modification of custom and usage.   It is inevitable in
the nature of things that a great amount of energy must
be wasted in preliminary work, which results only in
finding out what the question is; but we ought to have
some test which would show us whether we are going in
the proper direction and whether there is reasonable
probability that we shall accomplish something on the
line we are pursuing.   One such test is to notice whether
the topic converges to a simple issue or whether it dissolves into mere logomachy and word-juggling.

Now it is characteristic of the discussion of the various
forms of industrial war that they have lost definiteness,
instead of winning it, during the last years.   It has come
out of the discussion, as almost the sole result, that we
have a whole vocabulary of words of which we have no
settled definition, which different people use in very different senses (for example, labor and capital, monopoly,
competition, workingman, wages, cost of production),
and that all social theorems or principles are as yet so
obscure that a mist of transcendentalism and mysticism
hangs over them all, which renders them most inviting
to the crank.   One is at a loss how to go on with any
such discussion at all, for the reason that he can hardly
use the only terms which the language affords for expressing thoughts about it, without using terms which, within
his knowledge, have become parts of the jargon of pseudo-
science and bogus philosophy.

Such being the position of the matter in the world of
thought and discussion, while it is in daily experience a
matter affecting the interests and happiness of great
numbers of people who are brought into antagonism to
each other, any attempt to deal with it by legislation
must be the purest empiricism.   We are told that the
coming session of the German Parliament is to be occu-

pied with measures for the prevention of strikes. It will be an interesting experiment, and one on many accounts deserving of careful watching. The Emperor some weeks ago, in his speeches about the strike then existing, gave it to be understood that he could and would stop strikes, putting both masters and men in their proper places. He seems just now to have the key of the universe, and it will be interesting for us, who are at a safe distance, to stand by and see him use it. The experiment of State socialistic legislation and tyrannical anti-socialist legislation, both at the same time, is, to say the least, bold and interesting. It is not possible now to say what the question will be which will come before the Parliament. If it is: How can we put down strikes? the first incidental question will be: How do you know that you want to put down strikes?

There are only two ways in which strikes can be put down. The first is to make it a crime to strike and to punish it with pains and penalties. That way has been tried and is effete. That way was addressed to the employees. The other way must be addressed to the employers, and will consist in compelling them to pay what the employed ask for. At present, wages are fixed by a contract between two consenting parties. If either party wants to revise the contract — that is to say, to make a new one — they must both consent again, else there is a strike or a lock-out. How can this be prevented except by forcing that one to consent who is holding back? Then, however, his will is coerced, his interests are sacrificed, and his civil or social freedom is violated. Hence the obvious fallacy of arbitration. There is no time when a man is more supremely sovereign and independent than when he is making a contract, for then he is freely subjecting himself to conditions which he con-

234 ESSAYS OF WILLIAM GRAHAM SUMNER

siders satisfactory, for purposes which he considers worth
obtaining. It is only another of the confusions which
have been introduced into this subject that a juggle is
made here on the word "free." It is declared that the
contract is not free, because it is made under the existing
conditions of the market, which may be hard for one of
the parties — an objection which is entirely irrelevant,
since the only "freedom" which can here come into
account, where the proposition is to use civil and social
coercion, is civil and social freedom If, then, a man is
making a contract, how can anybody else judge for him
what conditions he shall submit to or what ends he
ought to consider worth attaining? His final and perfectly conclusive answer is: I will, or, I will not. Now
if one man can force another, by virtue of law and social
force, to enter into a contract which is not satisfactory
to him — that is to say, which is not the best one that he
thinks he can make — then the latter is a slave and the
relationship might serve as a definition of slavery. This
is as true if the victim is an employer as if he were an
employee.

Industrial war is, in fact, an incident of liberty. It is
an inconvenience; it is doubtful if it is an evil. The
greatest injustice about war is that it imposes loss and
harm on those who are not parties to it. If two nations
go to war, they interfere with all their neighbors by breaking up the regular currents of trade and industry and
cutting off the ten thousand relations of various kinds
which have sprung up during peace and which affect
the happiness and welfare of all mankind. It is so in
industrial war. Strikes and railroad wars cause loss and
inconvenience to thousands who are not parties to the
quarrel at all, because they upset all those social and
industrial relationships upon which the regularity and

security of modern society depend. They destroy the social organization which is our reliance nowadays for the supply of our needs. Indeed, this is the real strain upon which a strike relies for its hopes of success; and if there is any justification for legislation to prevent industrial war, it lies in this interest of the public, not in any interest of either of the parties. It is an interesting thing to notice that industrial war has arisen in modern society in proportion as greater State organization has modified the old form of chronic war and brigandage.

There is an interesting and important parallel to this transformation of one kind of social ill into another, attendant upon what we call progress, in another branch of the social organization. A century ago France was so thoroughly policed that violence or breach of public order was scarcely possible. In general, even now, anywhere on the continent of Europe, the man who first strikes a blow is held to be in the wrong, without much regard to provocation, because he violates public peace and order. In Russia any overt act of violence meets with very prompt suppression, without regard to the grievance which caused it. This may be the very worst tyranny and wrong, unless it is attended by a constant and effective redress of all grievances upon proper complaint. Now a modern election, such as we are accustomed to in this country, is a form of riot and disorder which would have set the whole police of France in agitation a century ago. A sarcastic critic might find many amusing analogies by which to sustain the proposition that a modern American election is only a revolution under legal form; that it is a fight of two factions for State power under legal form, but that it works by the same means and toward the same end as a palace revolution, only openly and avowedly. Such an assertion would be extravagant and untrue, but not devoid of foundation. Political liberty must have room in which to play. It will, in its moments of transition and new creation, lose the forms of disciplined and harmonious action and undergo crises of _disorder, struggle, and strife.

In the same manner industrial war is an attendant upon liberty. It has come just because industry has been unfettered and has been allowed to shape itself freely. How can it shape itself freely unless it works out the full effect of all the forces that are in it? It would be a fatal undertaking to endeavor to police elections in such a way as to put an end to those features of them which, from the standpoint of ordinary times, are disorderly; for he who policed would soon elect. The good sense of our people long ago recognized this fact, and within limits which are respected by this good sense, the comparative license of an election is endured, because it is worth what it costs.

The same is true with regard to industrial war. It is worth all that it costs to maintain industrial liberty. So far as individual interests are concerned, those who find themselves weak under liberty may be sure that they would find themselves very much weaker under any system of legal regulation. That, however, is a comparatively unimportant consideration. The most important consideration is that the industrial war is solving questions which can never be solved in any other way.

We are told, indeed, that they can be solved otherwise; some say by science, others by ethics and religion, others by the specific prescribed by some social philosopher. In regard to all such propositions we may observe at once that, although the philosophers and literary men should reach, by their discussion, a unanimous conclusion as to the principles of social dissolution and reconstruction, the men of this age will never put their inheritance of institutions and property in voluntary and unnecessary liquidation. It is well to remember that there are millions of people in the United States who do not know what the literary disputants and the various learned societies are talking about. The latter are led by their knowledge of the movement among themselves to judge of the effect on all outsiders, whereas the two are related very much like the ripples on the surface of the ocean and the great currents at its depths.

Then, again, even within the limits of the discussion, it may become plain to anyone who will take up and compare any two articles on this subject of industrial war that the writers are not agreed as to the fundamental assumptions which constitute the root and stock of their respective positions. For instance, when they talk about the labor question, they do not agree as to what makes the rate of wages. But how is it possible to advance a step in the discussion of any question about employers and employed without a definite doctrine of what it is that makes the rate of wages? In the discussions about railroads it is constantly assumed that there is some "cost" which can be taken as a basis for the definition of fair and reasonable rates. On the other hand, it is stoutly asserted that cost in this sense is a myth, and that no cost can be determined which will serve as a basis for any such computation. How can there be any deliberative solution of a practical question as to what railroads and shippers and legislators respectively ought to do, with such discord on the very first notions about the relations of the parties to each other inside the industrial organization? Again, in the discussion about trusts it is asserted that trusts adopt an arbitrary capitalization and then fix the prices of their products at such rates as to pay dividends on the paper capital. On the other hand, it is asserted that there are laws of the market which are imperative in their action and which make it utterly impossible for anybody to do that. In fact, the whole discussion revolves around this issue, without ever bringing it out as a definite, independent subject of debate. One or the other view is assumed implicitly, and the discussion moves over secondary and derived applications, while any chance of clearing the matter up is diminished by the odium which is imported into the discussion.

Indeed, there is another and still more fundamental difficulty than that last noticed. These questions all finally reach down to the notion which we entertain of the social organization and the facts as to what human society is. All schools of opinion talk about "nature," or what is "natural," and all of them ridicule each other's pretensions to know or to use the real natural order. It is here, in fact, that the great difficulty lies for any deliberative or theoretical solution of social questions. Our age has inherited the ruins of a half-dozen old philosophies and has invented a number of new ones. Each deduces an explanation of the social order from its own grand premises and an independent social science with its own guarantees does not exist. This does not stop the discussion, it only makes it all the more lively; but when one of us states his views, you can see that he is only rehearsing the platform of his school; and one who is well up in the doctrines of the schools can save time if each disputant will only say: I am a Comtist; I am a Darwinian; I am an evangelical Christian; I am an economist of the historical school, and so on. He knows all the rest if he has seen the label.

Far be it from me now to deride science in this field of study. My point is that we cannot wait for science to work out its results, because we must live to-day and to-morrow, and the day when public opinion will be founded on correct notions of the order of society, reduced to commonplace, and ingrained into the common mind, is at an indefinite distance; and that therefore, in the meantime, the thing to do is to abstain from empirical undertakings and to let the problems solve themselves under liberty, no matter if the process be attended by industrial war.

The industrial war is, in great measure, the entirely inevitable means by which redistributions of capital and labor are brought about. We boast very often about the modern achievements, without noticing the incidental effects which are not all pleasant. The world-wide organization is necessarily automatic and impersonal; that makes it mechanical and unfeeling in action. One of us is pursuing in peace and honesty the occupation to which he has become accustomed; he asks nothing better than to live his life out in modest and contented circumstances, but on the lines to which he has become accustomed. Formerly he could do it. It has become one of the commonest experiences for such a man, no matter what his occupation or social position may be, to find that he must change his occupation, or his investments, or his methods; forfeit his acquired skill, change his abode, acquire new habits, and seek other means of livelihood. He will be very apt to find that the first warning of this comes in the shape of a reduction in the price of his product, or in his dividends, or his salary, or his professional income, or his wages. He resents the change and resists it as long as he can, and this resistance takes the form of a battle with the members of that social group nearest to his own, to whose voluntary human action he attributes that injury to his own interest which is really due to "natural causes." Hence landlords and tenants, borrowers and lenders, producers and consumers, shippers and transporters, employers and employees are pushed against one another in collisions which are nothing but the social manifestation of great changes in the currents of trade and in the organization of production. Many railroad wars are interpreted as efforts of railroad managers to force trade into certain places, when they are really symptoms of the tendency of trade to certain places — a tendency which makes itself felt by the transporters in the first place and is transmitted by them to the local interests. In all such cases the rational thing to do would be to investigate the real significance of the war, but such an investigation has to contend, not only with the obscurity of the matter itself and the inadequacy of our scientific attainments for the task, but also with various developments of local pride and personal vanity, the worst lions which ever rise to bar the way of a labor bureau or a railroad commission. In the absence of such investigation, however, one thing is reasonably certain: that is, that any interference which would stop the war by enabling any party to escape for the time being the irksome change which is forced upon it by economic changes is sure to produce nothing but greater misery under a renewed and intenser necessity at a later time. That is the dilemma which repeats itself over and over again in the social developments of our time and brings up one after another of these "great social questions." If we go on we can see plainly before us that we have to encounter a threatening social peril.

We stop or try to turn back in order to avoid it; then we find either that it is impossible to turn back or that, if we do, we shall suffer still worse.

The irksomeness of industrial changes as an inevitable attendant of intense industrial activity such as we live under is a subject which would form an important chapter in some new popular ethics. We have been taught for a century that everything ought to go on with concurrent results, contributing to our enjoyment and satisfaction, without drawbacks of any kind; and those theories of social facts are always popular and are eagerly accepted which pretend to show that all things concur to make it nice and easy for us here. Industrial war is one of the penalties of adopting a notion so sweet and seductive, but so false to all the facts. Industrial war is a symptom of the social changes produced by the seething chaos into which all industrial relations have been thrown by great modern inventions. We want to develop the symptoms; we do not want to suppress them.

There is another feature of the industrial war which is of immense importance — its political side. What we call modern progress is to a great extent an effect of the extension of population from the crowded countries of Europe to the outlying continents, especially America; it is also an effect of the great inventions. The former provided more land; the latter increased power over the land acre by acre. The social effect of these two things has been the emancipation of the classes which had neither land nor capital. These forces have undermined the privileges of the classes which had the advantage under the mediæval system. They have modified class differences and brought about comparative equality. Politically, they have given the advantage to democratic forms and have carried power over to the "masses"; that is, to the classes powerful by numbers.

It is impossible in this place to trace the immeasurable social effects which are in the way of development, much less to show how mistaken is the received opinion about the causes of the social phenomena which we see about us, whose development has been so greatly accelerated during the nineteenth century. No one can be blind to the interplay of political power and economic interest in the industrial war. Socialism is nothing but a phase of that relation of the parts of the social organization, and its self-satisfied parading of itself as being at once the cause and the arbiter of the new social growth is among the humorous features of the situation.

It is inevitable, however, that the classes which constitute the masses should go on to win all the power which is thrown into their hands by the facts of the situation. In the long run this social antagonism, like those which have preceded it, will be reduced to new harmony; but never by the wit of man, only by the working out of the forces. A movement so vast and so new will have to construct its own institutions. It is vain to speculate as to what they will be. Such a movement will, of course, be attended by a vast chorus of bystanders; some shouting in honor of its triumph, some asserting that they always predicted it, an immense number claiming that they brought it about, some shaking their heads over it and predicting disaster. On the other hand, it is not sound philosophy to say that all other forces should be withdrawn and that the social revolution should go on without hindrance. No revolution is healthful and sound which does not contain all the elements, and the conservative elements must be included in their full force. How then can we have industrial peace? Why should we not have industrial war? Industrial war is a sign of vigor in society. It contains a promise of a sound solution. It is not possible to stop it if all the philosophers and statesmen in the world should agree to try it; and it will be wise philosophy and statesmanship not to try.

ON THE CASE OF A CERTAIN MAN
WHO IS NEVER THOUGHT OF

XI

ON THE CASE OF A CERTAIN MAN WHO IS NEVER THOUGHT OF

[1884]

THE type and formula of most schemes of philanthropy or humanitarianism is this: A and B put their heads together to decide what C shall be made to do for D. The radical vice of all these schemes, from a sociological point of view, is that C is not allowed a voice in the matter, and his position, character, and interests, as well as the ultimate effects on society through C's interests, are entirely overlooked. I call C the Forgotten Man. For once let us look him up and consider his case, for the characteristic of all social doctors is that they fix their minds on some man or group of men whose case appeals to the sympathies and the imagination, and they plan remedies addressed to the particular trouble; they do not understand that all the parts of society hold together and that forces which are set in action act and react throughout the whole organism until an equilibrium is produced by a readjustment of all interests and rights. They therefore ignore entirely the source from which they must draw all the energy which they employ in their remedies, and they ignore all the effects on other members of society than the ones they have in view. They are always under the dominion of the superstition of government, and forgetting that a government produces nothing at all, they leave out of sight the first fact to be remembered in all social discussion — that the state cannot get a cent for any man without taking it from some other man, and this latter must be a man who has produced and saved it. This latter is the Forgotten Man.

The friends of humanity start out with certain benevolent feelings towards "the poor," "the weak," "the laborers," and others of whom they make pets. They generalize these classes and render them impersonal, and so constitute the classes into social pets. They turn to other classes and appeal to sympathy and generosity and to all the other noble sentiments of the human heart. Action in the line proposed consists in a transfer of capital from the better off to the worse off. Capital, however, as we have seen, is the force by which civilization is maintained and carried on. The same piece of capital cannot be used in two ways. Every bit of capital, therefore, which is given to a shiftless and inefficient member of society who makes no return for it is diverted from a reproductive use; but if it was put to reproductive use, it would have to be granted in wages to an efficient and productive laborer. Hence the real sufferer by that kind of benevolence which consists in an expenditure of capital to protect the good-for-nothing is the industrious laborer. The latter, however, is never thought of in this connection. It is assumed that he is provided for and out of the account. Such a notion only shows how little true notions of political economy have as yet become popularized. There is an almost invincible prejudice that a man who gives a dollar to a beggar is generous and kind-hearted, but that a man who refuses the beggar and puts the dollar in a savings-bank is stingy and mean. The former is putting capital where it is very sure to be wasted, and where it will be a kind of seed for a long succession of future dollars, which must be wasted to ward off a greater strain on the sympathies than would have been occasioned by a refusal in the first place. Inasmuch as the dollar might have been turned into capital and given to a laborer who, while earning it, would have reproduced it, it must be regarded as taken from the latter. When a millionaire gives a dollar to a beggar, the gain of utility to the beggar is enormous and the loss of utility to the millionaire is insignificant. Generally the discussion is allowed to rest there. But if the millionaire makes capital of the dollar, it must go upon the labor market as a demand for productive services. Hence there is another party in interest — the person who supplies productive services. There always are two parties. The second one is always the Forgotten Man, and anyone who wants to understand truly the matter in question must go and search for the Forgotten Man. He will be found to be worthy, industrious, independent, and self-supporting. He is not, technically, "poor" or "weak"; he minds his own business and makes no complaint. Consequently the philanthropists never think of him and trample on him.

We hear a great deal of schemes for "improving the condition of the working-man." In the United States the farther down we go in the grade of labor, the greater is the advantage which the laborer has over the higher classes. A hod-carrier or digger here can, by one day's labor, command many times more days' labor of a carpenter, surveyor, bookkeeper, or doctor than an unskilled laborer in Europe could command by one day's labor. The same is true, in a less degree, of the carpenter, as compared with the bookkeeper, surveyor, and doctor. This is why the United States is the great country for the unskilled laborer. The economic conditions all favor that class. There is a great continent to be subdued and there is a fertile soil available to labor, with scarcely any need of capital. Hence the people who have the strong arms have what is most needed, and if it were not for social consideration, higher education would not pay. Such being the case, the working-man needs no improvement in his condition except to be freed from the parasites who are living on him. All schemes for patronizing "the working classes" savor of condescension. They are impertinent and out of place in this free democracy. There is not, in fact, any such state of things or any such relation as would make projects of this kind appropriate. Such projects demoralize both parties, flattering the vanity of one and undermining the self-respect of the other.

For our present purpose it is most important to notice that if we lift any man up we must have a fulcrum or point of reaction. In society that means that to lift one man up we push another down. The schemes for improving the condition of the working classes interfere in the competition of workmen with each other. The beneficiaries are selected by favoritism and are apt to be those who have recommended themselves to the friends of humanity by language or conduct which does not betoken independence and energy. Those who suffer a corresponding depression by the interference are the independent and self-reliant, who once more are forgotten or passed over; and the friends of humanity once more appear, in their zeal to help somebody, to be trampling on those who are trying to help themselves.

Trades-unions adopt various devices for raising wages, and those who give their time to philanthropy are interested in these devices and wish them success. They fix their minds entirely on the workmen for the time being *in* the trade and do not take note of any other *workmen*

as interested in the matter. It is supposed that the
fight is between the workmen and their employers, and
it is believed that one can give sympathy in that contest
to the workmen without feeling responsibility for anything farther. It is soon seen, however, that the employer adds the trades-union and strike risk to the other
risks of his business and settles down to it philosophically
because he has passed the loss along on the public. It
then appears that the public wealth has been diminished
and that the danger of a trade war, like the danger of a
revolution, is a constant reduction of the well-being of
all. So far, however, we have seen only things which
could *lower* wages — nothing which could raise them.
The employer is worried, but that does not raise wages.
The public loses, but the loss goes to cover extra risk,
and that does not raise wages.

Aside from legitimate and economic means,[1] a trades-
union raises wages by restricting the number of apprentices who may be taken into the trade. This device
acts directly on the supply of laborers, and that produces
effects on wages. If, however, the number of apprentices is limited, some are kept out who want to get in.
Those who are in have, therefore, made a monopoly and
constituted themselves a privileged class on a basis
exactly analogous to that of the old privileged aris-
tocracies. But whatever is gained by this arrangement
for those who are in is won at a greater loss to those
who are kept out. Hence it is not upon the masters nor
upon the public that trades-unions exert the pressure by
which they raise wages; it is upon other persons of the
labor class who want to get into the trades, but, not
being able to do so, are pushed down into the unskilled
labor class. These persons, however, are passed by en-

[1] Noted in Chapter VI of Sumner's *What Social Classes Owe to Each Other*.

tirely without notice in all the discussions about trades-unions. They are the Forgotten Men. But since they want to get into the trade and win their living in it, it is fair to suppose that they are fit for it, would succeed at it, would do well for themselves and society in it; that is to say, that of all persons interested or concerned, they most deserve our sympathy and attention.

The cases already mentioned involve no legislation. Society, however, maintains police, sheriffs, and various institutions, the object of which is to protect people against themselves — that is, against their own vices. Almost all legislative effort to prevent vice is really protective of vice, because all such legislation saves the vicious man from the penalty of his vice. Nature's remedies against vice are terrible. She removes the victims without pity. A drunkard in the gutter is just where he ought to be, according to the fitness and tendency of things. Nature has set up in him the process of decline and dissolution by which she removes things which have survived their usefulness. Gambling and other less mentionable vices carry their own penalties with them.

Now we never can annihilate a penalty. We can only divert it from the head of the man who has incurred it to the heads of others who have not incurred it. A vast amount of "social reform" consists in just this operation. The consequence is that those who have gone astray, being relieved from nature's fierce discipline, go on to worse, and that there is a constantly heavier burden for the others to bear. Who are the others? When we see a drunkard in the gutter we pity him. If a policeman picks him up, we say that society has interfered to save him from perishing. "Society" is a fine word, and it saves us the trouble of thinking. The industrious and sober workman, who is mulcted of a percentage of his day's wages to pay the policeman, is the one who bears the penalty. But he is the Forgotten Man. He passes by and is never noticed, because he has behaved himself, fulfilled his contracts, and asked for nothing.

The fallacy of all prohibitory, sumptuary, and moral legislation is the same. A and B determine to be teetotalers, which is often a wise determination, and sometimes a necessary one. If A and B are moved by considerations which seem to them good, that is enough. But A and B put their heads together to get a law passed which shall force C to be a teetotaler for the sake of D, who is in danger of drinking too much. There is no pressure on A and B. They are having their own way, and they like it. There is rarely any pressure on D. He does not like it, and evades it. The pressure all comes on C. The question then arises, Who is C? He is the man who wants alcoholic liquors for any honest purpose whatsoever, who would use his liberty without abusing it, who would occasion no public question and trouble nobody at all. He is the Forgotten Man again, and as soon as he is drawn from his obscurity we see that he is just what each one of us ought to be.

THE CASE OF THE FORGOTTEN MAN
FURTHER CONSIDERED

XII

THE CASE OF THE FORGOTTEN MAN
FURTHER CONSIDERED

[1884]

THERE is a beautiful notion afloat in our literature and in the minds of our people that men are born to certain "natural rights." If that were true, there would be something on earth which was got for nothing, and this world would not be the place it is at all. The fact is, that there is no right whatever inherited by man which has not an equivalent and corresponding duty by the side of it. The rights, advantages, capital, knowledge, and all other goods which we inherit from past generations have been won by the struggles and sufferings of past generations; and the fact that the race lives, though men die, and that the race can by heredity accumulate within some cycle its victories over nature, is one of the facts which make civilization possible. The struggles of the race as a whole produce the possessions of the race as a whole. Something for nothing is not to be found on earth.

If there were such things as natural rights, the question would arise, Against whom are they good? Who has the corresponding obligation to satisfy these rights? There can be no rights against nature, except to get out of her whatever we can, which is only the fact of the struggle for existence stated over again. The common assertion is that the rights are good against society; that is, that society is bound to obtain and secure them

[257]

for the persons interested.   Society, however, is only the
persons interested plus some other persons; and as
the persons interested have by the hypothesis failed to
win the rights, we come to this, that natural rights are
the claims which certain persons have by prerogative
against some other persons.   Such is the actual interpretation in practice of natural rights — claims which some
people have by prerogative on other people.

This theory is a very far-reaching one, and of course
it is adequate to furnish a foundation for a whole social
philosophy.   In its widest extension it comes to mean
that if any man finds himself uncomfortable in this world
it must be somebody else's fault, and that somebody is
bound to come and make him comfortable.   Now the
people who are most uncomfortable in this world — for
if we should tell all our troubles it would not be found
to be a very comfortable world for anybody — are those
who have neglected their duties, and consequently have
failed to get their rights.   The people who can be called
upon to serve the uncomfortable must be those who have
done their duty, as the world goes, tolerably well.   Consequently the doctrine which we are discussing turns
out to be in practice only a scheme for making injustice
prevail in human society by reversing the distribution
of rewards and punishments between those who have
done their duty and those who have not.

We are constantly preached at by our public teachers
as if respectable people were to blame because some
people are not respectable — as if the man who has done
his duty in his own sphere was responsible in some way
for another man who has not done his duty in his sphere.
There are relations of employer and employee which
need to be regulated by compromise and treaty.   There
are sanitary precautions which need to be taken in

factories and houses. There are precautions against fire which are necessary. There is care needed that children be not employed too young, and that they have an education. There is cared needed that banks, insurance companies, and railroads be well managed, and that officers do not abuse their trusts. There is a duty in each case on the interested parties to defend their own interest. The penalty of neglect is suffering. The system of providing for these things by boards and inspectors throws the cost of it, not on the interested parties, but on the tax-payers. Some of them, no doubt, are the interested parties, and they may consider that they are exercising the proper care by paying taxes to support an inspector. If so, they only get their fair deserts when the railroad inspector finds out that a bridge is not safe after it is broken down, or when the bank examiner comes in to find out why a bank failed after the cashier has stolen all the funds. The real victim is the Forgotten Man again — the man who has watched his own investments, made his own machinery safe, attended to his own plumbing, and educated his own children, and who, just when he wants to enjoy the fruits of his care, is told that it is his duty to go and take care of some of his negligent neighbors, or, if he does not go, to pay an inspector to go. No doubt it is often his interest to go or to send, rather than to have the matter neglected, on account of his own connection with the thing neglected and his own secondary peril; but the point now is, that if preaching and philosophizing can do any good in the premises, it is all wrong to preach to the Forgotten Man that it is his duty to go and remedy other people's neglect. It is not his duty. It is a harsh and unjust burden which is laid upon him, and it is only the more unjust because no one thinks of him when laying the burden so that it falls on him. The exhortations ought to be expended on the negligent — that they take care of themselves.

It is an especially vicious extension of the false doctrine above mentioned that criminals have some sort of a right against or claim on society. Many reformatory plans are based on a doctrine of this kind when they are urged upon the public conscience. A criminal is a man who, instead of working with and for the society, has turned against it and become destructive and injurious. His punishment means that society rules him out of its membership and separates him from its association, by execution or imprisonment, according to the gravity of his offense. He has no claims against society at all. What shall be done with him is a question of expediency to be settled in view of the interests of society — that is, of the non-criminals. The French writers of the school of '48 used to represent the badness of the bad men as the fault of "society." As the object of this statement was to show that the badness of the bad men was not the fault of the bad men, and as society contains only good men and bad men, it followed that the badness of the bad men was the fault of the good men. On that theory of course the good men owed a great deal to the bad men who were in prison and at the galleys on their account. If we do not admit that theory, it behooves us to remember that any claim which we allow to the criminal against the "state" is only so much burden laid upon those who have never cost the State anything for discipline or correction. The punishments of society are just, like those of God and nature — they are warnings to the wrong-doer to reform himself.

When public offices are to be filled numerous candidates at once appear. Some are urged on the ground that they are poor, or cannot earn a living, or want support while getting an education, or have female relatives dependent on them, or are in poor health, or belong in a particular district, or are related to certain persons, or have done meritorious service in some other line of work than that which they apply to do. The abuses of the public service are to be condemned on account of the harm to the public interest, but there is an incidental injustice of the same general character with that which we are discussing. If an office is granted by favoritism or for any personal reason to A, it cannot be given to B. If an office is filled by a person who is unfit for it, he always keeps out somebody somewhere who is fit for it; that is, the social injustice has a victim in an unknown person — the Forgotten Man — and he is some person who has no political influence, and who has known no way in which to secure the chances of life except to deserve them. He is passed by for the noisy, pushing, importunate, and incompetent.

I have said elsewhere, disparagingly, something about the popular rage against combined capital, corporations, corners, selling futures, etc. The popular rage is not without reason, but it is sadly misdirected, and the real things which deserve attack are thriving all the time. The greatest social evil with which we have to contend is jobbery. Whatever there is in legislative charters, watering stocks, and so on which is objectionable comes under the head of jobbery. Jobbery is any scheme which aims to gain, not by the legitimate fruits of industry and enterprise, but by extorting from somebody a part of his product under guise of some pretended industrial undertaking. Of course it is only a modification when the undertaking in question has some legitimate character, but the occasion is used to graft upon it devices for obtaining what has not been earned. Jobbery is the vice of plutocracy, and it is the especial form under which plutocracy corrupts a democratic and republican form of government.   The United States is deeply afflicted with it, and the problem of civil liberty here is to conquer it. It affects everything which we really need to have done to such an extent that we have to do without public objects which we need through fear of jobbery.   Our public buildings are jobs — not always, but often.   They are not needed, or are costly beyond all necessity or even decent luxury.   Internal improvements are jobs.   They are not made because they are needed to meet needs which have been experienced.   They are made to serve private ends, often incidentally the political interests of the persons who vote the appropriations.   Pensions have become jobs.   In England pensions used to be given to aristocrats, because aristocrats had political influence, in order to corrupt them.   Here pensions are given to the great democratic mass, because they have political power, to corrupt them.   Instead of going out where there is plenty of land and making a farm there, some people go down under the Mississippi River to make a farm, and then they want to tax all the people in the United States to make dikes to keep the river off their farms.   The California gold-miners have washed out gold and have washed the dirt down into the rivers and on the farms below.   They want the Federal Government to clean out the rivers now and restore the farms. The silver-miners found their product declining in value and they got the Federal Government to go into the market and buy what the public did not want, in order to sustain, as they hoped, the price of silver.   The Federal Government is called upon to buy or hire unsalable ships, to build canals which will not pay, to furnish capital for all sorts of experiments, and to provide capital for enterprises of which private individuals will win the profits. All this is called "developing our resources," but it is, in truth, the great plan of all living on each other.

The greatest job of all is a protective tariff. It includes the biggest log-rolling and the widest corruption of economic and political ideas. It was said that there would be a rebellion if the taxes were not taken off whisky and tobacco, which taxes were paid into the public Treasury. Just then the importations of Sumatra tobacco became important enough to affect the market. The Connecticut tobacco-growers at once called for an import duty on tobacco which would keep up the price of their product. So it appears that if the tax on tobacco is paid to the Federal Treasury there will be a rebellion, but if it is paid to the Connecticut tobacco-raisers there will be no rebellion at all. The farmers have long paid tribute to the manufacturers; now the manufacturing and other laborers are to pay tribute to the farmers. The system is made more comprehensive and complete and we are all living on each other more than ever.

Now the plan of plundering each other produces nothing. It only wastes. All the material over which the protected interests wrangle and grab must be got from somebody outside of their circle. The talk is all about the American laborer and American industry, but in every case in which there is not an actual production of wealth by industry there are two laborers and two industries to be considered — the one who gets and the one who gives. Every protected industry has to plead, as the major premise of its argument, that any industry which does not pay *ought* to be carried on at the expense of the consumers of the product, and as its minor premise, that the industry in question does not pay; that is, that it cannot reproduce a capital equal in value to that which it consumes plus the current rate of profit. Hence every such industry must be a parasite on some other industry. What is the other industry? Who is the other man? This, the real question, is always overlooked.

In all jobbery the case is the same. There is a victim somewhere who is paying for it all. The doors of waste and extravagance stand open, and there seems to be a general agreement to squander and spend. It all belongs to somebody. There is somebody who had to contribute it and who will have to find more. Nothing is ever said about him. Attention is all absorbed by the clamorous interests, the importunate petitioners, the plausible schemers, the pitiless bores. Now, who is the victim? He is the Forgotten Man. If we go to find him, we shall find him hard at work tilling the soil to get out of it the fund for all the jobbery, the object of all the plunder, the cost of all the economic quackery, and the pay of all the politicians and statesmen who have sacrificed his interests to his enemies. We shall find him an honest, sober, industrious citizen, unknown outside his little circle, paying his debts and his taxes, supporting the church and the school, reading his party newspaper, and cheering for his pet politician.

We must not overlook the fact that the Forgotten Man is not infrequently a woman. I have before me a newspaper which contains five letters from corset-stitchers who complain that they cannot earn more than seventy-five cents a day with a machine and that they have to provide the thread. The tax on the grade of thread used by them is prohibitory as to all importation, and it is the corset-stitchers who have to pay day by day out of their time and labor the total enhancement of price

due to the tax. Women who earn their own living probably earn on an average seventy-five cents per day of
ten hours. Twenty-four minutes' work ought to buy a
spool of thread at the retail price, if the American work-
woman were allowed to exchange her labor for thread
on the best terms that the art and commerce of to-day
would allow; but after she has done twenty-four minutes'
work for the thread she is forced by the laws of her country
to go back and work sixteen minutes longer to pay the
tax — that is, to support the thread-mill. The thread-
mill, therefore, is not an institution for getting thread
for the American people, but for making thread harder to
get than it would be if there were no such institution.

In justification, now, of an arrangement so monstrously
unjust and out of place in a free country, it is said that
the employes in the thread-mill get high wages and that,
but for the tax, American laborers must come down to
the low wages of foreign thread-makers. It is not true
that American thread-makers get any more than the
market rate of wages, and they would not get less if the
tax were entirely removed, because the market rate of
wages in the United States would be controlled then, as
it is now, by the supply and demand of laborers under
the natural advantages and opportunities of industry in
this country. It makes a great impression on the
imagination, however, to go to a manufacturing town and
see great mills and a crowd of operatives; and such a
sight is put forward, *under the special allegation that it
would not exist but for a protective tax*, as a proof that
protective taxes are wise. But if it be true that the
thread-mill would not exist but for the tax, then how
can we form a judgment as to whether the protective
system is wise or not unless we call to mind all the seam-
stresses, washer-women, servants, factory-hands, sales-

women, teachers, and laborers' wives and daughters, scattered in the garrets and tenements of great cities and in cottages all over the country, who are paying the tax which keeps the mill going and pays the extra wages? If the sewing-women, teachers, servants, and washer-women could once be collected over against the thread-mill, then some inferences could be drawn which would be worth something. Then some light might be thrown upon the obstinate fallacy of "creating an industry" and we might begin to understand the difference between wanting thread and wanting a thread-mill. Some nations spend capital on great palaces, others on standing armies, others on iron-clad ships of war. Those things are all glorious and strike the imagination with great force when they are seen, but no one doubts that they make life harder for the scattered insignificant peasants and laborers who have to pay for them all. They "support a great many people," they "make work," they "give employment to other industries." We Americans have no palaces, armies, or iron-clads, but we spend our earnings on protected industries. A big protected factory, if it really needs the protection for its support, is a heavier load for the Forgotten Men and Women than an iron-clad ship of war in time of peace.

It is plain that the Forgotten Man and the Forgotten Woman are the real productive strength of the country. The Forgotten Man works and votes — generally he prays — but his chief business in life is to pay. His name never gets into the newspapers except when he marries or dies. He is an obscure man. He may grumble sometimes to his wife, but he does not frequent the grocery, and he does not talk politics at the tavern. So he is forgotten. Yet who is there whom the states-man, economist, and social philosopher ought to think of before this man? If any student of social science comes to appreciate the case of the Forgotten Man, he will become an unflinching advocate of strict scientific thinking in sociology and a hard-hearted skeptic as regards any scheme of social amelioration. He will always want to know, Who and where is the Forgotten Man in this case, who will have to pay for it all?

The Forgotten Man is not a pauper. It belongs to his character to save something. Hence he is a capitalist, though never a great one. He is a "poor" man in the popular sense of the word, but not in a correct sense. In fact, one of the most constant and trustworthy signs that the Forgotten Man is in danger of a new assault is that "the poor man" is brought into the discussion. Since the Forgotten Man has some capital, anyone who cares for his interest will try to make capital secure by securing the inviolability of contracts, the stability of currency, and the firmness of credit. Anyone, therefore, who cares for the Forgotten Man will be sure to be considered a friend of the capitalist and an enemy of the poor man.

It is the Forgotten Man who is threatened by every extension of the paternal theory of government. It is he who must work and pay. When, therefore, the statesmen and social philosophers sit down to think what the state can do or ought to do, they really mean to decide what the Forgotten Man shall do. What the Forgotten Man wants, therefore, is a fuller realization of constitutional liberty. He is suffering from the fact that there are yet mixed in our institutions mediæval theories of protection, regulation, and authority, and modern theories of independence and individual liberty and responsibility. The consequence of this mixed state of things is that those who are clever enough to get into control use the paternal theory by which to measure their own rights — that is, they assume privileges — and they use the theory of liberty to measure their own duties; that is, when it comes to the duties, they want to be "let alone." The Forgotten Man never gets into control. He has to pay both ways. His rights are measured to him by the theory of liberty — that is, he has only such as he can conquer; his duties are measured to him on the paternal theory — that is, he must discharge all which are laid upon him, as is the fortune of parents. In a paternal relation there are always two parties, a father and a child; and when we use the paternal relation metaphorically, it is of the first importance to know who is to be father and who is to be child. The rôle of parent falls always to the Forgotten Man. What he wants, therefore, is that ambiguities in our institutions be cleared up and that liberty be more fully realized.

It behooves any economist or social philosopher, whatever be the grade of his orthodoxy, who proposes to enlarge the sphere of the "state," or to take any steps whatever having in view the welfare of any class whatever, to pursue the analysis of the social effects of his proposition until he finds that other group whose interests must be curtailed or whose energies must be placed under contribution by the course of action which he proposes, and he cannot maintain his proposition until he has demonstrated that it will be more advantageous, *both quantitatively and qualitatively*, to those who must bear the weight of it than complete non-interference by the state with the relations of the parties in question.

THE PROPOSED DUAL ORGANIZATION
OF MANKIND

XIII

THE PROPOSED DUAL ORGANIZATION OF MANKIND[1]

[1896]

RODBERTUS turned aside from his studies of taxation in the Roman Empire, which had shown him the Roman city exhausting and consuming the rest of the Roman world, to express the opinion that the history of the last three hundred years is a story of the exploitation of the outlying continents by the old centers of civilization. This was an attempt to describe summarily the significance for the human race of the opening up of new regions by exploration and colonization. The period during which the influences of the new extension of civilized settlements has been at work is so short that it is impossible to define with confidence its ultimate effects on the relation of the parts of the race to each other and on the fortunes of the race as a whole. Recent events, however, have forced this subject upon our attention, for the "Monroe doctrine," as it has been recently affirmed and construed, would be nothing less than a doctrine and policy which some people are disposed to force upon the new organization of the inhabitants of the globe produced by the discovery and settlement of the outlying continents. If anybody claims to be able now to take control of this most portentous evolution in the life of the human race, and to dictate the course which it is to take, it behooves us all to verify the doctrine and to test the programme of policy proposed.

[1] Reprinted from Appleton's Popular Science Monthly. Copyright, 1896, by D. Appleton and Company.

The era of geographical discovery and adventure passes for an era of glorious achievement by men; yet to what end did they care to know and reach the outlying parts of the earth?   One motive which led them was the gain of commerce.   The products of the Indies could be obtained in no other way, and the trade for them was as old as civilization.   The other great motive was to obtain new supplies of gold and silver, under an exaggerated and fallacious notion of the desirableness of those forms of wealth.   Starting from these motives the movement has run its own course of commerce, colonization, war, missionary enterprise, economic expansion, and social evolution for three centuries.   The discovery, colonization, and exploitation of the outlying continents have been the most important elements in modern history. We Americans live in one of the great commonwealths which have been created by it.   From our local and later, but comparatively old center of civilization, we are hard at work occupying and subduing one of these outlying continents; for in our own history we have been, first, one of the outlying communities which were being exploited, and then ourselves an old civilization exploiting outlying regions.

The process of extension from Europe has gone on with the majesty and necessity of a process of nature.   Nothing in human history can compare with it as an unfolding of the drama of human life on earth under the aspects of growth, reaction, destruction, new development, and higher integration.   The record shows that the judgments of statesmen and philosophers about this process from its beginning have been a series of errors, and that the policies by which they have sought to control and direct it have only crippled it and interrupted it by war, revolt, and dissension.   At the present time the process is going on under a wrangle of discordant ethical judgments about its nature and the rights of the parties in it. We are rebuked for the wrongs of the aborigines, the vices of civilization, the greed of traders, the mistakes of missionaries, land-grabbing, etc., yet we Americans and others are living to-day in the enjoyment of the fruits of these wrongs perpetrated a few years ago. The fact is, as the history clearly shows, that the extension of the higher civilization over the globe is a natural process in which we are all swept along in spite of our ethical judgments. Those men, civilized or uncivilized, who cannot or will not come into the process will be crushed under it. It is as impossible that the present and future exploitation of Africa should not go on as it is that the present inhabitants of Manhattan Island should return to Europe and let the red man come back to his rights again. The scope for reason and conscience in the matter lies in taking warning from the statesmen and philosophers who have been over-hasty in the past with their doctrines and policies of how the process must go on.

Looking at the movement of men from Europe to the outlying continents as a phenomenon in the development of private interests and welfare, it appears at once that the man who went out as a fortune-hunter and he who went out as a colonist are on a very different footing. The former might be said to aim at selfishly exploiting the outlying country because he hoped, after a few years, to return to Europe and there enjoy his gains. The same could not be said of the colonist, for he cast in his lot with the new country, hoping there to establish a new home for his descendants and to build up a new commonwealth.

If the same movement is regarded from the standpoint of the duties and interests of European states, it is evident that both the fortune-hunter and the colonist needed, at first, the support and protection of the state from which they went forth. The whole movement of discovery and settlement appears, in this point of view, as a manifestation of growing social power in western Europe, and the nations there are seen to have made, in the first instance, a great expenditure of energy and capital for which they never received any return. The relation was one of parenthood, and therefore one of sacrifice, on the part of the mother countries. This relation was, however, obscured by traditions and accepted notions of national aggrandizement and glory, and by notions about commerce which were accepted as axiomatic. These notions drove the great states into policies of conquest, exclusion, monopoly, and war with each other. As a consequence the whole grand movement came to be regarded by European statesmen from the standpoint of gain to European nations, and they adopted sordid measures for snatching this gain from each other. Those statesmen assumed that Europe was the head of the world, and they allotted the outlying regions among themselves with no regard for the aborigines and very little regard for the colonists. The body of relations which was established between the Old World and the New, under this theory, constituted the colonial system.

It cannot be denied that the colonial system stands in history as an attempt to exploit the outlying continents for the benefit of Europe. Thousands of lives and millions of capital were expended in the effort to perfect the system, and in that struggle to steal each other's colonies which the system caused. The logical outcome was the ambition of each competitor to win universal dominion for itself and to impose a balance-of-power policy on each of the others. The system had its doctrines too; some old, some new: "He who holds the sea will hold the land," "Trade follows the flag." The English colonial system was far less oppressive and more enlightened than that of any other nation. It alone was founded on real colonization and aimed to create new commonwealths. It was therefore the one under which the system first broke down, for it contained a fatal inconsistency in itself. It educated the colonists to independence, and it was certain that they would go alone as soon as they were strong enough to do so, if they thought that they were being exploited in the colonial relation. To such extent as this destiny was aimed at or unconsciously brought about, the construction of modern history put forward by Rodbertus fails to be correct.

It has become a commonplace of history that the revolt of the American colonies was a good thing for the colonies and for England. The question no longer has any other than speculative interest, and perhaps no speculation is more idle than that which deals with the possible consequences of some other course of history than that which actually took place; but if such speculation ever could be profitable, it would be upon this question: What would have been the consequences to human welfare if the English statesmen of 1775 could have risen to the nineteenth-century doctrine of colonies and if the whole English-speaking world could have remained united in sympathy and harmony? This question has so much practical value that it may help us to see the advantage there may be in a colonial relation where it still exists, and to see that there is no universal and dogmatic ground for independence which can be urged by a third party.

Independence was brought about on the Western continent; not to any important extent anywhere else. The

Spanish-American colonies had grievances against their
mother-country which fully justified their revolt; still, it
appears that they revolted chiefly from contagion and
imitation. They have never been able to obtain good
standing in the family of nations as independent commonwealths. The Panama Congress of 1824, in its original
plan, promised to be a very important incident in the
development of the relations of the New World to the
Old. It appeared for a time that the Western continent
might be organized as a unit in independence of, and
possible hostility to, the Eastern continent. The project
came to nothing. It was crushed in one of the hardest
political collisions in our history, that between the Adams
administration and the Jackson opposition. The theory
of it, however, remains behind and, under the name of
the Monroe doctrine, has remained as a vague and elastic
notion. The practical outcome of any attempt to realize
that doctrine must be to organize the world into a dual
system. Instead of the old notion of a world-unit ruled
from Europe as its head, we should have a dual world-
system, one part under the hegemony of Europe, the
other part under that of the United States. Is this a
rational or practicable plan of future development? Is
it not fantastic and arbitrary? If the United States
pretends to hold aloof from a share in the affairs of the
Eastern continent, and to demand that all European
states shall abstain from any share in the affairs of the
Western continent, is that anything more than a pose
and an affectation? Have we not within a year or two
been forced to take action in protection of our citizens in
China and Armenia? If Africa is opened up to commerce,
do we mean to hold aloof from a share in it? Are we not
already deeply interested in it so far as it has advanced?
We have interests in Madagascar which have already

drawn us into the proceedings there, and which promise to involve us still further.   We accepted a rôle in the war between China and Japan which was by no means that of an uninterested stranger.   Will anyone maintain that we could carry out the policy of abstention in respect to that part of the world?

On the other hand, so long as European nations own colonies in America, how can we rule the Western continent without coming in collision with them?   Even if we should dispossess them of those colonies, how would it be possible to rule the Western continent and to deny them any right to meddle in its affairs, so long as their citizens may visit the same for business or pleasure? The notion that the world can be so divided that we can rule one part and Europe the other, and thus never be brought in collision with each other, is evidently a silly whim.   We may talk about "Western civilization" or "American ideas," but these are only grandiloquent phrases.   Everybody knows that there is no civilization common to all America and different from that of Europe; there are no ideas common to all America and different from European ideas.   There has never been any sympathy between North and South America, and there are only few and comparatively feeble bonds of interest based on commerce or investments.   Either North or South America has far stronger bonds to Europe than they both have to each other.   As far as the external resemblance 'of "republics" is concerned, the South American states have hitherto only made republican government ridiculous.   The geographical neighborhood, on which stress is often laid, can be seen by a glance at the map to be non-existent.   If it existed it would be of little importance compared with economic distance, which is reckoned by cost, time, and facility of transportation.

The Western continents are divided from each other by race, religion, language, real political institutions, manners and customs, and above all, by tastes and habits. They entertain a strong dislike of each other. The United States could never establish a hegemony over the Western world until after long years of conquest. In their quarrels with European states it suits the South American states very well that the United States should act the cat's-paw for them, but it cannot be that their statesmen will be so short-sighted as to accept a protection which would turn into domination without a moment's warning; neither can it be possible that our statesmen will ever seriously commit us to a responsibility for the proceedings of South American states.

We may probe the ideas and projects which are grouped under this attempt at a dual organization of the world as we will, in no direction do we come upon anything but crude notions and inflated rhetoric. Such notions have hitherto proved very costly to the human race. President Cleveland, in his Venezuela message, sought a parallel for the Monroe doctrine in the balance-of-power doctrine. The parallel was unfortunate, if it had been true. The balance-of-power doctrine cost frightful expenditures of life and capital, and what was won by them? Where is the balance of power as it was understood in the eighteenth century or in Napoleon's time? A real parallel to the Monroe doctrine is furnished by the colonial system. The latter, as above shown, was the doctrine of the unity of the world under the headship of Europe. The former is the doctrine of the dualism of the world, with Europe at the head of one part and the United States at the head of the other. One of these conceptions of the new organization of the human race, which is to grow out of the colonization and settlement of the outlying countries, is as arbitrary as the other, and the new one can never be realized without far greater expenditure of life and property than the other. If history and science have any power over the convictions and actions of men, here is a good opportunity for proof of it, for if anything is proved by ecclesiastical and civil history it would seem to be the frightful cost of phrases and doctrines and of the whole cohort of phantasms which take the place of facts and relations in determining the actions of men. It is to these that men have always brought the heaviest sacrifices of their happiness, blood, and property. We have had in our own history the doctrines of no entangling alliances, state rights, nullification, manifest destiny, the self-expanding power of the Constitution, the higher law, secession, and as many more as rhetorical politicians have found necessary to save them the trouble of coming down to facts and law. How frightful has been the penalty for the people who have been deluded by some of these! Who knows on what day another of them may, by a turn of events, become politically important and call for its share of sacrifice? It is a wise rule of life for a man of education and sense not to allow his judgment to be taken captive by stereotyped catch-words, mottoes, and doctrines.

We have already a commercial system in which we have undertaken to surround ourselves by a wall of taxes so as to raise the prices of all manufactured products twenty-five to fifty per cent above the same prices in western Europe. That system has been adopted as a policy of prosperity to be produced by specific devices of legislation. We have applied it to the best part of the continent of North America. It is now proposed to restrict immigration so as to close the labor market of the same part of North America, in the belief that wages will thus be raised and that, if they are, a great advantage will be produced for the wages class. We have also a project before us to inclose all America in a barrier within which an arbitrary circulation of silver money may be secured, all relations with the money of the rest of the world being cut off. That these doctrines and projects all hang together, and are all coherent with the political notion of the dual division of the world, is obvious. The common element is in the narrow and distorted view of what is true and possible and desirable in social and economic affairs.

We have had before us, since the revolt of the English North American colonies, another conception of the organization of human society which is to come out of the extension of civilization to the outlying continents. It is, in fact, now embedded in international law and in the diplomacy of civilized states. That is why the advocates of the Monroe doctrine have been forced to meet the argument that their doctrine was not in international law by new spinnings of political metaphysics. They have to try to cover the fact that the Monroe doctrine is an attempt by the United States to define the rights of other nations. The modern conception, however, is that the states of the world are all united in a family of nations whose rights and duties toward each other are embodied in a code of international law. All states may be admitted into this family of nations whenever they accept this code, whether they have previously been considered "civilized" or not. The code itself is a product of the reasoning and moral convictions of civilized states, and it grows by precedents and usages, as cases arise for the application of the general principles which have been accepted as sound, because they conduce to peace, harmony, and smooth progress of affairs. The code has undergone its best developments in connection with the spread of enlightenment and the extension of industrialism. This is the only conception of the relation of parts of the human race to each other which is consistent with civilization and which is worthy of the enlightenment of our age. Any "doctrine" which is not consistent with it will sooner or later be set aside through the suffering of those who adhere to it.

THE FALLACY OF TERRITORIAL EXTENSION

XIV

THE FALLACY OF TERRITORIAL EXTENSION

[1896]

THE traditional belief is that a state aggrandizes itself by territorial extension, so that winning new land is gaining in wealth and prosperity, just as an individual would gain if he increased his land possessions. It is undoubtedly true that a state may be so small in territory and population that it cannot serve the true purposes of a state for its citizens, especially in international relations with neighboring states which control a large aggregate of men and capital. There is, therefore, under given circumstances, a size of territory and population which is at the maximum of advantage for the civil unit. The unification of Germany and Italy was apparently advantageous for the people affected. In the nineteenth century there has been a tendency to create national states, and nationality has been advocated as the true basis of state unity. The cases show, however, that the national unit does not necessarily coincide with the most advantageous state unit, and that the principle of nationality cannot override the historical accidents which have made the states. Sweden and Norway, possessing unity, threaten to separate. Austro-Hungary, a conglomerate of nationalities largely hostile to each other, will probably be held together by political necessity. The question of expedient size will always be one for the judgment and good sense of statesmen.

The opinion may be risked that Russia has carried out a policy of territorial extension which has been harmful to its internal integration. For three hundred years it has been reaching out after more territory and has sought the grandeur and glory of conquest and size. To this it has sacrificed the elements of social and industrial strength. The autocracy has been confirmed and established because it is the only institution which symbolizes and maintains the unity of the great mass, and the military and tax burdens have distorted the growth of the society to such an extent as to produce disease and weakness.

Territorial aggrandizement enhances the glory and personal importance of the man who is the head of a dynastic state. The fallacy of confusing this with the greatness and strength of the state itself is an open pitfall close at hand. It might seem that a republic, one of whose chief claims to superiority over a monarchy lies in avoiding the danger of confusing the king with the state, ought to be free from this fallacy of national greatness, but we have plenty of examples to prove that the traditional notions are not cut off by changing names and forms.

The notion that gain of territory is gain of wealth and strength for the state, after the expedient size has been won, is a delusion. In the Middle Ages the beneficial interest in land and the jurisdiction over the people who lived on it were united in one person. The modern great states, upon their formation, took to themselves the jurisdiction, and the beneficial interest turned into full property in land. The confusion of the two often reappears now, and it is one of the most fruitful causes of fallacy in public questions. It is often said that the United States owns silver-mines, and it is inferred that

the policy of the state in regard to money and currency
ought to be controlled in some way by this fact. The
"United States," as a subject of property rights and of
monetary claims and obligations, may be best defined
by calling it the "Fiscus." This legal person owns no
silver-mines. If it did, it could operate them by farming
them or by royalties. The revenue thus received would
lower taxes. The gain would inure to all the people in
the United States. The body politic named the United
States has nothing to do with the silver-mines except
that it exercises jurisdiction over the territory in which
they lie. If it levies taxes on them it also incurs expenses
for them, and as it wins no profits on its total income
and outgo, these must be taken to be equal. It renders
services for which it exacts only the cost thereof. The
beneficial and property interest in the mines belongs to
individuals, and they win profits only by conducting the
exploitation of the mines with an expenditure of labor
and capital. These individuals are of many nationalities. They alone own the product and have the use
and enjoyment of it. No other individuals, American
or others, have any interest, right, duty, or responsibility
in the matter. The United States has simply provided
the protection of its laws and institutions for the mine-
workers while they were carrying on their enterprise.
Its jurisdiction was only a burden to it, not a profitable
good. Its jurisdiction was a boon to the mine-workers
and certainly did not entail further obligation.

It is said that the boundary between Alaska and British
America runs through a gold field, and some people are
in great anxiety as to who will "grab it." If an American
can go over to the English side and mine gold there for
his profit, under English laws and jurisdiction, and an
Englishman can come over to the American side and mine

gold there for his profit, under American laws and jurisdiction, what difference does it make where the line falls?
The only case in which it would make any difference is
where the laws and institutions of the two states were not
on equal stages of enlightenment.

This case serves to bring out distinctly a reason for
the old notion of territorial extension which is no longer
valid. In the old colonial system, states conquered
territories or founded colonies in order to shut them
against all other states and to exploit them on principles
of subjugation and monopoly. It is only under this
system that the jurisdiction is anything but a burden.

If the United States should admit Hawaii to the Union,
the Fiscus of the former state would collect more taxes
and incur more expenses. The circumstances are such
that the latter would probably be the greater. The
United States would not acquire a square foot of land
in property unless it paid for it. Individual Americans
would get no land to till without paying for it and would
win no products from it except by wisely expending their
labor and capital on it. All that they can do now.
So long as there is a government on the islands, native
or other, which is competent to guarantee peace, order,
and security, no more is necessary, and for any outside
power to seize the jurisdiction is an unjustifiable aggression. That jurisdiction would be the best founded which
was the most liberal and enlightened, and would give
the best security to all persons who sought the islands
upon their lawful occasions. The jurisdiction would, in
any case, be a burden, and any state might be glad to
see any other state assume the burden, provided that it
was one which could be relied upon to execute the charge
on enlightened principles for the good of all. The best
case is, therefore, always that in which the resident popu-

lation produce their own state by the institutions of self-government.

What private individuals want is free access, under order and security, to any part of the earth's surface, in order that they may avail themselves of its natural resources for their use, either by investment or commerce. If, therefore, we could have free trade with Hawaii while somebody else had the jurisdiction, we should gain all the advantages and escape all the burdens. The Constitution of the United States establishes absolute free trade between all parts of the territory under its jurisdiction. A large part of our population was thrown into indignant passion because the Administration rejected the annexation of Hawaii, regarding it like the act of a man who refuses the gift of a farm. These persons were generally those who are thrown into excitement by any proposition of free trade. They will not, therefore, accept free trade with the islands while somebody else has the trouble and burden of the jurisdiction, but they would accept free trade with the islands eagerly if they could get the burden of the jurisdiction too.

Canada has to deal with a race war and a religious war, each of great virulence, which render governmental jurisdiction in the Dominion difficult and hazardous. If we could go to Canada and trade there our products for those of that country, we could win all for our private interests which that country is able to contribute to the welfare of mankind, and we should have nothing to do with the civil and political difficulties which harass the government. We refuse to have free trade with Canada. Our newspaper and congressional economists prove to their own satisfaction that it would be a great harm to us to have free trade with her now, while she is outside the jurisdiction under which we live; but, within a few months, we have seen an eager impulse of public opinion toward a war of conquest against Canada. If, then, we could force her to come under the same jurisdiction, by a cruel and unprovoked war, thus bringing on ourselves the responsibility for all her civil discords and problems, it appears to be believed that free trade with her would be a good thing.

The case of Cuba is somewhat different. If we could go to the island and trade with the same freedom with which we can go to Louisiana, we could make all the gains, by investment and commerce, which the island offers to industry and enterprise, provided that either Spain or a local government would give the necessary security, and we should have no share in political struggles there. It may be that the proviso is not satisfied, or soon will not be. Here is a case, then, which illustrates the fact that states are often forced to extend their jurisdiction whether they want to do so or not. Civilized states are forced to supersede the local jurisdiction of uncivilized or half-civilized states, in order to police the territory and establish the necessary guarantees of industry and commerce. It is idle to set up absolute doctrines of national ownership in the soil which would justify a group of population in spoiling a part of the earth's surface for themselves and everybody else. The island of Cuba may fall into anarchy. If it does, the civilized world may look to the United States to take the jurisdiction and establish order and security there. We might be compelled to do it. It would, however, be a great burden, and possibly a fatal calamity to us. Probably any proposition that England should take it would call out a burst of jingo passion against which all reasoning would be powerless. We ought to pray that England would take it. She would govern it well, and everybody would have free access to it for the purposes of private interest, while our Government would be free from all complications with the politics of the island. If we take the jurisdiction of the island, we shall find ourselves in a political dilemma, each horn of which is as disastrous as the other: either we must govern it as a subject province, or we must admit it into the Union as a state or group of states. Our system is unfit for the government of subject provinces. They have no place in it. They would become seats of corruption, which would react on our own body politic. If we admitted the island as a state or group of states, we should have to let it help govern us. The prospect of adding to the present senate a number of Cuban senators, either native or carpet-bag, is one whose terrors it is not necessary to unfold. Nevertheless it appears that there is a large party which would not listen to free trade with the island while any other nation has the jurisdiction of it, but who are ready to grab it at any cost and to take free trade with it, provided that they can get the political burdens too.

This confederated state of ours was never planned for indefinite expansion or for an imperial policy. We boast of it a great deal, but we must know that its advantages are won at the cost of limitations, as is the case with most things in this world. The fathers of the Republic planned a confederation of free and peaceful industrial commonwealths, shielded by their geographical position from the jealousies, rivalries, and traditional policies of the Old World and bringing all the resources of civilization to bear for the domestic happiness of the population only. They meant to have no grand state-craft or "high politics," no "balance of power" or "reasons of state," which had cost the human race so much. They meant to offer no field for what Benjamin Franklin called the "pest of glory." It is the limitation of this scheme of the state that the state created under it must forego a great number of the grand functions of European states; especially that it contains no methods and apparatus of conquest, extension, domination, and imperialism. The plan of the fathers would have no controlling authority for us if it had been proved by experience that that plan was narrow, inadequate, and mistaken. Are we prepared to vote that it has proved so? For our territorial extension has reached limits. which are complete for all purposes and leave no necessity for "rectification of boundaries." Any extension will open questions, not close them. Any extension will not make us more secure where we are, but will force us to take new measures to secure our new acquisitions. The preservation of acquisitions will force us to reorganize our internal resources, so as to make it possible to prepare them in advance and to mobilize them with promptitude. This will lessen liberty and require discipline. It will increase taxation and all the pressure of government. It will divert the national energy from the provision of self-maintenance and comfort for the people, and will necessitate stronger and more elaborate governmental machinery. All this will be disastrous to republican institutions and to democracy. Moreover, all extension puts a new strain on the internal cohesion of the preexisting mass, threatening a new cleavage within. If we had never taken Texas and Northern Mexico we should never have had secession.

The sum of the matter is that colonization and territorial extension are burdens, not gains. Great civilized states cannot avoid these burdens. They are the penalty of greatness because they are the duties of it. No state can successfully undertake to extend its jurisdiction unless its internal vitality is high, so that it has surplus energy to dispose of. Russia, as already mentioned, is a state which has taken upon itself tasks of this kind beyond its strength, and for which it is in no way competent. Italy offers at this moment the strongest instance of a state which is imperiling its domestic welfare for a colonial policy which is beyond its strength, is undertaken arbitrarily, and has no proper motive. Germany has taken up a colonial policy with great eagerness, apparently from a notion that it is one of the attributes of a great state. To maintain it she must add a great navy to her great military establishment and increase the burdens of a population which is poor and heavily taxed and which has not in its territory any great natural resources from which to draw the strength to bear its burdens. Spain is exhausting her last strength to keep Cuba, which can never repay the cost unless it is treated on the old colonial plan as a subject province to be exploited for the benefit of the mother-country. If that is done, however, the only consequence will be another rebellion and greater expenditure. England, as a penalty of her greatness, finds herself in all parts of the world face to face with the necessity of maintaining her jurisdiction and of extending it in order to maintain it. When she does so she finds herself only extending law and order for the benefit of everybody. It is only in circumstances like hers that the burdens have any compensation.

THE CONQUEST OF THE UNITED STATES BY SPAIN

XV

THE CONQUEST OF THE UNITED STATES BY SPAIN

[1898]

DURING the last year the public has been familiar-ized with descriptions of Spain and of Spanish methods of doing things until the name of Spain has become a symbol for a certain well-defined set of notions and policies. On the other hand, the name of the United States has always been, for all of us, a symbol for a state of things, a set of ideas and traditions, a group of views about social and political affairs. Spain was the first, for a long time the greatest, of the modern imperialistic states. The United States, by its historical origin, its traditions, and its principles, is the chief representative of the revolt and reaction against that kind of a state. I intend to show that, by the line of action now proposed to us, which we call expansion and imperialism, we are throwing away some of the most important elements of the American symbol and are adopting some of the most important elements of the Spanish symbol. We have beaten Spain in a military conflict, but we are submitting to be conquered by her on the field of ideas and policies. Expansionism and imperialism are nothing but the old philosophies of national prosperity which have brought Spain to where she now is. Those philosophies appeal to national vanity and national cupidity. They are seductive, especially upon the first view and the most superficial judgment, and therefore it cannot be denied that they are very strong for popular effect. They are delusions, and they will lead us to ruin unless we are hard-headed enough to resist them. In any case the year 1898 is a great landmark in the history of the United States. The consequences will not be all good or all bad, for such is not the nature of societal influences. They are always mixed of good and ill, and so it will be in this case. Fifty years from now the historian, looking back to 1898, will no doubt see, in the course which things will have taken, consequences of the proceedings of that year and of this present one which will not all be bad, but you will observe that that is not a justification for a happy-go-lucky policy; that does not affect our duty to-day in all that we do to seek wisdom and prudence and to determine our actions by the best judgment which we can form.

War, expansion, and imperialism are questions of statesmanship and of nothing else. I disregard all other aspects of them and all extraneous elements which have been intermingled with them. I received the other day a circular of a new educational enterprise in which it was urged that, on account of our new possessions, we ought now to devote especial study to history, political economy, and what is called political science. I asked myself, Why? What more reason is there for pursuing these studies now on behalf of our dependencies than there was before to pursue them on behalf of ourselves? In our proceedings of 1898 we made no use of whatever knowledge we had of any of these lines of study. The original and prime cause of the war was that it was a move of partisan tactics in the strife of parties at Washington. As soon as it seemed resolved upon, a number of interests began to see their advantage in it and hastened to further it. It was necessary to make appeals to the public which would bring quite other motives to the support of the enterprise and win the consent of classes who would never consent to either financial or political jobbery. Such appeals were found in sensational assertions which we had no means to verify, in phrases of alleged patriotism, in statements about Cuba and the Cubans which we now know to have been entirely untrue.

Where was the statesmanship of all this? If it is not an established rule of statecraft that a statesman should never impose any sacrifices on his people for anything but their own interests, then it is useless to study political philosophy any more, for this is the alphabet of it. It is contrary to honest statesmanship to imperil the political welfare of the state for party interests. It was unstatesmanlike to publish a solemn declaration that we would not seize any territory, and especially to characterize such action in advance as "criminal aggression," for it was morally certain that we should come out of any war with Spain with conquered territory on our hands, and the people who wanted the war, or who consented to it, hoped that we should do so.

We talk about "liberty" all the time in a big and easy way, as if liberty was a thing that men could have if they want it, and to any extent to which they want it. It is certain that a very large part of human liberty consists simply in the choice either to do a thing or to let it alone. If we decide to do it, a whole series of consequences is entailed upon us in regard to which it is exceedingly difficult, or impossible, for us to exercise any liberty at all. The proof of this from the case before us is so clear and easy that I need spend no words upon it. Here, then, you have the reason why it is a rule of sound statesmanship not to embark on an adventurous policy. A statesman could not be expected to know in advance

that we should come out of the war with the Philippines
on our hands, but it belongs to his education to warn
him that a policy of adventure and of gratuitous enterprise would be sure to entail embarrassments of some
kind.   What comes to us in the evolution of our own
life and interests, that we must meet; what we go to
seek which lies beyond that domain is a waste of our
energy and a compromise of our liberty and welfare.
If this is not sound doctrine, then the historical and
social sciences have nothing to teach us which is worth
any trouble.

There is another observation, however, about the war
which is of far greater importance: that is, that it was a
gross violation of self-government.   We boast that we
are a self-governing people, and in this respect, particularly, we compare ourselves with pride with older nations.
What is the difference after all?   The Russians, whom
we always think of as standing at the opposite pole of
political institutions, have self-government, if you mean
by it acquiescence in what a little group of people at the
head of the government agree to do.   The war with
Spain was precipitated upon us headlong, without reflection or deliberation, and without any due formulation of
public opinion.   Whenever a voice was raised in behalf
of deliberation and the recognized maxims of statesmanship, it was howled down in a storm of vituperation and
cant.   Everything was done to make us throw away
sobriety of thought and calmness of judgment and to
inflate all expressions with sensational epithets and
turgid phrases.   It cannot be denied that everything in
regard to the war has been treated in an exalted strain
of sentiment and rhetoric very unfavorable to the truth.
At present the whole periodical press of the country
seems to be occupied in tickling the national vanity to

the utmost by representations about the war which are extravagant and fantastic. There will be a penalty to be paid for all this. Nervous and sensational newspapers are just as corrupting, especially to young people, as nervous and sensational novels. The habit of expecting that all mental pabulum shall be highly spiced, and the corresponding loathing for whatever is soberly truthful, undermines character as much as any other vice. Patriotism is being prostituted into a nervous intoxication which is fatal to an apprehension of truth. It builds around us a fool's paradise, and it will lead us into errors about our position and relations just like those which we have been ridiculing in the case of Spain.

There are some now who think that it is the perfection of statesmanship to say that expansion is a fact and that it is useless to discuss it. We are told that we must not cross any bridges until we come to them; that is, that we must discuss nothing in advance, and that we must not discuss anything which is past because it is irretrievable. No doubt this would be a very acceptable doctrine to the powers that be, for it would mean that they were relieved from responsibility, but it would be a marvelous doctrine to be accepted by a self-governing people. Senator Foraker has told us that we are not to keep the Philippines longer than is necessary to teach the people self-government. How one man can tell what we are to do before the constitutional authorities have decided it, I do not know. Perhaps it is a detail in our new method of self-government. If his assurances are to be trusted, we are paying $20,000,000 for the privilege of tutoring the Tagals up to liberty and self-government. I do not believe that, if the United States undertakes to govern the islands, it will ever give them up except to superior force, but the weakening of imperialism shown by this gentleman's assurances, after a few days of mild debate in the senate, shows that agitation of the subject is not yet in vain.   Then again, if we have done anything, especially if we have acted precipitately, it is a well-recognized course of prudent behavior to find out where we are, what we have done, and what the new situation is into which we have come.   Then, too, we must remember that when the statesman lays a thing down the historian takes it up, and he will group it with historical parallels and contrasts.   There is a set of men who have always been referred to, in our Northern states, for the last thirty years, with especial disapproval.   They are those Southerners who, in 1861, did not believe in secession, but, as they said, "went with their states."   They have been condemned for moral cowardice.   Yet within a year it has become almost a doctrine with us that patriotism requires that we should hold our tongues while our interests, our institutions, our most sacred traditions, and our best established maxims have been trampled underfoot.   There is no doubt that moral courage is the virtue which is more needed than any other in the modern democratic state, and that truckling to popularity is the worst political vice.   The press, the platform, and the pulpit have all fallen under this vice, and there is evidence that the university also, which ought to be the last citadel of truth, is succumbing to it likewise. I have no doubt that the conservative classes of this country will yet look back with great regret to their acquiescence in the events of 1898 and the doctrines and precedents which have been silently established. Let us be well assured that self-government is not a matter of flags and Fourth of July orations, nor yet of strife to get offices.   Eternal vigilance is the price of that as of every other political good.   The perpetuity of self-government depends on the sound political sense of the people, and sound political sense is a matter of habit and practice. We can give it up and we can take instead pomp and glory. That is what Spain did. She had as much self-government as any country in Europe at the beginning of the sixteenth century. The union of the smaller states into one big one gave an impulse to her national feeling and national development. The discovery of America put into her hands the control of immense territories. National pride and ambition were stimulated. Then came the struggle with France for world-dominion, which resulted in absolute monarchy and bankruptcy for Spain. She lost self-government and saw her resources spent on interests which were foreign to her, but she could talk about an empire on which the sun never set and boast of her colonies, her gold-mines, her fleets and armies and debts. She had glory and pride, mixed, of course, with defeat and disaster, such as must be experienced by any nation on that course of policy; and she grew weaker in her industry and commerce and poorer in the status of the population all the time. She has never been able to recover real self-government yet. If we Americans believe in self-government, why do we let it slip away from us? Why do we barter it away for military glory as Spain did?

There is not a civilized nation which does not talk about its civilizing mission just as grandly as we do. The English, who really have more to boast of in this respect than anybody else, talk least about it, but the Phariseeism with which they correct and instruct other people has made them hated all over the globe. The French believe themselves the guardians of the highest and purest culture, and that the eyes of all mankind are fixed on Paris, whence they expect oracles of thought and taste. The Germans regard themselves as charged with a mission, especially to us Americans, to save us from egoism and materialism. The Russians, in their books and newspapers, talk about the civilizing mission of Russia in language that might be translated from some of the finest paragraphs in our imperialistic newspapers. The first principle of Mohammedanism is that we Christians are dogs and infidels, fit only to be enslaved or butchered by Moslems. It is a corollary that wherever Mohammedanism extends it carries, in the belief of its votaries, the highest blessings, and that the whole human race would be enormously elevated if Mohammedanism should supplant Christianity everywhere. To come, last, to Spain, the Spaniards have, for centuries, considered themselves the most zealous and self-sacrificing Christians, especially charged by the Almighty, on this account, to spread true religion and civilization over the globe. They think themselves free and noble, leaders in refinement and the sentiments of personal honor, and they despise us as sordid money-grabbers and heretics. I could bring you passages from peninsular authors of the first rank about the grand rôle of Spain and Portugal in spreading freedom and truth. Now each nation laughs at all the others when it observes these manifestations of national vanity. You may rely upon it that they are all ridiculous by virtue of these pretensions, including ourselves. The point is that each of them repudiates the standards of the others, and the outlying nations, which are to be civilized, hate all the standards of civilized men. We assume that what we like and practice, and what we think better, must come as a welcome blessing to Spanish-Americans and Filipinos. This is grossly and obviously untrue. They hate our ways. They are hostile to our ideas. Our religion, language, institutions, and manners offend them. They like their own ways, and if we appear amongst them as rulers, there will be social discord in all the great departments of social interest. The most important thing which we shall inherit from the Spaniards will be the task of suppressing rebellions. If the United States takes out of the hands of Spain her mission, on the ground that Spain is not executing it well, and if this nation in its turn attempts to be school-mistress to others, it will shrivel up into the same vanity and self-conceit of which Spain now presents an example. To read our current literature one would think that we were already well on the way to it. Now, the great reason why all these enterprises which begin by saying to somebody else, We know what is good for you better than you know yourself and we are going to make you do it, are false and wrong is that they violate liberty; or, to turn the same statement into other words, the reason why liberty, of which we Americans talk so much, is a good thing is that it means leaving people to live out their own lives in their own way, while we do the same. If we believe in liberty, as an American principle, why do we not stand by it? Why are we going to throw it away to enter upon a Spanish policy of dominion and regulation?

The United States cannot be a colonizing nation for a long time yet. We have only twenty-three persons to the square mile in the United States without Alaska. The country can multiply its population by thirteen; that is, the population could rise above a billion before the whole country would be as densely populated as Rhode Island is now. There is, therefore, no pressure of population, which is the first condition of rational expansion, unless we could buy another territory like the Mississippi Valley with no civilized population in it. If we could do that it would postpone the day of over-population still further, and make easier conditions for our people in the next generations. In the second place, the islands which we have taken from Spain never can be the residence of American families, removing and settling to make their homes there. The climatic conditions forbid it. Although Spaniards have established themselves in Spanish America, even in the tropics, the evils of Spanish rule have largely arisen from the fact that Spaniards have gone to the colonies as adventurers, eager to make fortunes as quickly as possible, that they might return to Spain to enjoy them. That the relation of our people to these possessions will have that character is already apparent. It is, therefore, inaccurate to speak of a colonial system in describing our relation to these dependencies, but as we have no other term, let us use this one and inquire *what kind of a colonial system we are to establish.*

I. Spain stands, in modern history, as the first state to develop and apply a colonial system to her outlying possessions. Her policy was to exclude absolutely all non-Spaniards from her subject territories and to exploit them for the benefit of Spain, without much regard for the aborigines or the colonists. The cold and unnecessary cruelty of the Spaniards to the aborigines is appalling, even when compared with the treatment of the aborigines by other Europeans. A modern economist stands aghast at the economic measures adopted by Spain, as well in regard to her domestic policy as to her colonies. It seems as if those measures could only have been inspired by some demon of folly, they were so destructive to her prosperity. She possesses a large literature from the last three centuries, in which her publicists discuss with amazement the question whether it was a blessing or a curse to get the Indies, and why, with all the supposed conditions of prosperity in her hands, she was declining all the time. We now hear it argued that she is well rid of her colonies, and that, if she will devote her energies to her internal development and rid her politics of the corruption of colonial officials and interests, she may be regenerated. That is a rational opinion. It is the best diagnosis of her condition and the best prescription of a remedy which the occasion has called forth. But what, then, will happen to the state which has taken over her colonies? I can see no answer except that that nation, with them, has taken over the disease and that *it* now is to be corrupted by exploiting dependent communities just as she has been. That it stands exposed to this danger is undeniable.

It would not be becoming to try, in a paragraph, to set forth the causes of the decadence of Spain, and although the economic history of that country has commanded such attention from me as I could give to it consistently with other obligations, yet I could not feel prepared to do any justice to that subject; but one or two features of the history can be defined with confidence, and they are such as are especially instructive for us.

In the first place Spain never intended, of set purpose, to ruin the material prosperity of herself or her colonies. Her economic history is one long lesson to prove that any prosperity policy is a delusion and a path to ruin. There is no economic lesson which the people of the United States need to take to heart more than that. In the second place the Spanish mistakes arose, in part, from confusing the public treasury with the national wealth. They thought that, when gold flowed into the public treasury, that was the same as an increase of wealth of the people. It really meant that the people

were bearing the burdens of the imperial system and that
the profits of it went into the public treasury; that is,
into the hands of the king. It was no wonder, then,
that as the burdens grew greater the people grew poorer.
The king spent the revenues in extending the imperial
system in Germany, Italy, and the Netherlands, so that
the revenues really became a new cause of corruption
and decay. The only people who were well off, in the
midst of the increasing distress, were the ecclesiastics
and nobles, who were protected by entails and charters,
which, in their turn, were a new cause of restriction and
destruction to the industries of the country. As to the
treatment of the aborigines in the outlying possessions of
Spain, the orders from the home government were as
good as could possibly be desired. No other European
government issued any which were nearly so enlightened
or testified to such care about that matter. Spanish
America is still covered with institutions founded by
Spain for the benefit of the aborigines, so far as they
have not been confiscated or diverted to other uses.
Nevertheless the Spanish rule nearly exterminated the
aborigines in one hundred and fifty years. The Pope
gave them into servitude to the Spaniards. The Spaniards regarded them as savages, heretics, beasts, not
entitled to human consideration. Here you have the
great explanation of man's inhumanity to man. When
Spaniards tortured and burned Protestants and Jews it
was because, in their minds, Protestants and Jews were
heretics; that is to say, were beyond the pale, were
abominable, were not entitled to human consideration.
Humane men and pious women felt no more compunc-
tions at the sufferings of Protestants and Jews than we
would at the execution of mad dogs or rattlesnakes.
There are plenty of people in the United States to-day

who regard negroes as human beings, perhaps, but of a different order from white men, so that the ideas and social arrangements of white men cannot be applied to them with propriety. Others feel the same way about Indians. This attitude of mind, wherever you meet with it, is what causes tyranny and cruelty. It is this disposition to decide off-hand that some people are not fit for liberty and self-government which gives relative truth to the doctrine that all men are equal, and inasmuch as the history of mankind has been one long story of the abuse of some by others, who, of course, smoothed over their tyranny by some beautiful doctrines of religion, or ethics, or political philosophy, which proved that it was all for the best good of the oppressed, therefore the doctrine that all men are equal has come to stand as one of the corner-stones of the temple of justice and truth. It was set up as a bar to just this notion that we are so much better than others that it is liberty for them to be governed by us.

The Americans have been committed from the outset to the doctrine that all men are equal. We have elevated it into an absolute doctrine as a part of the theory of our social and political fabric. It has always been a domestic dogma in spite of its absolute form, and as a domestic dogma it has always stood in glaring contradiction to the facts about Indians and negroes and to our legislation about Chinamen. In its absolute form it must, of course, apply to Kanakas, Malays, Tagals, and Chinese just as much as to Yankees, Germans, and Irish. It is an astonishing event that we have lived to see American arms carry this domestic dogma out where it must be tested in its application to uncivilized and half-civilized peoples. At the first touch of the test we throw the doctrine away and adopt the Spanish doctrine. We are

told by all the imperialists that these people are not fit
for liberty and self-government; that it is rebellion for
them to resist our beneficence; that we must send fleets
and armies to kill them if they do it; that we must devise
a government for them and administer it ourselves; that
we may buy them or sell them as we please, and dispose
of their "trade" for our own advantage. What is that
but the policy of Spain to her dependencies? What can
we expect as a consequence of it? Nothing but that it
will bring us where Spain is now.

But then, if it is not right for us to hold these islands
as dependencies, you may ask me whether I think that
we ought to take them into our Union, at least some of
them, and let them help to govern us. Certainly not.
If *that* question is raised, then the question whether they
are, in our judgment, fit for self-government or not is
in order. The American people, since the Civil War,
have to a great extent lost sight of the fact that this
state of ours, the United States of America, is a confederated state of a very peculiar and artificial form.
It is not a state like the states of Europe, with the
exception of Switzerland. The field for dogmatism in our
day is not theology, it is political philosophy. "Sovereignty" is the most abstract and metaphysical term in
political philosophy. Nobody can define it. For this
reason it exactly suits the purposes of the curbstone
statesman. He puts into it whatever he wants to get
out of it again, and he has set to work lately to spin out
a proof that the United States is a great imperialistic
state, although the Constitution, which tells us just what
it is and what it is not, is there to prove the contrary.

The thirteen colonies, as we all know, were independent
commonwealths with respect to each other. They had
little sympathy and a great deal of jealousy. They came

into a union with each other upon terms which were stipulated and defined in the Constitution, but they united only unwillingly and under the pressure of necessity. What was at first only a loose combination or alliance has been welded together into a great state by the history of a century. Nothing, however, has altered that which was the first condition of the Union; *viz.*, that all the states members of it should be on the same plane of civilization and political development; that they should all hold the same ideas, traditions, and political creed; that their social standards and ideals should be such as to maintain cordial sympathy between them. The Civil War arose out of the fact that this condition was imperfectly fulfilled. At other times actual differences in standpoint and principle, or in ideals and opinion, have produced discord within the confederation. Such crises are inevitable in any confederated state. It is the highest statesmanship in such a system to avoid them, or smooth them over, and above all, never to take in voluntarily any heterogeneous elements. The prosperity of such a state depends on closer and closer sympathy between the parts in order that differences which arise may be easily harmonized. What we need is more intension, not more extension.

It follows, then, that it is unwisdom to take into a State like this any foreign element which is not congenial to it. Any such element will act as a solvent upon it. Consequently we are brought by our new conquests face to face with this dilemma: we must either hold them as inferior possessions, to be ruled and exploited by us after the fashion of the old colonial system, or we must take them in on an equality with ourselves, where they will help to govern us and to corrupt a political system which they do not understand and in which they cannot participate. From that dilemma there is no escape except to give them independence and to let them work out their own salvation or go without it. Hayti has been independent for a century and has been a theater of revolution, tyranny, and bloodshed all the time. There is not a Spanish-American state which has proved its capacity for self-government as yet. It is a fair question whether any one of them would have been worse off than it is to-day if Spanish rule had been maintained in it. The chief exception is Mexico. Mr. Lummis, an American, has recently published a book on Mexico, in which he tells us that we would do well to go to school to Mexico for a number of important public interests, but Mexico has been, for ten or fifteen years, under a dictator, and the republican forms have been in abeyance. What will happen there when the dictator dies nobody knows. The doctrine that we are to take away from other nations any possessions of theirs which we think that we could manage better than they are managing them, or that we are to take in hand any countries which we do not think capable of self-government, is one which will lead us very far. With that doctrine in the background, our politicians will have no trouble to find a war ready for us the next time that they come around to the point where they think that it is time for us to have another. We are told that we must have a big army hereafter. What for; unless we propose to do again by and by what we have just done? In that case our neighbors have reason to ask themselves whom we will attack next. They must begin to arm, too, and by our act the whole western world is plunged into the distress under which the eastern world is groaning. Here is another point in regard to which the conservative elements in the country are making a great mistake to allow all this militarism and imperialism to go on without protest. It will be established as a rule that, whenever political ascendency is threatened, it can be established again by a little war, filling the minds of the people with glory and diverting their attention from their own interests. Hard-headed old Benjamin Franklin hit the point when, referring back to the days of Marlborough, he talked about the "pest of glory." The thirst for glory is an epidemic which robs a people of their judgment, seduces their vanity, cheats them of their interests, and corrupts their consciences.

This country owes its existence to a revolt against the colonial and navigation system which, as I have said, Spain first put in practice. The English colonial system never was even approximately so harsh and tyrannical as that of Spain. The first great question which arose about colonies in England was whether they were parts of the possessions of the king of England or part of the dominion of the crown. The constitutional difference was great. In the one case they were subject to the king and were not under the constitutional guarantees; in the other case they were subject to the Parliament and were under the constitutional guarantees. This is exactly the same question which arose in the middle of this century in this country about territories, and which helped to bring on the Civil War. It is already arising again. It is the question whether the Constitution of the United States extends over all men and territory owned by the United States, or whether there are to be grades and planes of rights for different parts of the dominions over which our flag waves. This question already promises to introduce dissensions amongst us which will touch the most vital elements in our national existence.

The constitutional question, however, goes even deeper than this. Of the interpretation of clauses in the Constitution I am not competent to speak, but the Constitution is the organic law of this confederated state in which we live, and therefore it is the description of it as it was planned and as it is. The question at stake is nothing less than the integrity of this state in its most essential elements. The expansionists have recognized this fact by already casting the Constitution aside. The military men, of course, have been the first to do this. It is of the essence of militarism that under it military men learn to despise constitutions, to sneer at parliaments, and to look with contempt on civilians. Some of the imperialists are not ready to go quite so fast as yet. They have remonstrated against the military doctrine, but that only proves that the military men see the point at issue better than the others do. Others say that if the legs of the Constitution are too short to straddle the gulf between the old policy and the new, they can be stretched a little, a view of the matter which is as flippant as it is in bad taste. It would require too much time to notice the various contemptuous and jaunty references to the Constitution which every day brings to our notice, and from the same class, at least, who, two years ago, were so shocked at a criticism of the *interpretation* of the Constitution which was inserted in the Chicago platform.

The question of imperialism, then, is the question whether we are going to give the lie to the origin of our own national existence by establishing a colonial system of the old Spanish type, even if we have to sacrifice our existing civil and political system to do it. I submit that it is a strange incongruity to utter grand platitudes about the blessings of liberty, etc., which we are going to impart to these people, and to begin by refusing to extend the Constitution over them, and still more, by throwing the Constitution into the gutter here at home. If you take away the Constitution, what is American liberty and all the rest? Nothing but a lot of phrases.

Some will answer me that they do not intend to adopt any Spanish colonial system; that they intend to imitate the modern English policy with respect to colonies. The proudest fact in the history of England is that, since the Napoleonic wars, she has steadily corrected abuses, amended her institutions, redressed grievances, and so has made her recent history a story of amelioration of all her institutions, social, political, and civil. To do this she has had to overcome old traditions, established customs, vested rights, and all the other obstacles which retard or prevent social improvement. The consequence is that the traditions of her public service, in all its branches, have been purified, and that a body of men has grown up who have a noble spirit, high motives, honorable methods, and excellent standards. At the same time the policy of the country has been steadily growing more and more enlightened in regard to all the great interests of society. These triumphs of peace are far greater than any triumphs of war. It takes more national grit to correct abuses than to win battles. England has shown herself very willing indeed to learn from us whatever we could teach, and we might learn a great deal from her on matters far more important than colonial policy. Her reform of her colonial policy is only a part, and perhaps a consequence, of the improvements made elsewhere in her political system.

We have had some experience this last summer in the attempt to improvise an army. We may be very sure that it is equally impossible to improvise a colonial system. The present English colonial system is aristocratic.

It depends upon a large body of specially trained men, acting under traditions which have become well established, and with a firm *esprit de corps*. Nobody can get into it without training. The system is foreign to our ideas, tastes, and methods. It would require a long time and radical changes in our political methods, which we are not as yet at all disposed to make, to establish any such thing here, and then it would be an imitation. Moreover, England has three different colonial systems, according to the development of the resident population in each colony or dependency, and the selection of the one of these three systems which we will adopt and apply involves all the difficulties which I have been discussing.

There is, however, another objection to the English system. A great many people talk about the revenue which we are to get from these possessions. If we attempt to get any revenues from them we shall repeat the conduct of England towards her colonies against which they revolted. England claimed that it was reasonable that the colonies should pay their share of imperial expenses which were incurred for the benefit of all. I have never been able to see why that was not a fair demand. As you know, the colonies spurned it with indignation, on the ground that the taxation, being at the discretion of a foreign power, *might* be made unjust. Our historians and publicists have taught us that the position of the colonists was right and heroic, and the only one worthy of freemen. The revolt was made on the *principle* of no taxation, not on the size of the tax. The colonists would not pay a penny. Since that is so, we cannot get a penny of revenue from the dependencies, even for their fair share of imperial expenditures, without burning up all our histories, revising all the great principles of our heroic period, repudiating our great men of that period,

and going over to the Spanish doctrine of taxing dependencies at the discretion of the governing State. Already
one of these dependencies is in arms struggling for liberty
against us. Read the threats of the imperialists against
these people, who dare to rebel against us, and see whether
I am misstating or exaggerating the corruption of imperialism on ourselves. The question is once more,
whether we are prepared to repudiate the principles
which we have been insisting on for one hundred and
fifty years, and to embrace those of which Spain is the
oldest and most conspicuous representative, or not.

In regard to this matter of taxation and revenue, the
present English colonial system is as unjust to the mother-
country as the old system was to the colonies, or more
so. The colonies now tax the mother-country. She
pays large expenses for their advantage, for which they
return nothing. They set up tax barriers against her
trade with them. I do not believe that the United States
will ever consent to any such system, and I am clear in
the opinion that they never ought to. If the colonies
ought not to be made tributary to the mother-country,
neither ought the mother-country to be made tributary
to them. The proposition to imitate England's colonial
policy is evidently made without the necessary knowledge
of what it means, and it proves that those who thrust
aside prudent objections by declaring off-hand that we
will imitate England have not any serious comprehension
of what it is that they propose to us to do.

The conclusion of this branch of the subject is that it
is fundamentally antagonistic to our domestic system to
hold dependencies which are unfit to enter into the Union.
Our system cannot be extended to take them in or adjusted to them to keep them out without sacrificing its
integrity. If we take in dependencies which, as we now

agree, are not fit to come in as states, there will be constant political agitation to admit them as states, for such agitation will be fomented by any party which thinks that it can win votes in that way. It was an enormous blunder in statecraft to engage in a war which was sure to bring us into this predicament.

II. It seems as if this new policy was destined to thrust a sword into every joint in our historical and philosophical system. Our ancestors revolted against the colonial and navigation system, but as soon as they got their independence, they fastened a navigation system on themselves. The consequence is that our industry and commerce are to-day organized under a restrictive system which is the direct offspring of the old Spanish restrictive system, and is based on the same ideas of economic policy; *viz.*, that statesmen can devise a prosperity policy for a country which will do more for it than a spontaneous development of the energy of the people and the resources of the territory would do. On the other hand, inside of the Union we have established the grandest experiment in absolute free trade that has ever existed. The combination of the two is not new, because it is just what Colbert tried in France, but it is original here and is an interesting result of the presence in men's minds of two opposite philosophies, the adjustment of which has never yet been fought out. The extension of our authority over these new territories forces the inconsistency between our internal and our external policy out of the field of philosophy into that of practical politics. Wherever the boundary line of the national system falls we have one rule inside of it and another outside of it. Are the new territories to be taken inside or to be treated as outside? If we develop this dilemma, we shall see that it is of the first importance.

If we treat the dependencies as inside the national system, we must have absolute free trade with them. Then if, on the policy of the "open door," we allow all others to go to them on the same terms as ourselves, the dependencies will have free trade with all the world, while we are under the restrictive system ourselves. Then, too, the dependencies can obtain no revenues by import duties.

If we take the other branch of the dilemma and treat the dependencies as outside of our national policy, then we must shut out their products from our market by taxes. If we do this on the policy of the "open door," then any taxes which the islands lay upon imports from elsewhere they must also lay upon imports from us. Then they and we will be taxing each other. If we go upon the protectionist policy, we shall determine our taxes against them and theirs against other nations, and we shall let them lay none against us. That is exactly the Spanish system. Under it the colonies will be crushed between the upper and the nether millstone. They will revolt against us for just the same reason for which they revolted against Spain.

I have watched the newspapers with great interest for six months, to see what indications were presented of the probable currents of opinion on the dilemma which I have described. There have been but few. A few extreme protectionist newspapers have truculently declared that our protective system was to be extended around our possessions, and that everybody else was to be excluded from them. From a number of interviews and letters, by private individuals, I select the following as expressing well what is sure to be the view of the unregenerate man, especially if he has an interest to be protected as this writer had.

"I am opposed to the 'open door' policy, as I understand it. To open the ports of our new territories free to the world would have the effect of cheapening or destroying many of the benefits of territorial acquisition, which has cost us blood and money. As a nation we are well qualified to develop and handle the trade of our new possessions, and by permitting others to come in and divide the advantages and profits of this trade we not only wrong our own citizens, who should be given preference, but exhibit a weakness that ill becomes a nation of our prominence."

This is exactly the view which was held in Spain, France, Holland, and England in the eighteenth century, and upon which the navigation system, against which our fathers revolted, was founded. If we adopt this view we may count upon it that we shall be embroiled in constant wars with other nations, which will not consent that we should shut them out of parts of the earth's surface until we prove that we can do it by force. Then we shall be parties to a renewal of all the eighteenth century wars for colonies, for supremacy on the sea, for "trade," as the term is used, for world supremacy, and for all the rest of the heavy follies from which our fathers fought to free themselves. That is the policy of Russia and France at the present time, and we have before our eyes proofs of its effect on the peace and welfare of mankind.

Our modern protectionists have always told us that the object of their policy is to secure the home market. They have pushed their system to an extravagant excess. The free traders used to tell them that they were constructing a Chinese wall. They answered that they wished we were separated from other nations by a gulf of fire. Now it is they who are crying out that they are shut in by a Chinese wall. When we have shut all the world out, we find that we have shut ourselves in. The protective system is applied especially to certain selected lines of production. Of course these are stimulated out of proportion to the requirements of the community, and so are exposed to sharp fluctuations of high profits and over-production. At great expense and loss we have carried out the policy of the home market, and now we are called upon at great expense and loss to go out and conquer territory in order to widen the market. In order to have trade with another community the first condition is that we must produce what they want and they must produce what we want. That is the economic condition. The second condition is that there must be peace and security and freedom from arbitrary obstacles interposed by government. This is the political condition. If these conditions are fulfilled, there will be trade, no matter whether the two communities are in one body politic or not. If these conditions are not fulfilled, there will be no trade, no matter what flag floats. If we want more trade we can get it any day by a reciprocity treaty with Canada, and it will be larger and more profitable than that of all the Spanish possessions. It will cost us nothing to get it. Yet while we were fighting for Puerto Rico and Manila, and spending three or four hundred millions to get them, negotiations with Canada failed through the narrow-mindedness and bigotry which we brought to the negotiation. Conquest can do nothing for trade except to remove the political obstacles which the conquered could not, or would not, remove. From this it follows that the only justification for territorial extension is the extension of free and enlightened policies in regard to commerce. Even then extension is an irksome necessity. The question always is, whether you are taking an asset or a liability. Land grabbing means properly taking territory and shutting all the rest of the world out of it, so as to exploit it ourselves. It is not land grabbing to take it and police it and throw it open to all. This is the policy of the "open door." Our external commercial policy is, in all its principles, the same as that of Spain. We had no justification, on that ground, in taking anything away from her. If we now seek to justify ourselves, it must be by going over to the free policy; but, as I have shown, that forces to a crisis the contradiction between our domestic and our external policy as to trade. It is very probable, indeed, that the destruction of our restrictive system will be the first good result of expansion, but my object here has been to show what a network of difficulties environ us in the attempt to establish a commercial policy for these dependencies. We have certainly to go through years of turmoil and political bitterness, with all the consequent chances of internal dissension, before these difficulties can be overcome.

III. Another phenomenon which deserves earnest attention from the student of contemporaneous history and of the trend of political institutions is the failure of the masses of our people to perceive *the inevitable effect of imperialism on democracy.* On the twenty-ninth of last November [1898] the Prime Minister of France was quoted in a cable dispatch as follows: "For twenty-eight years we have lived under a contradiction. The army and democracy subsist side by side. The maintenance of the traditions of the army is a menace to liberty, yet they assure the safety of the country and its most sacred duties."

That antagonism of democracy and militarism is now coming to a crisis in France, and militarism is sure to

win, because the French people would make any other
sacrifice rather than diminish their military strength.
In Germany the attempt has been going on for thirty
years to establish constitutional government with parlia-
mentary institutions. The parts of the German system
are at war with each other. The Emperor constantly
interferes with the operation of the system and utters
declarations which are entirely personal. He is not
responsible and cannot be answered or criticised. The
situation is not so delicate as in France, but it is exceedingly unstable. All the desire of Germans for self-government and civil liberty runs out into socialism, and socialism
is repressed by force or by trickery. The conservative
classes of the country acquiesce in the situation while
they deplore it. The reason is because the Emperor is
the war lord. His power and authority are essential to
the military strength of the State in face of its neighbors.
That is the preponderating consideration to which everything else has to yield, and the consequence of it is that
there is to-day scarcely an institution in Germany except
the army.

Everywhere you go on the continent of Europe at
this hour you see the conflict between militarism and
industrialism. You see the expansion of industrial power
pushed forward by the energy, hope, and thrift of men,
and you see the development arrested, diverted, crippled,
and defeated by measures which are dictated by military
considerations. At the same time the press is loaded
down with discussions about political economy, political
philosophy, and social policy. They are discussing poverty, labor, socialism, charity, reform, and social ideals,
and are boasting of enlightenment and progress, at the
same time that the things which are done are dictated
by none of these considerations, but only by military

interests. It is militarism which is eating up all the products of science and art, defeating the energy of the population and wasting its savings. It is militarism which forbids the people to give their attention to the problems of their own welfare and to give their strength to the education and comfort of their children. It is militarism which is combating the grand efforts of science and art to ameliorate the struggle for existence.

The American people believe that they have a free country, and we are treated to grandiloquent speeches about our flag and our reputation for freedom and enlightenment. The common opinion is that we have these things because we have chosen and adopted them, because they are in the Declaration of Independence and the Constitution. We suppose, therefore, that we are sure to keep them and that the follies of other people are things which we can hear about with complacency. People say that this country is like no other; that its prosperity proves its exceptionality, and so on. These are popular errors which in time will meet with harsh correction. The United States is in a protected situation. It is easy to have equality where land is abundant and where the population is small. It is easy to have prosperity where a few men have a great continent to exploit. It is easy to have liberty when you have no dangerous neighbors and when the struggle for existence is easy. There are no severe penalties, under such circumstances, for political mistakes. Democracy is not then a thing to be nursed and defended, as it is in an old country like France. It is rooted and founded in the economic circumstances of the country. The orators and constitution-makers do not make democracy. They are made by it. This protected position, however, is sure to pass away. As the country fills up with population, and the task of getting a living out of the ground becomes more difficult, the struggle for existence will become harder and the competition of life more severe. Then liberty and democracy will cost something, if they are to be maintained.

Now what will hasten the day when our present advantages will wear out and when we shall come down to the conditions of the older and densely populated nations? The answer is: war, debt, taxation, diplomacy, a grand governmental system, pomp, glory, a big army and navy, lavish expenditures, political jobbery — in a word, imperialism. In the old days the democratic masses of this country, who knew little about our modern doctrines of social philosophy, had a sound instinct on these matters, and it is no small ground of political disquietude to see it decline. They resisted every appeal to their vanity in the way of pomp and glory which they knew must be paid for. They dreaded a public debt and a standing army. They were narrow-minded and went too far with these notions, but they were, at least, right, if they wanted to strengthen democracy.

The great foe of democracy now and in the near future is plutocracy. Every year that passes brings out this antagonism more distinctly. It is to be the social war of the twentieth century. In that war militarism, expansion and imperialism will all favor plutocracy. In the first place, war and expansion will favor jobbery, both in the dependencies and at home. In the second place, they will take away the attention of the people from what the plutocrats are doing. In the third place, they will cause large expenditures of the people's money, the return for which will not go into the treasury, but into the hands of a few schemers. In the fourth place, they will call for a large public debt and taxes, and these things especially tend to make men unequal, because any social burdens bear more heavily on the weak than on the strong, and so make the weak weaker and the strong stronger. Therefore expansion and imperialism are a grand onslaught on democracy.

The point which I have tried to make in this lecture is that expansion and imperialism are at war with the best traditions, principles, and interests of the American people, and that they will plunge us into a network of difficult problems and political perils, which we might have avoided, while they offer us no corresponding advantage in return.

Of course "principles," phrases, and catch-words are always invented to bolster up any policy which anybody wants to recommend. So in this case. The people who have led us on to shut ourselves in, and who now want us to break out, warn us against the terrors of "isolation." Our ancestors all came here to isolate themselves from the social burdens and inherited errors of the old world. When the others are all over ears in trouble, who would not be isolated in freedom from care? When the others are crushed under the burden of militarism, who would not be isolated in peace and industry? When the others are all struggling under debt and taxes, who would not be isolated in the enjoyment of his own earnings for the benefit of his own family? When the rest are all in a quiver of anxiety, lest at a day's notice they may be involved in a social cataclysm, who would not be isolated out of reach of the disaster? What we are doing is that we are abandoning this blessed isolation to run after a share in the trouble.

The expansionists answer our remonstrances on behalf of the great American principles by saying that times have changed and that we have outlived the fathers of

the republic and their doctrines. As far as the authority
of the great men is concerned, that may well be sacrificed
without regret. Authority of persons and names is a
dangerous thing. Let us get at the truth and the right.
I, for my part, am also afraid of the great principles,
and I would make no fight on their behalf. In the ten
years before the Revolution our ancestors invented a fine
lot of "principles" which they thought would help their
case. They repudiated many of them as soon as they
got their independence, and the rest of them have since
made us a great deal of trouble. I have examined them
all critically, and there is not one of them which I consider
sound, as it is popularly understood. I have been denounced as a heretic on this account by people who now
repudiate them all in a sentence. But this only clears
the ground for the real point. There is a consistency of
character for a nation as well as for a man. A man
who changes his principles from week to week is destitute
of character and deserves no confidence. The great men
of this nation were such because they embodied and
expressed the opinion and sentiments of the nation in
their time. Their names are something more than clubs
with which to knock an opponent down when it suits
one's purpose, but to be thrown away with contempt
when they happen to be on the other side. So of the
great principles; whether some of us are skeptical about
their entire validity and want to define and limit them
somewhat is of little importance. If the nation has
accepted them, sworn by them, founded its legislation
on them, imbedded them in the decisions of its courts,
and then if it throws them away at six months' warning,
you may depend upon it that that nation will suffer in
its moral and political rectitude a shock of the severest
kind. Three years ago we were ready to fight Great

Britain to make her arbitrate a quarrel which she had with Venezuela. The question about the Maine was one of the fittest subjects for arbitration that ever arose between two nations, and we refused to listen to such a proposition. Three years ago, if you had said that any proposition put forth by anybody was "English," he might have been mobbed in the streets. Now the English are our beloved friends, and we are going to try to imitate them and adopt their way of doing things. They are encouraging us to go into difficulties, first because our hands will be full and we shall be unable to interfere elsewhere, and secondly, because if we are in difficulties we shall need allies, and they think that they will be our first choice as such. Some of our public journals have been pouring out sentimental drivel for years about arbitration, but last summer they turned around and began to pour out sentimental drivel about the benefits of war. We congratulate ourselves all the time on the increased means of producing wealth, and then we take the opposite fit and commit some great folly in order to prove that there is something grander than the pursuit of wealth. Three years ago we were on the verge of a law to keep immigrants out who were not good enough to be in with us. Now we are going to take in eight million barbarians and semi-barbarians, and we are paying twenty million dollars to get them. For thirty years the negro has been in fashion. He has had political value and has been petted. Now we have made friends with the Southerners. They and we are hugging each other. We are all united. The negro's day is over. He is out of fashion. We cannot treat him one way and the Malays, Tagals, and Kanakas another way. A Southern senator two or three days ago thanked an expansionist senator from Connecticut for enunciating doctrines which proved that, for the last thirty years, the Southerners have been right all the time, and his inference was incontrovertible. So the "great principles" change all the time; or, what is far more important, the phrases change. Some go out of fashion, others come in; but the phrase-makers are with us all the time. So when our friends the expansionists tell us that times have changed, what it means is that they have a whole set of new phrases which they want to force into the place of the old ones. The new ones are certainly no more valid than the old ones. All the validity that the great principles ever had they have now. Anybody who ever candidly studied them and accepted them for no more than they were really worth can stand by them now as well as ever. The time when a maxim or principle is worth something is when you are tempted to violate it.

Another answer which the imperialists make is that Americans can do anything. They say that they do not shrink from responsibilities. They are willing to run into a hole, trusting to luck and cleverness to get out. There are some things that Americans cannot do. Americans cannot make $2 + 2 = 5$. You may answer that that is an arithmetical impossibility and is not in the range of our subject. Very well; Americans cannot collect two dollars a gallon tax on whisky. They tried it for many years and failed. That is an economic or political impossibility, the roots of which are in human nature. It is as absolute an impossibility on this domain as the former on the domain of mathematics. So far as yet appears, Americans cannot govern a city of one hundred thousand inhabitants so as to get comfort and convenience in it at a low cost and without jobbery. The fire department of this city is now demoralized by political jobbery — and Spain and all her possessions are not worth as much to you and me as the efficiency of the fire department of New Haven. The Americans in Connecticut cannot abolish the rotten borough system. The English abolished their rotten borough system seventy years ago, in spite of nobles and landlords. We cannot abolish ours in spite of the small towns. Americans cannot reform the pension list. Its abuses are rooted in the methods of democratic self-government, and no one dares to touch them. It is very doubtful indeed if Americans can keep up an army of one hundred thousand men in time of peace. Where can one hundred thousand men be found in this country who are willing to spend their lives as soldiers; or if they are found, what pay will it require to induce them to take this career? Americans cannot disentangle their currency from the confusion into which it was thrown by the Civil War, and they cannot put it on a simple, sure, and sound basis which would give stability to the business of the country. This is a political impossibility. Americans cannot assure the suffrage to negroes throughout the United States; they have tried it for thirty years and now, contemporaneously with this war with Spain, it has been finally demonstrated that it is a failure. Inasmuch as the negro is now out of fashion, no further attempt to accomplish this purpose will be made. It is an impossibility on account of the complexity of our system of State and Federal government. If I had time to do so, I could go back over the history of negro suffrage and show you how curbstone arguments, exactly analogous to the arguments about expansion, were used to favor it, and how objections were thrust aside in this same blustering and senseless manner in which objections to imperialism are met. The ballot, we were told, was an educator and would solve all difficulties in its own path as by magic. Worse still, Americans cannot assure life, liberty, and the pursuit of happiness to negroes inside of the United States. When the negro postmaster's house was set on fire in the night in South Carolina, and not only he, but his wife and children, were murdered as they came out, and when, moreover, this incident passed without legal investigation or punishment, it was a bad omen for the extension of liberty, etc., to Malays and Tagals by simply setting over them the American flag. Upon a little serious examination the off-hand disposal of an important question of policy by the declaration that Americans can do anything proves to be only a silly piece of bombast, and upon a little reflection we find that our hands are quite full at home of problems by the solution of which the peace and happiness of the American people could be greatly increased. The laws of nature and of human nature are just as valid for Americans as for anybody else, and if we commit acts we shall have to take consequences, just like other people. Therefore prudence demands that we look ahead to see what we are about to do, and that we gauge the means at our disposal, if we do not want to bring calamity on ourselves and our children. We see that the peculiarities of our system of government set limitations on us. We cannot do things which a great centralized monarchy could do. The very blessings and special advantages which we enjoy, as compared with others, bring disabilities with them. That is the great fundamental cause of what I have tried to show throughout this lecture, that we cannot govern dependencies consistently with our political system, and that, if we try it, the State which our fathers founded will suffer a reaction which will transform it into another empire just after the fashion of all the old ones. That is what imperialism means. That is what it will be; and the democratic republic, which has been, will stand in history, like the colonial organization of earlier days, as a mere transition form.

And yet this scheme of a republic which our fathers formed was a glorious dream which demands more than a word of respect and affection before it passes away. Indeed, it is not fair to call it a dream or even an ideal; it was a possibility which was within our reach if we had been wise enough to grasp and hold it. It was favored by our comparative isolation, or, at least, by our distance from other strong states. The men who came here were able to throw off all the trammels of tradition and established doctrine. They went out into a wilderness, it is true, but they took with them all the art, science, and literature which, up to that time, civilization had produced. They could not, it is true, strip their minds of the ideas which they had inherited, but in time, as they lived on in the new world, they sifted and selected these ideas, retaining what they chose. Of the old-world institutions also they selected and adopted what they chose and threw aside the rest. It was a grand opportunity to be thus able to strip off all the follies and errors which they had inherited, so far as they chose to do so. They had unlimited land with no feudal restrictions to hinder them in the use of it. Their idea was that they would never allow any of the social and political abuses of the old world to grow up here. There should be no manors, no barons, no ranks, no prelates, no idle classes, no paupers, no disinherited ones except the vicious. There were to be no armies except a militia, which would have no functions but those of police. They would have no court and no pomp; no orders, or ribbons, or decorations, or titles. They would have no public debt. They repudiated with scorn the notion that a public debt is a public blessing; if debt was incurred in war it was to be paid in peace and not entailed on posterity. There was to be no grand diplomacy, because they intended to mind their own business and not be involved in any of the intrigues to which European statesmen were accustomed. There was to be no balance of power and no "reason of state" to cost the life and happiness of citizens. The only part of the Monroe doctrine which is valid was their determination that the social and political systems of Europe should not be extended over any part of the American continent, lest people who were weaker than we should lose the opportunity which the new continent gave them to escape from those systems if they wanted to. Our fathers would have an economical government, even if grand people called it a parsimonious one, and taxes should be no greater than were absolutely necessary to pay for such a government. The citizen was to keep all the rest of his earnings and use them as he thought best for the happiness of himself and his family; he was, above all, to be insured peace and quiet while he pursued his honest industry and obeyed the laws. No adventurous policies of conquest or ambition, such as, in the belief of our fathers, kings and nobles had forced, for their own advantage, on European states, would ever be undertaken by a free democratic republic. Therefore the citizen here would never be forced to leave his family or to give his sons to shed blood for glory and to leave widows and orphans in misery for nothing. Justice and law were to reign in the midst of simplicity, and a government which had little to do was to offer little field for ambition. In a society where industry, frugality, and prudence were honored, it was believed that the vices of wealth would never flourish.

We know that these beliefs, hopes, and intentions have been only partially fulfilled.   We know that, as time has gone on and we have grown numerous and rich, some of these things have proved impossible ideals, incompatible with a large and flourishing society, but it is by virtue of this conception of a commonwealth that the United States has stood for something unique and grand in the history of mankind and that its people have been happy. It is by virtue of these ideals that we have been "isolated," isolated in a position which the other nations of the earth have observed in silent envy; and yet there are people who are boasting of their patriotism, because they say that we have taken our place now amongst the nations of the earth by virtue of this war.   My patriotism is of the kind which is outraged by the notion that the United States never was a great nation until in a petty three months' campaign it knocked to pieces a poor, decrepit, bankrupt old state like Spain.   To hold such an opinion as that is to abandon all American standards, to put shame and scorn on all that our ancestors tried to build up here, and to go over to the standards of which Spain is a representative.

THE PREDOMINANT ISSUE

XVI

THE PREDOMINANT ISSUE

[1900]

EACH of the two great parties in the present campaign is trying to force on the other a "predominant issue" to which the other will not agree. The predominant issue, not for a campaign or a year, is expansion and all that goes with it. It will not be settled by speeches or votes. It will have to work itself out in history. The political history of the United States for the next fifty years will date from the Spanish war of 1898. The attempt to absorb into the body politic of the United States communities of entirely foreign antecedents, nationality, religion, language, *mores*, political education, institutions — in short, of a different culture and social education from ours — must be regarded as a far more serious venture than it is now popularly supposed to be. Out of it will arise one question after another, and they will be of a kind to produce political convulsions amongst us. The predominant issue, in a far wider sense than the wranglings of a presidential campaign, is how to let go of what we seized. No discussion such as occurs in a campaign ever clears up an issue; for one reason, because the discussion is carried on, not to get at the truth or wisdom of the case, but to win a party victory. It is an interesting study to notice how such a discussion results in set phrases and stereotyped assertions which bar the way to any real understanding of the issue. Let it be our object now to try to define the issue under expansion, imperialism, and militarism, which stands before the American people as the chief political interest of the immediate future.

There are few of us who have not heard it said, after the failure of a mercantile or manufacturing firm, that the cause of failure was that they had "spread out too much." The story is generally one of success within a field of effort, then of enthusiasm and ambition over-mastering prudence and moderation, then of excessive burdens and failure. On the other hand, we are familiar enough with cases in which business enterprise and courage sustain enormous growth and expansion. It appears, therefore, that expansion, as such, is neither good nor bad. The question is one of conditions, cir-cumstances, powers. It is a question of policy which must be decided by wisdom and prudence. It follows that it is never a question which can be settled by prece-dent. Every new case of expansion has its own cir-cumstances. Enthusiasm would have no place in the plan if it was to win the confidence of bankers and in-vestors. Impatience of prudent foresight, and irritation at demands to see the grounds for expecting success, would not recommend the project to wise business men. Mere megalomania — a desire to get a big thing to brag about — would not be regarded as a good basis for the enterprise.

At least two of our large cities have recently expanded their boundaries. A leading newspaper of Chicago has explained the financial distress of that city by the extent to which it has included unimproved suburbs.[1] The people of greater New York seem to have many doubts whether their expansion was wise and prudent.[2] No

[1] Chicago Tribune in the New York Times, September 4, 1900.
[2] Comptroller's statements and newspaper comments thereon about September 22, 1900.

doubt both cities were chiefly influenced by megalomania, although it may very probably appear, after twenty-five years, in the case of New York, that it was well to secure the consolidation before greater difficulties accumulated in the way of it, and that the ultimate interest of all concerned was really served by it.

If it is proposed to a railroad company to buy or lease another line, shall they not look to see whether it will be a burden or an advantage? To buy a lawsuit is not always an act of folly. John Jacob Astor did it with great profit, but he took care to get the best information and legal advice which could be obtained before he did it.

Expansion, therefore, is not a disease, of which it can be said that it is always a calamity; nor is it a growth of which it can be said that it is always an advantage. How can it be doubted that territorial expansion for a state presents the same kind of a problem, with similar danger of . delusions, fallacies, and pitfalls of vanity? Expansion may lower national vitality and hasten decay.

Any state or nation has life necessities to meet as time goes on. It was a life necessity of the German nation fifty years ago to form a unified state, and the same was true of Italy. The cost was great, but it had to be met. The alternative was stagnation and decay. The Russians say that it is a life necessity for them to get better access to the sea, but the case is by no means so clear. Probably the real philosophy of the American Revolution is that it was a life necessity of the Anglo-American colonies to become independent. It matters little, therefore, that the alleged reasons for the revolt, in history, law, and political philosophy, will not bear examination.

This doctrine of life necessity is dangerous. Unless it be handled with great caution and conscientiousness and be checked by a close and positive adherence to facts, it may easily degenerate into the old "reason of state" and furnish an excuse for any political crime. It is a grand thing to soar over epochs and periods of history, deducing political generalizations and sweeping "laws of history," but it is futile and to be condemned unless it is done upon a basis of mature scholarship and with great reserve and care. Such deductions deserve no attention unless they are restricted to simple phenomena and are above all suspicion of party interest.

The acquisition of Louisiana by the United States was a clear and simple case of life necessity. If Spain claimed that, as possessor of New Orleans, she might of right close the Mississippi River, it was a life necessity of the people of the United States to take New Orleans from her by purchase or war. Her views of public law and international rights and colonies then brought her into collision with us. The purchase of the whole western half of the valley was never contemplated by anybody here; it was proposed by France. If the purchase was wise, it was because the city could not be obtained otherwise, and we have a case which establishes the doctrine of "meeting the consequences" at the same time that it limits and defines it. The arguments of the Federalists against the purchase were all good, so far as they were not partisan, at that time, but the railroad and the telegraph took away all their force afterwards. Neither party could foresee the railroads or telegraphs. The purchase of Louisiana entailed the question of extending slavery, but the statesmen of 1803, doing what our interests then required, could properly leave the consequences to be met when they arose, and they are not to be blamed if those consequences were unwisely met when they came.

The acquisition of Florida was not in obedience to a State necessity so clear and great as the acquisition of New Orleans, but Florida was geographically a part of our territory and Spain discharged her international duties with respect to it in such manner that our relations with her were always bad. There was a great interest to acquire Florida, if it could be done by peaceful purchase.

The acquisition of Texas and California was a very different matter. The two cases are generally conjoined, but they were very different and the whole story is one of those which a nation ignores in its own annals while vigorously denouncing similar episodes in the history of other states. The current argument now to justify what was done then is to point to Texas and the other states, to the harbor of San Francisco, the gold-mines, and the Pacific Railroad, and to say that we should have had none of these but for what was done in 1848. This is as if a man who had stolen a fortune fifty years ago should justify himself by saying that he would not otherwise have had the land, houses, ships, and stocks, which he has had and enjoyed. Public and private property are not to be put on the same plane, and this comparison is good only for the particular point for which it is adduced; namely, that the pleasure and profit obtained from spoliation never can justify it. Nevertheless, there is some force in the doctrine of "manifest destiny." Manifest destiny is far more sound than the empty and silly talk of the last two years about "Destiny." Manifest destiny includes a rational judgment about the relations which now exist compared with those which will probably arise in the future, but "Destiny" has nothing rational in it. To invoke it in public affairs is a refusal to think or to be governed by reason. Destiny is a name for the connection which unites the series of consequences upon an act like the war with Spain, and it is invoked to prevent us from going back to see whether the consequences do not prove that that act was wrong and foolish.

There was room to argue, in 1845, that it was the plain course of the future that the United States should occupy and develop California: it was a contiguous territory; it lay between the United States and the Pacific and contained the best harbor on the coast; it was in hands which were not developing it; it was almost uninhabited, so that the subjugation of dissatisfied people, although not entirely absent, was not an important feature. The claim of a group of people to hold a part of the earth's surface is never absolute. Every group holds its territory by force and holds it subject to the obligation to exploit it and make it contributory to the welfare of mankind. If it does not do this it will probably lose the territory by the conquest of a more energetic people. This is manifest destiny. It is another dangerous doctrine, if it is used without a candid heed to its limitations. It has been abused twice recently: first, an absolute right to territory has been set up on behalf of the Boers, who really challenged the English as to the manifest destiny of South Africa; second, in our own relations with Spain we have heard arguments that, if one state thinks that another is not making good use of its territory, the former may dispossess the latter. In so far, then, as state necessity in the weaker form of manifest destiny may be judged to apply to California, that case of expansion could be justified.

If now we turn to our recent expansion and apply the doctrine of state necessity to it, there might be some argument in favor of the acquisition of Cuba. It is contiguous to our territory and there is a slight but unimportant military advantage in owning it. No necessity for owning it was ever experienced; that is to say, no conviction that we needed it was ever forced upon us by experience of loss, disadvantage, injury, or incapacity of any kind, from not possessing it, as in the case of the Mississippi River. The American people were indifferent to it up to 1898. We had no grievance against Spain. No folly or wrong which she had committed had reached us, as in the case of Florida. Yet it was with reference to Cuba that we went to war with her, and we have bound ourselves to make Cuba independent; that is, to put her out of our jurisdiction and sacrifice any interest which we have in possessing the island. It is as safe as any political prediction can be that we shall never again give up the jurisdiction over Cuba. Our national vanity is at stake in it now, and there is some rational ground for holding it.

As to Puerto Rico and the Philippines the great ground for dissent from what has been done is that action did not proceed from any rational motive connected with the growth and ramifications of the interests of the American people. The action was gratuitous and adventurous. While it was not called for by any care for our interests it involved us in risks and obligations. A new doctrine of constructive obligation has been invented which is false and dangerous. A prominent newspaper recently argued that we are bound to protect the Chinese Christian converts because we allowed missionaries to be sent to China under our protection. This is but a specimen of the way in which false dogmas grow when statesmen begin to act from motives which are entirely foreign to statecraft. The arguments in favor of expansion all have the character of after-thoughts invented to excuse or defend acts which were resolved upon for other reasons. At the present moment perhaps not a single voter wants the United States to acquire a part of China. Why not? If anyone was asked, he probably would say that it is out of our way, that it would involve us in trouble, that it is not necessary for our interests, that it would be foolish, since it would show a lack of judgment as to when a thing is wise and when it is not. If any voter had been asked on January 1, 1898, whether he desired that the United States should acquire the Philippine Islands, would he not have made the same reply, with impatient scorn that anyone should bother him with such a senseless proposition? How did the battle of Manila Bay alter any factor which entered into the wisdom of acquiring the Philippines as a question of rational statesmanship? If that battle had never taken place, and the Philippine islanders had continued their revolution until they drove out the Spaniards, what would Americans have cared what government they set up or how they got along with it? Why should we care now, even if a naval battle between us and the Spaniards did take place in Manila Bay? No one is so foolish as really to believe in these constructive obligations, if there were no other elements in the case, but the national vanity is now enlisted, and vanity leads nations into folly just as it does individuals.

Upon a positive analysis, therefore, the case of recent expansion is shown to be different from all the earlier cases which are cited to justify it precisely in the most essential fact, the interest of the American people as the efficient motive.

All expansion includes the question whether we shall treat the inhabitants of new possessions as we treat each other, or on some inferior footing; whether we shall govern them by our will or let them share in governing themselves and us. This dilemma is insoluble under our system of government. We shall struggle with it through the next generation, and it will force a change in our system of government. This is why the present expansion, taking in elements which are foreign and uncongenial, is no parallel to cases of expansion into uninhabited territory. The inhabitants of the new possessions have interests, ideas, tastes, wills, and unless we kill them all, their human traits will enter into the problem. If we take them into full fellowship, imagine what the "Spanish Gang" will be and do in Congress within twenty years! It would be madness to put our interests into such jeopardy, and it would be fatal to the political system under which we have lived to take that course. The other branch of the dilemma is imperialism and it is no less fatal to our political system.

Specifically, it is imperialism for the Congress of the United States to rule any people who are outside of the United States and not under the guarantees of the Constitution of the United States. Congress owes its existence to the Constitution, which defines the rights and duties of Congress. Congress has no existence or authority outside of the sway and the restrictions of the political system to which that document gives order, nor outside of the commonwealth of which that document prescribes the structure and functions. The answer which is made to this statement is that the United States is a sovereign state, like any other state, and with all the powers which any state of the first rank has. That is imperialism, for it disregards the historical and legal facts about the Constitution of the United States and the novel and unique political system created under it, in order to go off and find a basis of interpretation for

the American Federal Commonwealth in the precedents
and analogies of the Roman Empire and the modern
European military monarchies. Here is an issue which
is sharp enough. Here is something which may properly
be called "Americanism"; namely, the novel and unique
political system under which we have lived and loyalty
to the same, and the issue is nothing less than whether
to go on and maintain it or to discard it for the European
military and monarchical tradition. It must be a complete transformation of the former to try to carry on
under it two groups of political societies, one on a higher;
the other on a lower plane, unequal in rights and powers;
the former, in their confederated capacity, ruling the
latter perhaps by military force.

Then again, imperialism is a philosophy. It is the
way of looking at things which is congenial to people who
are ruling others without constitutional restraints, and it
is the temper in which they act. History offers plenty
of examples of it and the most striking ones are furnished
by democracies and republics. The Greek cities with
their colonies and dependent allies, the Roman republic,
the Italian city republics, showed what tyranny one
commonwealth is capable of when it rules another. We
showed it ourselves in the reconstruction period. You
cannot get a governing state to listen, think, repent,
confess, and reform. It is more vain than a despot.
Is it not a "free" government? Can "we" be tyrants
or do any wrong? Already we have had ample manifestations of this temper amongst ourselves. We have
juggled away so much of our sacred political dogmas as
troubles us, although we cling to such as we can still
make use of. We fret and chafe now at the "Constitution," of which, two years ago, we made a fetish. We
fly into a rage at anybody who dissents and call him

"rebel" and "traitor," as strikers shout "scab" at anyone who chooses to hold an opinion of his own. It is
one of the worst symptoms of change that the American
sense of humor, which has, in the past, done such good
service in suppressing political asininity, now makes
default. If it was still efficient we should not hear of
"traitors" who choose to vote no, or of "rebels" who
never owed allegiance, or of the doctrine that those who
oppose a war are responsible for the lives lost in it, or
that a citizen may criticise any action of his government
except a war. The evil of imperialism is in its
reaction on our own national character and institutions,
on our political ideas and creed, on our way of managing our public affairs, on our temper in political
discussion.

Imperialism is one way of dealing with the problem
forced upon us by expansion to embrace uncongenial
groups of people. Militarism is a method of carrying
out that policy. The President will not wear a crown,
and Congress will not introduce universal military service next winter. Derision of such fears is cheap, since
nobody entertains them. In this world it is the little
beginnings which tell; it is the first steps at the parting
of the ways which are decisive. Militarism is a system.
It may go with a small armament, or be absent with
a large one, as in England. It is militarism when a
European king always wears a military uniform. It
represents an idea. The predominant idea in the State
is, perhaps necessarily, its military strength, and the
king, as the representative of the State, keeps this ever
before himself and others. This is a way of looking at
State affairs, and it colors everything else. Therefore it
is militarism when military officers despise civilians and
call them "pekins," lawyers, grocers, philistines, etc.;

when they never go about without sabres by their sides; when they push civilians off the sidewalk and cut their heads open with the sabre if they remonstrate. It is militarism when railroads are built as military strategy requires, not as trade requires. Militarism and industrialism are two standpoints which are widely separated, from which the modern State has two very different aspects, and from which almost every question of policy will have two different presumptions to start with. Under militarism the foremost question is: Will it increase our power to fight? Under industrialism it is: Will it increase the comfort of our people? Of every new invention militarism asks: How can it be rendered useful for military purposes? Industrialism asks: How will it increase our power over nature to supply our needs? Militarism is also a philosophy and temper which is accordant with imperialism. It consists in aggression and domination instead of conciliation and concession. It is militarism to "jam things through" without consideration for the feelings and interests of other people, except so far as they can strike back, whether it is done in a legislature or on the field of battle. Militarism is pugnacity, preference for fighting methods, faith in violence, strenuosity, ruthlessness, cynical selfishness as far as one dare indulge it. It is entirely opposed to the American temper which has been developed by industrialism and which does not believe in fighting methods, although it recognizes the fact that men must fight sometimes, and that when the occasion comes they ought to fight with all their might. Militarism means one law for ourselves and another for everybody else; the great dogmas of the Declaration of Independence were good when we wanted to be independent of somebody else; they have no validity when somebody else wants to be

independent of us. Aguinaldo was a patriot when he
was fighting Spain; he is a rebel when he is fighting us.
Militarism is the neglect of rational motives and interests
and the surrender of one's mind and will to whimsical
points of vanity and anger.

We have advanced far on this road when we propose
to sit in judgment on the fitness of other people for self-
government. What are the criteria of this fitness?
Who knows whether we possess it ourselves? Any nation
possesses it only more or less. The legislature of New
York apparently does not think that the city of New
York possesses it. In the period of 1783 to 1789 many
contemporary observers saw good reason to doubt whether
the United States of North America possessed it, and
even distinguished fathers of the republic have left on
record their own misgivings about it. Thirty years ago
we gave the suffrage to newly emancipated negro slaves,
and gave them not only self-government, but the political
control of the States in which they lived. It was the
gravest political heresy of that period to doubt if they
were "fit for self-government," and no question of that
sort was ever formulated in public discussion. There is
something ludicrous in the attitude of one community
standing over another to see whether the latter is "fit
for self-government." Is lynching, or race-rioting, or
negro-burning, or a row in the legislature, or a strike with
paralyzed industry, or a disputed election, or a legislative
deadlock, or the murder of a claimant-official, or counting
in unelected officers, or factiousness, or financial corruption and jobbery, proof of unfitness for self-government?
If so, any State which was stronger than we might take
away our self-government on the ground that we were
unfit for it. It is, therefore, simply a question of *power*,
like all the other alleged grounds of interference of one

political body with another, such as humanity, sympathy, neighborhood, internal anarchy, and so on. We talk as if we were going to adjudicate the fitness of another body politic for self-government, as a free, open, and categorical question, when to decide it one way means that we shall surrender *power*, and when not even flagrant civil war could really be held to prove unfitness.

It does not improve the matter any to speak of a "stable government." A leading newspaper recently said that the thing to do is to establish "what may properly be regarded *by us* rather than Cuba as a stable government." This is the attitude of imperialism and militarism, and the issue involved between those of us who approve of it and those who do not is whether the American people ought, in their own interest, to engage in this kind of an enterprise with respect to anybody. All governments perish. None, therefore, is stable beyond more or less. What degree of duration suffices? There is no issue which is capable of adjudication. There is, in fact, no political issue between the parties in respect to their policy. Both use the same phrase. Mr. Bryan would be as slow to wound the national vanity as Mr. McKinley; the patronage and power in the dependencies are as dear to his followers as to Mr. McKinley's.

There is an issue, however, and the chief difficulty connected with it is that it is too deep and philosophical for easy popular discussion. It is nothing less than the standpoint, the philosophy, and the temper of our political system; that is to say, it is the integrity of our political system. Every step we take brings up new experiences which warn us that we are on a wrong path. The irritation and impatience of the expansionists testify to their own uneasiness at what we are doing. It is not to be expected that any appeal to reason can guide the course of events. Experience of trouble, war, expense, corruption, quarrels, scandals, etc., may produce weariness and anger and determine action. The issue will, therefore, press upon us for years to come.

The expansionists ask what we think ought to be done. It is they who are in power and have our fate in their hands, and it belongs to them to say what shall be done. This they have not done. They are contented with optimistic platitudes which carry no responsibility and can be dropped to-morrow as easily as "criminal aggression" and our "plain duty." It is unquestionably true that there is no fighting against the accomplished fact, although it is rare audacity to taunt the victims of misgovernment with their own powerlessness against it, as if that was an excuse for it. We were told that we needed Hawaii in order to secure California. What shall we now take in order to secure the Philippines? No wonder that some expansionists do not want to "scuttle out of China." We shall need to take China, Japan, and the East Indies, according to the doctrine, in order to "secure" what we have. Of course this means that, on the doctrine, we must take the whole earth in order to be safe on any part of it, and the fallacy stands exposed. If, then, safety and prosperity do not lie in this direction, the place to look for them is in the other direction: in domestic development, peace, industry, free trade with everybody, low taxes, industrial power. We ought not only to grant independence to these communities, which are both geographically and socially outside of us, but we ought to force it upon them as soon as a reasonable time has been granted to them to organize such a political system as suits them. After that they should go on their own way on their own responsibility, and we should turn our attention to our own interests, and the development of our own country, on those lines of political policy which our traditions set for us and of which our experience has been so satisfactory.

OUR COLLEGES BEFORE THE COUNTRY

XVII

OUR COLLEGES BEFORE THE COUNTRY

[1884]

THERE is no subject which is to-day so submerged in cant and humbug as education. Both primary and secondary education are suffering from this cause, but in different ways. Primary education is afflicted by the cant and humbug of progress and innovation, and secondary education is afflicted by the cant and humbug of conservatism and toryism. The former affliction is less grievous than the latter, because it pertains to life — may proceed from an excess of vitality; the latter pertains to death and leads down to it.

It is not my present intention to discuss primary education, but it belongs to my subject to notice one fact in the relation of secondary to primary education. There is a notion prevalent in college circles that the colleges have an important public duty to perform in marking out the line of study for the preparatory schools, and in keeping them up to their duty. It seems to me that this is a mischievous notion. The high-schools and academies of the country are doing their duty far better than the colleges are doing theirs. The teachers in the schools have as high a standard of duty as the teachers in the colleges, and the former have more care and zeal to devise and adopt good methods than the latter. Methods of instruction are yet employed in college which have long been discarded in the schools, and, if either has anything to learn from the other, it is the colleges which need instruc-

tion from the schools.   The colleges, by their requirements, do exercise a certain control over the curriculum
of the schools.   It is an open question whether this control
is generally beneficial to the education of the young men
of the country.   If the colleges have prescribed courses
of study, and if the schools have to follow a prescribed
course of study leading up to it, then a few gentlemen
with strong prejudices and limited experience of life
obtain power to set up a canon of what things may be
taught and learned in the country.   That such a power has
been possessed and used, that it still remains to a great
extent unbroken, and that it is purely mischievous, I
take to be facts beyond contradiction.   In no civilized
country is mandarinism in education so strong as in the
United States.   Its stronghold is in the colleges, and they
use such control as they possess to establish it in the
schools.   One great gain of the reform which is now needed
in the colleges would be that they would confine themselves
to their own functions and leave the academies and high-
schools to follow their own legitimate development.

I ought not to speak as if there had been no improvement in American colleges within a generation.   It is
well known that, both by founding new institutions and
reforming old ones, great improvements have been made.
A great college has a life of its own.   It grows by its own
vital powers and pushes on even the most timid or reac-
tionary of its *personnel*.   Probably bigotry and stupidity
could kill it in time.   One knows of ancient seats of
learning which have met that fate.   But it does not
come all at once.   Still, I believe that if the question
whether the college course had been valuable, had been
raised in a class of graduates twenty or fifty years ago,
more would have said that they looked back upon it
as a grand advantage than would say so now.

It is affirmed, and from such evidence as has come to my knowledge I believe it to be true, that the youth of the country do not care for a university education as the youth of former generations did. They consider that a high-school education is education enough. They do not look upon the colleges as offering anything of high and specific value which it is worth four years' time and a large expenditure of capital to get. Of course there has always been a large class of people who despised a culture which they never understood. The present temper of the youth and their parents is, as I understand it, a very different thing. They look upon the colleges as the gate of admission to a caste of people who are technically "educated" and "cultivated," who have a kind of free-masonry of culture amongst themselves, but who are not educated or cultivated, if we take those words in any liberal and rational sense, any better than large masses of people who are not college graduates, and so not members of the gild of the learned. Facts are indisputable that free and generous familiarity with the best thought and knowledge of the time, as well as intellectual power, activity, and elasticity, are displayed by men who have never visited a university, but have devoted time judiciously to intellectual pursuits. Therefore a notion has found place that college training only confers artificial accomplishments which serve to mark the members of the learned caste. Once it was thought that the only learning fit for a gentleman was heraldry, and that his only accomplishments should be those of arms, music, and gallantry. A flunkey once said that a certain woman could not be a lady: she played the piano so well that she must have been educated for a governess. In the old gilds a man could only become a master by producing a very costly and useless masterpiece. A belle in Siam lets her finger-nails grow inches long, so that she cannot even dress herself, and everyone who sees her knows that she is helpless and elegant. All these instances, heterogeneous as they are, have elements in common with each other and with the traditional work of our colleges. They present the notion that what is useful is vulgar, that useless accomplishments define a closed rank of superior persons, and that entrance into that rank should be made difficult. However, we live in a day and a country where these notions have only a feeble footing. Our people are likely to turn away with a smile and go on to things which are of use and importance, and no elegance of rhetoric and poetry, devising subtle and far-fetched explanations of the real utility of classical accomplishments, will avail to hold them. Such I take to be the significance of the fact that the youth do not appreciate a college education or feel an eager desire for it as their fathers did. I have heard it argued that it is a great misfortune that the boys should be contented with a high-school education and should not care to go to college; also that something should be done to persuade them to seek a college education. I do not so argue. A college or school ought to stand on its own footing as a blessing to anybody who can get its advantages, and its advantages ought to be so obvious and specific that they should advertise themselves. If a college does not offer such advantages that anyone who can may gladly seize them, then the young men may better not enter it. If special inducements are necessary to persuade men to go to college, then the condemnation of the college is pronounced. It has no reason to exist.

It is no doubt true that a classical education once gave a man a positive and measurable advantage in the

career which he might choose in life. At a time when
the sciences which teach us to know the world in which
we live were still in their infancy; when the studies by
which the mind is trained to high, strict, and fearless
thinking were as yet undeveloped; when history was
still only a record of curious and entertaining incidents
in war and diplomacy; when modern civil institutions
were yet in many respects below the standard of the
ancients, and still on the same military basis; when no
notion of law had yet found footing in the conception
of society; — at such a time no doubt study of classical
types and models was valuable; ideas were obtained from
an old treasure-house which could not have been obtained
from the experience of actual life; literary culture was
the only possible discipline; grammar stood first as a
training in thought and expression; formal logic was a
practical tool; perhaps even introspective metaphysics
was not entirely a scholastic and dialectic exercise. In
those times a young man who possessed a classical education, with a few touches of metaphysics and theology
to finish it off, was put on a true superiority to his uneducated contemporaries as regarded his stock of ideas, his
powers of expression, his horizon of knowledge, and the
general liberality of his attitude towards life. He felt
this his whole life long. It made him earnestly grateful
to the institution which had educated him. Every young
man who grew up saw distinctly the superior advantages
which a college man possessed, and, if he felt at all fit for it,
was eager to win the same advantage. There certainly
never has been, in the United States, any appreciation
of the rose-water arguments about "culture" which are
now put forward in defense of classical training. We,
when we were boys, sought classical training because it
was *the* training which then put the key of life in our

hands, and because we saw positive and specific advantages which we could obtain by it.

At the present time all is altered, and the changes which have come about have made necessary a great change in the character of our colleges, in their courses of study, and in their whole attitude towards the public. I do not say that they need to come into direct and close relations with the life of the nation to-day: I say that they must take heed to themselves lest they fall out of that intimate relation to the life of the nation in which they once stood, and out of which they have no importance or value at all. A college which is a refuge for mere academicians, threshing over the straw of a dead learning, is no better than a monastery. Men who believe that they can meet the great interests of mankind which to-day demand satisfaction, by a complacent reference to what satisfied them when they were young, are simply building for themselves a fool's paradise.

It must be said here that college officers are, for many reasons, unfit for college management. They are exposed to all the pitfalls of every pedagogue. They have to guard themselves against the vices of dogmatism, pedantry, hatred of contradiction, conceit, and love of authority. They, of course, come each to love his own pursuit beyond anything else on earth. Each thinks that a man who is ignorant of *his* specialty is a barbarian. As a man goes on in life under this discipline he becomes more self-satisfied and egotistical. He has little contact with active life; gets few knocks; is rarely forced into a fight or into a problem of diplomacy; gets to hate care or interruption, and loves routine. Men of this type, of course, are timid, and even those traits which are most admirable in the teacher become vices in the executive officer. Such men are always over-fond of *a priori* reasoning and fall helpless the moment they have to face a practical undertaking. They have the whole philosophy of heaven and earth reduced, measured out, and done up in powders, to be prescribed at need. They know just what ought to be studied, in what amount and succession of doses. That is to say, they are prepared to do any amount of mischief at a juncture when the broadest statesmanship is needed to guide the development of a great institution. Certainly the notion that any body of men can now regulate the studies of youth by what was good for themselves twenty, forty, or sixty years ago is one which is calculated to ruin any institution which they control. It is always a hard test of the stuff men are made of when they are asked to admit that a subject of which they have had control would profit by being taken out of their control and intrusted to liberty.

On the other hand, the system of heterogeneous and nondescript electives, jumbled together without coordination of any kind, and offered to the choice of lazy youth, can never command the confidence of sober teachers. A university ought to teach everything which anybody wants to know. Such is the old idea of a university — a universe of letters. It ought to give complete liberty in the choice of a *line* or *department* of study, but it ought to prescribe rigidly what studies must be pursued in the chosen department by anyone who wants its degree. A Yale diploma ought not to mean that a man knows everything, for that would be absurd; nor that he knows "something about the general principles" of all those things which "every educated man ought to know," for this is a formula for superficiality and false pretense. It ought to mean that he has acquired knowledge in some one line of study, suffi-

cient to entitle him to be enrolled amongst the graduates
of the institution, and the college ought to define strictly
the kind and quantity of attainment which it considers
sufficient, in that line or department, to earn its
degree.

Now, however, the advocates of the old classical culture, ignoring or ignorant of all the change which has
come over human knowledge and philosophy within
fifty years, come forward to affirm that that culture
still is the best possible training for our young men and
the proper basis for the work of our colleges. How do
they know it? How can anybody say that one thing
or another is just what is needed for education? Can
we not break down this false and stupid notion that it
is the duty of a university, not to teach whatever anyone wants to know, but to prescribe to everybody what
he ought to want to know? Some years ago, at a school
meeting in one of our cities, a gentleman made an argument against the classics. A distinguished clergyman
asked him across the room whether he had ever studied
the classics. He replied that he had not. "I thought
not," replied the clergyman, as he sat down. He was
thought to have won a great victory, but he had not.
His opponent should have asked him whether he had
ever studied anything else. Where is the man who has
studied beyond the range of the classical culture who
retains his reverence for that culture as superior to all
other for the basis of education? No doubt a man of
classical training often looks back with pleasure and
gratitude to his own education and feels that it has been
of value to him; but when he draws an inference, either
that no other course of discipline would have been worth
more to himself, or that no other discipline can be generally more useful as a basis of education, he forms a judg-

ment on a comparison one branch of which is to him unknown.

I am not in the same position on this question as that held by certain other writers of the day. I may say that I profited fairly by a classical education. I believe that I am in a position to form a judgment as to how much is truth and how much is humbug in the rhapsodies about the classics to which we are treated. The historical sciences and language will always have great value for certain classes of scholars. Clergymen will always need the ancient languages as a part of their professional training. Teachers in certain departments will always need them. No professor of modern languages could be considered equipped for his work if he were unacquainted with Greek and Latin. Philologists and special students in the science of language contribute in a high degree and in an indispensable manner to the stock of our knowledge. Literary men and some kinds of journalists, classes who are sure in the future to seek a more special and detailed training than they have enjoyed in the past, will find utility in classical study. All these classes need, not less Greek and Latin than hitherto, but more. One evil result of trying to force the classics on everybody is that those for whom the classics have value cannot get as much of them as they need. Of modern languages, two at least are to-day indispensable to an educated man. As nations come nearer to each other, and as their literatures grow richer and richer, the need of being able to step over the barrier of language becomes greater. It is easy for anyone who watches the course of things to see how, from one decade to another, the necessity of learning the modern languages makes itself more distinctly felt. Those languages were formerly accomplishments. Now they are necessities for anyone who intends to pursue literary or scientific work, or even practical work in many departments. Hence language will always enter into the scope of education, especially in its elementary stageş. Latin has especial utility and advantage. If one wanted to learn three or four modern languages, it might pay him to learn Latin first, and Latin will always have value for an introduction to the ancient classical world. Greek is a rich and valuable accomplishment to any man of literary or philological tastes, or to an orator or public debater, or to anyone who needs the art of interpretation. I know of no study which will in general develop gifts of expression, or chasten literary style, like the study of Greek. That language more than any other teaches the delicate power of turns in the phrase, of the collocation of words, of emphasis, of subtle shading in synonyms and adjectives. Then, too, surely no student of politics and political economy can pass over the subject-matter of Aristotle, or Demosthenes and the orators, nor the life and polity of the Greek State.

When, however, all this is admitted in regard to the uses of a classical training, what does it prove in regard to the claims of the classics to be made the basis of all higher education or the toll which everyone must pay before he can be admitted to the gild of the learned? Nothing at all. I have known splendid Greek scholars who could not construct a clear and intelligible argument of six sentences. They always became entangled in subtleties of phrase and super-refinement of words. I have known other great Greek scholars who wrote an English which was so dull that scarcely anyone could read it. On the other hand, there are men whose names are household words wherever the English language is spoken because they can say what they mean in clear,

direct, and limpid English, although they have never had
any classical culture at all. I have known whole classes
to graduate at our colleges who had never read a line
of Aristotle, and who had not a single correct notion
about the life and polity of the Greeks. Men graduate
now all the time who know nothing of Greek history and
polity but the fragments which they pick out of the
notes on the authors which they read. It is grotesque to
talk about the recondite charms and graces of classical
culture when one knows what it amounts to for all but
here and there one. It is a rare thing for a man to graduate who has read Grote or Curtius, although he has
studied Greek for five or six years. Anyone who reads no
Greek and never goes to college, but reads Grote or
Curtius, knows far more of Greek life, polity, and culture
than any but the most exceptional college graduate. I
do not believe that this was formerly true. It appears
that faithful students in former times used such means
as then existed for becoming familiar with classical life
and history far more diligently than is now customary.
Classical studies, having sunk to a perfunctory character,
now stand in the way of faithful study of anything.

I go further, and if the classics are still proposed as
the stem of a liberal education, to be imposed upon every
student who seeks a university training, I argue that
classical culture has distinct and mischievous limitations.
The same may no doubt be said of any other special
culture, and whenever any other culture is put forward
as possessing some exclusive or paramount value, it will
be in order to show that fact. I do not doubt that I
gained great profit from a classical training. Part of
the profit I was conscious of. I think it very likely that
I won other profit of which I was unconscious. I know
that it cost me years of discipline to overcome the limita-

tions of the classical training and to emancipate my mind from the limited range of processes in which it had been trained. For the last ten years I have taught political economy to young men of twenty-one years or thereabouts who had been prepared for me by training in a curriculum based on classics. They have acquired certain facilities. They have a facility in "recitation" which is not always produced by familiarity with the subject. The art of recitation is an art all by itself. Very often it is all a man has won from his college training. Sometimes it consists in beating out a little very thin, so as to make it go a great way; sometimes it consists in "going on one's general information," and profiting to the utmost by any hint in the question; sometimes it consists in talking rapidly about something else than the question. Some men never can come to a point, but soar in lofty circles around and over the point, showing that they have seen it from a distance; others present rags and tags of ideas and phrases, showing that they have read the text and that here and there a word has stuck in the memory without sequence or relation. The habit of reading classics with a "pony" for years has produced these results. Many of these men must be regarded with pity because their mental powers have been miseducated for years, and when they try to acquire something, to make it their own, to turn it into a concise and correct statement and utter it again, they cannot do it. They have only acquired some tricks of speech and memory.

The case of men who have studied honestly, but who have been educated almost exclusively on grammar, is different. No doubt they have gained a great deal, but I find that they hardly ever know what a "law" is in the scientific sense of the word. They think that it is like a rule in grammar, and they are quite prepared to find it followed by a list of exceptions. They very often lack vigor and force in thinking. They either accept authority too submissively, if the notion which is presented does not clash with any notions they had received before, or if they argue, they do so on points of dialectical ingenuity. They do not join issue closely and directly, and things do not fall into order and range in their minds. They seem to be quite contented to take things and hold them in a jumble. It is rare to find one who has scholarship enough to look up a historical or biographical reference. It is generally assumed by them that if "no lesson has been given out" they have nothing to do. One of the most peculiar notions is that a "lecture" has no such importance as a "recitation"; that to cut the former is of no consequence, but that to cut the latter is serious. In short, the habits and traditions in which men have been trained when they reach senior year in college are such that they are yet boys in responsibility, and, although they are very manly and independent in many respects, they are dependent and unmanly in their methods of study, in their conceptions of duty, in their scholarship, and in their code of conduct in all that effects the institution. It has been claimed for the classics that they give guidance for conduct. This is, to me, the most amazing claim of all, for, in my experience and observation, the most marked fact about classical culture is that it gives no guidance in conduct at all.

In contrast with what I have stated, it is most important to notice that, in every class, men distinguish themselves in political economy who have been very poor scholars in the classics and have lost whatever mental drill a classical training might have given.

I shall be asked whether I attribute the facts which I have mentioned about the mental habits of students to the study of the classics. Evidently many of them are attributable to a system of school discipline continued until a too advanced age, and to a puerile system of discipline. Others are due to a text-book and recitation-with-marks system which breeds into a man unscholarly ideas and methods. But I affirm from my own experience and observation that the most serious of the mental faults and bad intellectual habits which I have described are caused by a training which is essentially literary, grammatical, and metaphysical. No doubt it is true that a large fraction of the men will shirk work; that they are slovenly in all their mental habits; that they will be as idle as they dare; that they seize gladly upon a chance to blame somebody else or "the system" for their own shortcomings. These facts, however, belong only to the imperfection of all things earthly. They are true; but if they are put forward as an excuse for routine and neglect on the part of university authorities, then those authorities simply lower themselves to the level of the bad students. A rigid discipline in prescribed tasks, with especial care for the dull scholars, is in place for youth up to a certain age, but in any good system of education the point must be judiciously chosen at which this system shall yield to a system of individual responsibility. The point at which this change should be made is certainly some years before the point at which young men become men by the laws of their country. That more responsibility would bring out more character is beyond question. The present method of prolonging tutelage and inculcating character by big doses of "moral science" is certainly a failure. I maintain that it is an impertinence for any authority whatever to withhold from young men twenty years of age anything which they desire to learn, or to impose upon them anything whatever which the authority in question thinks they ought to know.

The tendency of classical studies is to exalt authority, and to inculcate reverence for what is written rather than for what is true. Men educated on classics are apt to be caught by the literary form, if it is attractive. They are fond of paradoxes, and will entertain two contradictory ideas, if only each come in a striking literary dress. They think that they prove something when they quote somebody who has once said it. If anyone wants to keep out "new ideas," he does well to cling to classical studies. They are the greatest barrier to new ideas and the chief bulwark of modern obscurantism. The new sciences have produced in their votaries an unquenchable thirst and affection for what is *true* in fact, word, character, and motive. They have taught us to appreciate and weigh evidence and to deal honestly with it. Here a strong contrast with classical training has been developed, not because classical training led men to be false, but because the scientific love of truth is something new and intense. Men of classical training rarely develop the power to go through from beginning to end of a course of reasoning on a straight line. They go on until they see that they are coming out at a result which they do not like. Then they make a bend and aim for a result which they do like, not regarding the broken continuity, or smoothing it over as carefully as possible. Classical training, in the world of to-day, gives a man a limited horizon. There is far more beyond it than within it. He is taught to believe that he has sounded the depths of human knowledge when he knows nothing about its range or amount. If anyone wants to find prime specimens of the Philistinism which Matthew Arnold hates, he should seek them among the votaries of the culture which Matthew Arnold loves. The popular acuteness long ago perceived this, and the vile doctrines of anti-culture have sprung up and grown just in proportion as culture has come to have an artificial and technical definition, as something foreign to living interests.

An American college ought to be the seat of all the learning which would be of value to an American man in the American life of to-day. It ought to offer that training which would draw out and discipline the mental powers which are to-day useful. It ought to offer to its pupils an opportunity of becoming acquainted with all which is, or is coming to be, in the great world of thought, and it ought to offer such opportunities that those who profited by them faithfully would be highly trained men, drilled and disciplined for any of the tasks of life. If a college were such a place as this, its usefulness would be recognized at once. Every young man in the country would desire, if possible, to enjoy its advantages, because he would feel that, if he could get a college education, he would be as it were lifted upon a higher plane for all the work of his subsequent life, no matter what career he might choose. His ambition would have won a new footing. In the competition of life he would have won new skill and new weapons. No college can possibly take any such place if it "clings to the classics." In face of the facts it is ludicrous to talk about maintaining the old classical culture. We might as well talk of wearing armor or studying alchemy. During the last fifty years all the old sciences have been reconstructed and a score of new ones have been born. Shall a man be educated now at our highest seats of learning and not become acquainted with these facts and doctrines which are revolutionizing the world of knowledge? Shall he only be allowed a bit here and a fragment there, or spend his best years in pursuits which end in themselves? In every journal or conversation, and in many sermons, topics are treated which belong to the substance of modern thinking. Shall the colleges ignore these topics, or only refer to them in order to preach them down?

History does not any longer mean what it meant twenty years ago. As a disciplinary pursuit it has changed entirely from any exercise of memory to an analysis and investigation of relations and sequences. Constitutional history has grown into a great branch of study of the highest importance to the student of law, political science, jurisprudence, and sociology. It has totally altered the point of view and mode of conceiving of those subjects since the days when the study of them began with the classical authors. The years spent on Greek grammar and literature would be priceless to the whole mass of our youth if they could be spent on this study. Sociology is still in its infancy. Only its most elementary notions are, as yet, available for purposes of education. It is sure to grow into a great science, and one of the first in rank as regards utility to the human race. It is plain that progress in other directions is producing problems in society which we cannot meet because our social science is not proportionately advanced. Biology is a science which is still young and new, but, with its affiliated sciences, it holds the key to a number of our most important problems and to a new philosophy destined to supersede the rubbish of the schools. Physics in all its subdivisions, dynamics, anthropology, archæology, and a host of other sciences, with new developments in mathematics, offer just the stimulus which is proper and necessary to draw out youthful energies and to awaken youthful enthusiasm. The studies which I have mentioned and others are ready at our hand to-day to give our young men intellectual training and high scholarship and to carry them on to heights of enjoyment and useful activity of which they have no conception. In the mean time they are studying Latin and Greek, and the college authorities are boasting that they cling to the old curriculum and to classical culture.

Our colleges cannot maintain themselves in any such position before the country. They must have the best possible learning, and they must impart it freely. They cannot do this if they "run themselves" or live on their reputation. There is nothing else which now calls for such high statesmanship as the guidance of our old colleges into the new duties and functions which they ought to fulfill. It is a task which calls for great sagacity and good judgment, but above all, for constant study and care. There is here one remarkable consideration by way of encouragement. A great university can be subjected to experiments without any harm at all. It is a great mistake to think that an experiment, if it fails, will leave permanent evils behind. It will not do so. Every academic year stands by itself. Every year it is possible to begin anew, adopting a new plan or recurring to an old one, and no harm at all is done. No one proposes to do away with the study of the classics. For those who desire to pursue that study we desire far fuller opportunities than now exist. The assault is aimed entirely at the pre-eminent and privileged position which is claimed for the classics. We desire that the universities should offer equal chances for a liberal education on the basis of any of the other great lines of study. If it should prove, upon experiment, that men educated in other sciences could not hold their own in life in competition with the classically educated, there would undoubtedly be a revival of classical study and a return to it by those who were seeking an education.

BIBLIOGRAPHY

BIBLIOGRAPHY

1872 THE BOOKS OF THE KINGS, by K. C. W. F. Bähr. Translated, Enlarged, and Edited. . . . Book 2, by W. G. Sumner, in Lange, J. P. A commentary on the Holy Scripture. . . . New York, Scribner, Armstrong & Company, 1866–82, 26 vols., VI, 312 pp.

1874 A HISTORY OF AMERICAN CURRENCY. New York, H. Holt & Company, iv, 391 pp., two fold diagram.

1875 AMERICAN FINANCE. Boston, Williams.

1876 MONETARY DEVELOPMENT. (In Woolsey, T. D., and others, First Century of the Republic. New York, Harper & Brothers.)
Politics in America, 1776 to 1876. North American Review, Vol. 122, Centennial number, pp. 47–87.

1877 LECTURES ON THE HISTORY OF PROTECTION IN THE UNITED STATES. . . . New York, published for the New York Free Trade Club by G. P. Putnam & Sons, 64 pp. Contents: The National Idea and the American System, Broad Principles Underlying the Tariff Controversy, The Origin of Protection in this Country, The Establishment of Protection in this Country, Vacillation of the Protective Policy in this Country.

1878 EARLE, A. L. OUR REVENUE SYSTEM. Preface by W. G. Sumner. New York, published for the Free Trade Club by G. P. Putnam & Sons, 2 p. L., xi, 47 pp. (Economic Monograph No. V.)
MONEY AND ITS LAWS. International Review, January and February pp. 75–81.

1879 BIMETALLISM. Princeton Review, November, pp. 546–578.

378 BIBLIOGRAPHY

1880 THE THEORY AND PRACTICE OF ELECTIONS. *Ibid.*, March, pp. 262–286, and July, pp. 24–41.

1881 ELECTIONS AND CIVIL SERVICE REFORM. *Ibid.*, January, pp. 129–148.

1881 THE ARGUMENT AGAINST PROTECTIVE TAXES. *Ibid.*, March, pp. 241–259.

SOCIOLOGY. *Ibid.*, November, pp. 303–323.

1882 ANDREW JACKSON AS A PUBLIC MAN. Boston, New York, Houghton Mifflin & Company. vi, 402 pp. (American Statesmen). Edited by T. T. Morse, Jr.

WAGES. Princeton Review, November, pp. 241–262.

PROTECTIVE TAXES AND WAGES. Philadelphia Tariff Commission, 21 pp. Caption title.

POLITICAL ECONOMY AND POLITICAL SCIENCE. Comp. by W. G. Sumner, D. A. Wells, W. E. Foster, R. L. Dugdale, and G. H. Putnam. New York Society for Political Education. Cover title, 36 pp. Economic Tracts No. 2.

1883 WHAT THE SOCIAL CLASSES OWE TO EACH OTHER. New York, Harper & Bros., 2 p. I., (7)–169 pp.

1884 OUR COLLEGES BEFORE THE COUNTRY. Princeton Review, March, pp. 127–140.

PROBLEMS IN POLITICAL ECONOMY. New York, 12mo., 125 pp.

SOCIOLOGICAL FALLACIES. North American Review, June, pp. 574–579.

1885 SHALL SILVER BE DEMONETIZED? *Ibid.*, June, pp. 485–489.

COLLECTED ESSAYS IN POLITICAL AND SOCIAL SCIENCE. New York, 173 pp.

PROTECTIONISM. New York, 12mo., 170 pp.

1886 INDUSTRIAL WAR. Forum, September, pp. 1–8.

MR. BLAINE ON THE TARIFF. North American Review, October, pp. 398–405.

1887 WHAT MAKES THE RICH RICHER AND THE POOR POORER? Popular Science Monthly, January, pp. 289–296.

1887 THE INDIANS IN 1887. Forum, May, pp. 254–262.
STATE INTERFERENCE. North American Review, August,
pp. 109–119.

1888 TRUSTS AND TRADE UNIONS. The Independent, V.
40, pp. 482–483.

1888 THE FALL IN SILVER AND INTERNATIONAL COMPETI-
TION. Rand McNally's Banker's Monthly, February,
pp. 47–48.
THE FIRST STEPS TOWARDS A MILLENNIUM. Cosmo-
politan, March, pp. 32–36.

1889 DO WE WANT INDUSTRIAL PEACE? Forum, Decem-
ber, pp. 406–416.
WHAT IS CIVIL LIBERTY? Popular Science Monthly,
July, pp. 289–303.

1890 ALEXANDER HAMILTON ("Makers of America"). New
York, 12mo., 280 pp., Dodd, Mead & Co.

1891 LIBERTÉ DES ÉCHANGES. Nouveau Dictionnaire d'Eco-
nomie Politique, vol. 2, pp. 138–166, Guillaumin et
Cie Paris.
THE FINANCIER AND THE FINANCES OF THE AMERICAN
REVOLUTION. New York, 2 vol., 8mo., 309 and 330 pp.

1892 ROBERT MORRIS ("Makers of America"). New York,
12mo., 172 pp.

1894 ABSURD EFFORT TO MAKE THE WORLD OVER. Forum,
V. 17, pp. 92–102.

1896 BANKS OF ISSUE IN THE UNITED STATES. Forum, V. 22,
pp. 182–191.
THE FALLACY OF TERRITORIAL EXTENSION. Forum, V.
21, pp. 414–419.
HISTORY OF BANKING IN THE UNITED STATES (In Dods-
worth, A. W., ed. A History of Banking in all the
Leading Nations. New York, published by Journal
of Commerce and Commercial Bulletin, 4 V. v.l.,
3 p. l., ix to xv, 385 pp.).
THE PROPOSED DUAL ORGANIZATION OF MANKIND.
Popular Science Monthly, V. 49, pp. 432–439.

1896 THE SINGLE GOLD STANDARD, Chautauquan, V. 24, pp. 72–77.

1898 THE COIN SHILLING OF MASSACHUSETTS BAY. Yale Review, V. 7, pp. 247–280.
THE SPANISH DOLLAR AND THE COLONIAL SHILLING. American Historical Review. V. 3, pp. 607–619.

1899 THE CONQUEST OF THE UNITED STATES BY SPAIN. Yale Law Journal, V. 8, No. 4, pp. 168–193.

1901 ANTHRACITE COAL INDUSTRY, by Peter Roberts. Introduction by W. G. Sumner. New York, London, Macmillan Co., XII, pp., 11., 261 pp.
THE PREDOMINANT ISSUE. Burlington, Vt. Reprinted from the International Monthly, V. 2, pp. 496–509.
SPECIMENS OF INVESTMENT SECURITIES FOR CLASS ROOM USE. New Haven, The E. P. Judd Co., 32 pp.
THE YAKUTS. Abridged from the Russian of Sieroshevski. Journal of Anthropological Institute of Great Britain and Ireland, V. 31, pp. 65–110.

1902 JUSTIFICATION OF WEALTH. Independent, V. 54, pp. 1036–1040.
SUICIDAL FANATICISM IN RUSSIA. Popular Science Monthly, V. 60, pp. 442–447.

1904 THE FALLACIES OF SOCIALISM. Colliers Weekly, October 29, pp. 12–13.

1906 ADDRESS AT DINNER OF THE COMMITTEE ON TARIFF REFORM OF THE TARIFF REFORM CLUB IN THE CITY OF NEW YORK, 1906. 7 pp. Series 1906, No. 4.

1907 FOLKWAYS: A Study of the Sociological Importance of Usages, Manners, Customs, Mores, and Morals. Boston, Ginn & Co., V., 692 pp.
SOCIOLOGY AS A COLLEGE SUBJECT. American Journal of Sociology, V. 12, pp. 597–599.

1909 MORES OF THE PRESENT AND THE FUTURE. Yale Review, V. 18, pp. 233–245.
THE FAMILY AND SOCIAL CHANGE. American Journal of Sociology, V. 14, pp. 577–591.

1909 THE STATUS OF WOMEN IN CHALDEA, EGYPT, INDIA, ETC., TO THE TIME OF CHRIST. Forum, V. 42, pp. 113–136.
WITCHCRAFT. Forum, V. 41, pp. 410–423.
1910 RELIGION AND THE MORES. American Journal of Sociology, V. 15, pp. 577–591.
1911 WAR ("War and Other Essays"). Yale University Press.
WAR. Yale Review, (new series). V. 1, pp. 1–27.